A Deer Hunter's History Book

Twentieth-century woodland adventures from within and around the Blue Ridge Wilderness area.

Robert J. Elinskas

Printed in the United States of America

ISBN 0-9771017-0-3

Cover photo:
Frank, Stanley and Gerry Lanphear, Raquette Lake, 1920s

DEDICATION

This book is dedicated to Amy, my much better half,
who once said she would never marry a hunter.
For her undying support of everything I do
and for always keeping the home fires burning.

Bob & Amy Elinskas

TABLE OF CONTENTS

ACKNOWLEDGEMENTS

When I first began writing this book, I thought I knew quite a lot about the Blue Ridge area. It turned out that actually, I knew very little. My research led me to many new acquaintances, and I learned that these people loved and cared for the mountains as I do. Without their gracious help, a book of this kind could never have been written. Some people had a great deal of knowledge to contribute, and they gave it all with a good heart. Others had only a fact or two, or the guidance on where to get them. This also helped immensely.

Special recognition is given to Glade Keith, who answered so many questions, both by phone and personal visits. Glade was my primary source of inspiration and he provided so much material on those early years.

Major contributions to this text were generously given by Ernest Blanchard, Ed Goulet, Ed Mitchel, Frank, Gerry and Edgar Lanphear, Vern Turner, James Turner, Elva and Edgar Brown, Tony Dipino, Ned Welch, Nelson J. Kling, Warren Ramsdell, Royce Wells, George McCane, Ce'line Karraker, Dick and Ethel Fletcher, David S. York, Jay Manchester, Kenneth, Paul and William Larkin, Bob Gates, Marjorie Anderson, Bill Morrison, and Richard Lesser. To these people I will always be eternally grateful.

A special and heartfelt thank you goes out to Laura and Lelan York, Caroline Keith, Peter, Anthony and Frank Dipino, David J. York, Daryl Eaton, Harrison and Josephine Hall, Evelyn Thompson, Mary Doherty, Jamie Roblee, Ralph Burnham, Peter Roll, Janice Bonifield, Linda McCane, Milton Pope, Jeff and Kathy Savadel, Don Adams and Mike Arcurri.

Many research questions were diligently answered by Gerald Pepper – Adirondack Museum Librarian, Bill Zullo – Indian Lake historian, John and Mable Fish – Indian Lake Museum and Finch & Pruyn Industries.

The remembrances, tales, and testimony that follow were given as truthfully and sincerely as possible. There are many accounts given that were obvious violations of the law. They were not recorded to embarrass or offend anyone, but only to record what happened or went on during that particular time frame.

THE INSPIRATION

It was in July of 1987 that my wife, Amy and I, were touring the Adirondack Museum at Blue Mountain Lake, with our four children, Bob Jr., Dan, Rick, and Suzanne. Just before noon we decided to get a light lunch at the snack bar. It was one of those beautiful, blue sky summer days, with excellent haze-free visibility. The table we selected gave us a good view of the wilderness off to the southwest. This was my deer hunting country, and I knew intimately most of the bumps and dips that were laid out before us like a giant, rumpled, green carpet.

It was part of the Blue Ridge Wilderness Area, one of 15 Wilderness areas created in 1972 by the Adirondack Park Agency, in consultation with the D.E.C. The Blue Ridge Wilderness roughly consists of all the property between the Cedar River on the south, to the Eckford Chain and Raquette Lake's east shoreline on the north, and from Route 30 between Blue Mountain and Indian Lake, westerly to the Sagamore Road, Sagamore Lake, Lake Kora, and southerly to the Cedar River Flow. The predominant form of Blue Ridge rose from the center of this area, and runs east and west for a total distance of six miles. It rises to a maximum height of 3,497 feet on its east end, and it peaks out again at 3,436 feet near its west end. Both peaks are wooded so they afford no view.

I tried to point out to my children some of the places I had been to and where I had killed some of the bucks they would remember seeing or hearing about. They looked and thought they might be seeing some of the landmarks I was pointing to, but in reality, it was just one big green mass of woodlands. We went back to the business of eating our lunch and discussing some of the things we had already seen at the museum.

Occasionally, I would glance back towards Blue Ridge and the low lying hills nearby. I'd been through an awful lot of that country, but not all of it. The old familiar thought of the hunter came to mind, "If those hills could only talk, what stories they could tell!" I had been hunting that area for most of 31 years, and had some beautiful memories from hunting seasons past. They are the kind of memories that stay with you, "Till you die." I started looking over the high slopes of the ridge again, when I was brought back to the museum with a "Let's get going Dad!"

Five years later I was in the North Brookfield area, and I stopped in to visit with Glade and Lucy Keith at their farm on the Gorton Lake Road. Glade is 88 and has lived on the farm all his life. After the usual gossip about local news and people we know, the conversation turned to the upcoming Adirondack deer season. I summed things up by saying, "We sure have had some good times up there over the years. Your brother, Parks, used to tell some awful good stories." "Yes," Glade agreed, "he did tell some good ones.

It's too bad we have to take them with us when we die." Parks died July 4, 1964.

"It was a good visit," I thought as I drove back to Utica, but visits with Glade and Lucy were always good. My thoughts drifted back over our conversations, and Glade's last remark kept glaring at me, "It's too bad we have to take our stories with us when we die!"

Glade has been hunting in the Blue Ridge area now for 67 years. Some of our other hunters have hunted the region since the '30s, '40s, and myself the '50s. Hunting out of an Adirondack tent camp is an annual tradition. Some of our hunting and woodland experiences are retold every year as part of it. It never occurred to me that someday we would lose all this to time.

THE BOOK

The motivation to write a book was building within me. I have always enjoyed reading a good book, especially ones pertaining to our Adirondack Mountains. However, most authors seemed to skip lightly over the subject of deer hunting.

Aside from the major historical happenings that take place in a given period, there are many less significant occurrences that happen to enrich or motivate our lives. Many of these are wildlife or woods related and are sure to come up in the conversations between the local population and seasonal residents over a friendly cup of coffee. The book I have assembled is modeled after this theme.

The first part of the book chronicles Glade Keith and his first trips into the Adirondack Park. It describes the people he came to know and how he eventually establishes a seasonal deer hunting camp at Loon Brook.

As the years passed and I became old enough to hunt, I was invited up to try my luck in the Adirondacks. Our local hunting stories were at times supplemented with rumors of a big buck or bear taken at one of the peripheral hunting lodges or perhaps one of the great camps, so they were also included in my manuscript. We were all part of the Blue Ridge environment.

The last portion of the book deals with the adventures we shared out of my own deer hunting tent at Loon Brook. Gathering material for this book and the many personal interviews involved was a labor of love. I thoroughly enjoyed each and every visit.

So, now, if you enjoy a good Adirondack visit, sit down, relax and read what the happenings were in the 20th century around the Blue Ridge Wilderness area. Let the old-timers tell you their stories just like they told me. This is a history book from a deer hunter's point of view!

GLADE KEITH

Glade Keith was born at North Brookfield, N.Y., on June 27, 1904. His parents, Ralph and Caroline, were of Scottish ancestry. He had one brother, Parks, who was two years older. They were raised in the farm country environment and were given the responsibilities of farm chores at an early age. Both boys enjoyed a fascination for small game hunting and target shooting. Glade became highly interested in firearms and began collecting them.

His inspiration for collecting came from Albert (Bert) Ramsdel. Bert was the local postmaster and he and his wife Alice also ran a general store. Bert was an avid collector who would talk to Glade about collecting and also show and explain his own extensive collection to him. Glade was particularly interested in muzzle loaders. By the age of fifteen he had several fine rifles and shotguns in his collection. In time, Glade became a gun trader and collector, having attended gun shows all over the Northeast. In his early days, it was his practice to take off on a two- or three-day trip every so often and search out the local gun traders in small communities across the State. Each trip would be in a different area and most times he would make a deal or two that would make the whole effort well worthwhile.

When Glade was fourteen, his cousin, Gene Perkins, got a seasonal job at Blue Mountain Lake. Gene was the son of Emit and Lottie Perkins. They operated a farm on the Guiles Road, in the town of Brookfield. Gene was an acquaintance of Louisa and Waldo Faulkner, who were formerly from the York Hill area of Brookfield. Louisa and Wally had only recently opened up Faulkner's Inn at Blue Mountain Lake. Gene was seventeen years older than Glade. He would go up to Faulkner's Inn in early May and work right through until the end of the hunting season. When the season was over he would come back to the farm in Brookfield to spend the winter. Almost always he would bring home a nice set of whitetail antlers, as well as a fresh supply of hunting and fishing stories to tell. Glade used to listen attentively to every one of them, soaking in the information and looking over the deer antlers. As the years went by Gene could tell that Glade had a keen interest in trying his luck at deer hunting.

AN INVITATION TO HUNT THE ADIRONDACKS

In 1924, Parks and Glade lost both their parents in the same year. The boys would work the farm together now. In 1925, Gene invited Glade up to Blue Mountain Lake to hunt the last week of deer season.

It was only within the last twenty years that the Adirondack country had opened up to the automobile traveler. The old stage roads were being widened and improved. Every year many miles of new roads were being constructed or improved for the growing number of new cars.

Local newspapers would commonly carry accounts of newly established businesses, development of new roads, and adventures of the traveling sportsman. Of particular interest to Glade as his interest in hunting developed, were the glowing accounts of successful deer hunters that had visited the area and returned with their game by way of the rail lines. The successful hunters would ship their deer or bear back by Railway Express Agency and it would be accurately weighed in order to determine the correct shipping charges. The following excerpts were taken from the Utica Daily Press, Saturday morning, October 31, 1914:

WOODS ARE NOW RIGHT FOR DEER

The call of camp and trail takes many hundreds of hunters into northern N.Y. forests. The big game season of northern N.Y. is on and day by day there flows woodswards through Utica a steady stream of moccasined men, pack baskets, and guns, while each Adirondack train brings to this city its quota of many pointed bucks. Last night the Adirondack train brought in twenty-two good bucks, and the afternoon train of Thursday, brought in eighteen. Probably the best buck of the season was brought in at Carthage with a weight of 298 lbs. This is among some of the biggest bucks killed in recent years. The average weight is far below this figure, but deer weighing 250 lbs. are not uncommon in the express company's tally sheets.

MANY DEER TAKEN IN SARANAC LAKE AREA

The largest buck of the season was brought in by two boys, Fred Bailey and Francis Demers. The big fellow tipped the scales at 337 lbs. twenty-four hours after being killed and field dressed. He was gray-whiskered, with a magnificent pair of antlers.

Many other articles on hunting adventures appeared seasonally in the Utica newspapers including pictures. One picture showed a hunter with his buck and was captioned, "The reason for it all — New York's noblest forest dweller, the mighty buck of the Adirondack Mountains." Gene Perkins didn't have to ask Glade a second time, Glade would be at Blue Mountain Lake for the last week of the Adirondack deer season.

Later in the year, a friend of Glade's, Roy Brantingham, stopped by the house for a visit. He told Glade that Colgate College, in Hamilton, New York, was looking for more workers to help install steam lines at the College before winter set in. They were paying big money too — sixty cents per hour. Glade thought it might be a good way to pick up some extra cash, but only until his trip to Blue Mountain came up.

A letter from Gene told Glade he could meet him at the residence of Ernie Blanchard, a well-known professional guide in that area. Ernie had only recently lost his wife. He had made arrangements with a woman to care for his children while he was off in the woodland camps guiding hunting clients, but he needed someone to look after the house and livestock. Gene had agreed to do this until the end of deer season. Glade's plan was to head north right after work on Friday afternoon. Roy Brantingham had agreed to give him a ride up and then drive home as soon as he had dropped Glade off. Glade would hunt the area out of Ernie's house and then return with Gene at the end of the season.

FIRST TRIP TO BLUE MOUNTAIN LAKE

The days are short in November, so by the time Roy and Glade got as far as Utica in Roy's Model "T" it was already getting dark. They took Route 8 to Poland and then headed north toward Speculator. This was entirely new country to both men since neither of them had traveled into the Adirondack area before this. They both had the spirit for adventure though, and were eager to see whatever the headlights might expose that evening on their trip. They had talked with a fellow earlier in the week who was familiar with the route to Speculator. He said on the way up they would pass through Hoffmeister, so on the way up they kept expecting to see the village of Hoffmeister. The road wound on and on and only once did they see the glow of an electric light out near the road but there appeared to be nothing around. Many miles later they saw a man out near the road by his car. They stopped and asked him how much farther it was into Speculator. He said only three miles or so. Then Glade asked him where Hoffmeister was. He said, "Do you remember seeing an electric light out near the road about twenty miles back?" "Yes." "Well, that was Hoffmeister." "Hmmm, that was Hoffmeister?"

Roy and Glade drove into Speculator and then on towards Indian Lake. The road at that time was little more than a single lane dirt and sand trail through the woods with an occasional boulder sticking up through the middle of it. It was quite a challenge driving it in the daytime, let alone driving it for the first time in the middle of the night. When they got into Indian Lake, it was quite late at night, but they managed to spot someone out stirring around when they got into town.

Roy stopped and asked for directions into Blue Mountain Lake. They were told that the road into Blue Mountain was currently under construction and was not passable all the way. Construction crews would let the mail truck go through once a day, but that's all. He advised them to go to North Creek and then Minerva, Newcomb, Long Lake, and then south to Blue Mountain. That sounded like an awful long detour when they were only 11 miles from Blue Mountain.

Roy decided to see how far they could get in his Model "T". They headed off towards Blue Mountain and went quite a long way on a real good road. They were starting to think that they had gotten some bad advice in Indian Lake when across from flow 34 (the Lake Durant area now) the road was closed with barricades. They got out and saw that the road had been cut right across. It looked like they could get down into it alright but getting up the bank on the far side was questionable. They drove down into the cut, but the car just couldn't get a good bite on the sandy banks on the far side, so they had to quit. They guessed that they couldn't be very far away from town so they grabbed Glade's gear and started walking.

When they got to the end of flow 34, they took the left hand turn (now Durant

Road) that headed over towards Faulkner's Inn. It was now about 4 a.m. and the first house they came to had a light on. They stopped to ask for directions. The men of the house were just getting up for breakfast and then a day of deer hunting. Roy and Glade told them that they were heading for Ernie Blanchard's house and then they told them of their adventure coming up, and their misadventure in the roadcut.

Glade said the guys were "friendly and real good to us." They hooked up a team of horses to a sled and then took us across lots behind the houses and up on the mountain to Ernie's house. It was about five a.m. when they got there and got Gene Perkins out of bed. They had some breakfast, caught up on the news, and by sunrise they were back at the roadcut and Roy's car. With a little pushing and shoving on the old Ford, they got him back up the bank he had driven down and on his way back to Hamilton.

Now that it was daylight, Glade took his first good look at the central Adirondack country. He could see spruce-topped mountains in almost every direction and an ashen-gray hardwood forest covering the mountain sides and lower hills. Spruce-lined valleys defined the low lands and the reflection of water from a few distant lakes and ponds shown faintly in the distance. There was no farmland or patchwork of farm fields and hedge rows here, but a seemingly unbroken sea of wilderness. Gene would hunt with Glade whenever he could, but he had some daily chores that had to be taken care of there at the house.

CARLTON KING

Gene took Glade up the hill to Ernie's next door neighbor, Carlton King, and introduced him. Carlton was one of the local deer hunting guides and it was Gene's hope that Glade might hunt with Carlton at times during the coming week. Glade and Carlton seemed to hit it off right away, so after an hour or so of visiting, Carlton invited Glade to go deer hunting with him the next day.

The next morning Carlton drove Glade over to an area called the "hay marsh." The hay marsh was in the area of Mud Pond and is located about half way between Blue Mountain and the west end of Long Lake. Glade said it was a long series of mostly dry beaver meadows that were bordered with alders and spruce trees. You could see a long way off down the meadows, several hundred yards in some places. They saw lots of deer, alright, but they seemed to be pretty spooky. Most of the shots they had at bucks were long ones and the deer were moving fast. It was a good day out but they came back empty-handed.

While visiting with Carlton, Glade learned that earlier in the season he had made an agreement with a party from Seneca Falls, New York. The group wanted Carlton to guide them for a week's hunt. Carlton showed them a camping location with good water nearby for drinking and enough windfalls to supply the camp with firewood. The next morning he took the party out and showed them several good runs to watch and basically how to work them. By the end of the day the party had two big bucks hanging close by their tent. As soon as the bucks were hung, they paid Carlton one day's pay and told him they wouldn't be needing his help anymore. "Didn't we agree on one week's work?" asked Carlton. "We can handle this ourselves, we really don't need a guide anymore!" Carlton wasn't happy about that turn of events, but he let them be.

The next morning, the Seneca Falls hunters were all out in the woods looking for more deer. When they got back to their campsite in the afternoon, they found that their tent had caught fire and burned to the ground destroying everything in it. The two big bucks that were hanging close by had all the hair burnt off from them and their antlers were charred black. Carlton said, "Gosh, I don't know how it could have happened, but they really should be more careful with fire the next time!"

Carlton King enjoyed his social drinking. One evening he was sitting in an Indian Lake bar. He knew most of the fellows in the barroom as friends and acquaintances, but there was at least one that he didn't know. The deer season would be opening in a few days and Carlton was known to open it for himself a few days earlier than the official date. When asked by one of his friends if he'd been out, "lookin' around," he openly admitted to hanging up a couple of nice bucks that very day. The stranger who was seated at the bar immediately turned to Carlton and said, "Do you know who I am?"

"Don't believe I do," replied Carlton. "I'm a State game protector, assigned to this district," came the reply. Carlton returned with, "Do you know who I am?" "Not yet!" "Well, I'm the biggest damn liar in Hamilton County!"

The trail head for climbing Blue Mountain used to start right from Carlton King's front yard, across from the Adirondack Museum. In his later years, Carlton used to sell gasoline, sandwiches and soft drinks there. He would also rent parking spaces to the mountain climbers for a small fee.

During the next few days Glade hunted with both Carlton and Gene. They hunted the Terrill Pond, Salmon Pond and Salmon River areas. The lands they hunted on belonged to the Finch & Pruyn Paper Company, and hunters using the property were supposed to purchase a permit to hunt it. They never saw anyone out checking permits, so they didn't bother to buy any. Glade also noted that the "hounding law" was passed in 1897, forbidding the use of dogs as an aid in hunting deer. However, he could hear dogs, apparently chasing deer, almost every day off in that country.

CHARLES BLANCHARD

Ernie Blanchard's father, Charles, lived right across the road from Ernie's house on Blue Mountain. One evening, Glade decided to go across the street and pay the old guide a visit. As soon as he entered the house, Glade spotted an old Civil War musket leaning up against a wall. Glade's first words were, "That looks like a twice captured musket!" Charlie answered with, "I know darn well it is because I captured it myself the second time!" Charlie had served in the Civil War with Company One, 25th Mass. Infantry. He went on to say that near the end of his service tour, he came onto a Confederate soldier and got the drop on him. Charlie said, "Throw down your rifle," and he did. He then brought the soldier and his rifle back to the Union camp. The soldier was locked up, and Charlie kept his rifle.

Charlie also told him that just after his discharge from the army, he was spending a day in New York City before heading home. While out shopping, he couldn't help but notice a young man watching him. Eventually the man came over and introduced himself. He said he had guessed by Charlie's dress and appearance that he had just been discharged from the army. Charlie said, "Yes, that's right." They talked about his tour of service for a while and then the stranger offered him one thousand dollars if he would serve his tour of duty for him. Charlie said, "No," he'd had a belly full of it! Three weeks later, the war was over, but he still had no regrets.

Charlie Blanchard was born in 1842, in Barnard, Vermont. In 1873, he and his wife, Harriet, moved to Raquette Lake, New York, where he made his living renting cabins and providing services to sportsmen in season and caretaking in the off season. Charlie was very active right into his old age. He was often noted for leaving a set of snowshoe tracks in the snow on Blue Mountain Lake as "straight as an arrow," whenever he crossed the lake in winter on his way to the post office.

LOUISA & WALLY FAULKNER

Another evening Gene brought Glade down to meet Louisa and Waldo (Wally) Faulkner. They were both from the Brookfield area, but Glade had never really met them before. Wally and Louisa were married on 10 May 1899. Louisa was a school teacher and Wally farmed some, but he was usually involved in buying and selling farm stock, farm machinery, and whatever else he figured he might make money on.

About 1912 Louisa accepted a teaching position at Blue Mountain Lake so the couple moved north. Wally took right up with his wheeling-and-dealing style. Sometimes he would buy livestock in Mayfield and then he would hire local resident, Art Gates, to help him herd them up the mountain roads to Blue Mountain. It used to take them two real long days to make this trip.

In 1913, Wally and Art Gates walked a herd of cattle from Blue Mountain Lake to the Alexis York farm on York Hill in Brookfield, a distance of just over 100 miles. He took them down through the winter trail to Raquette Lake, and on to Old Forge, Utica and south to Waterville.

It took them quite a lot longer to make this trip that it did the Mayfield trip. Wally had bought the cattle in the early fall at a real good price and was taking them south where winter food was more abundant and he could turn a good profit. When they finally got into Waterville, they called down to the farm to let them know they were coming with the cattle. Alexis sent his oldest son, Lelan, who was only 10 years old at the time, down to meet them with a wagon and a team of horses. Lelan met up with them near Sangerfield, still about six miles distant from the farm. Lelan can plainly remember seeing them both. They were tired, sore and very dirty, and boy, were they ever glad to see his wagon! Their feet and toes were blistered up. To Lelan's knowledge, they never did that trip again.

Since Wally was always looking for something he could turn a profit on, it was only natural that his eye would spot the towering shell of the old Prospect House. In 1915, the Prospect House and its property were sold to Waldo Faulkner of Blue Mountain Lake and Gilbert Kelly of Syracuse. They dismantled the hotel and sold the furnishings and most of the lumber and building materials for good prices. Wally then took over the cottage and most of the property.

FAULKNER'S INN

The cottage was a good sized building in itself. It was formerly the residence of F.C. Durant, the Turnicliff family and Howard Durant. Wally and Louisa used some of the lumber from the Prospect House to remodel and add onto the cottage. They opened it up for business as Faulkner's Inn. Louisa managed the business. She was a tireless worker and ran a tight ship. She also did all the plumbing work and a lot of the carpentry herself. She was considered to be the strong person in their marriage. She had bright red hair and her brother, Fritz, who was very proud of her, would often say, "She wasn't given that red hair for nothing!" Of course, Wally was a hard worker too, but he was often dressed in tattered work clothing, knee-high rubber boots and almost always in a need of a shave. Louisa would often shoo him away from the dining guests and out of the public eye until he would dress more appropriately.

As part of the improvements to the cottage, Wally bought and installed as one unit, a large D.C. power system. It was powered by a General Motors four-cylinder engine, and it had a huge battery bank. The unit was fully automatic. Whenever the batteries would get low on charge, the G.M. motor would start up and run the charging unit until the batteries were recharged. Wally had purchased this unit brand new; it wasn't the old Edison unit that had provided power for the Prospect House.

Faulkner's Inn enjoyed a good business right from the start. As mentioned earlier, the automobile tourists and sportsmen were coming up in larger numbers every year. Louisa set a fine table for guests. Wally had put in a large vegetable garden on the hill above the Inn, and he managed it very well. In season, it provided much of the table fare served up at the Inn. The seed potatoes came from the Alexis York Farm. Ernie Blanchard's oldest son, Ernest, can remember eating many Sunday dinners there when he was a young lad. He said, "They had the best tasting sweet corn and potatoes that I've ever had in my life."

The Inn had a big walk-in cooler with an adjoining ice house. Whenever they needed more ice in the cooler, they would walk into the ice house and drag in another block. They stored many tons of ice every winter to supply the lodge through its operating season. In addition to the lodge, Wally also built three rental cottages. One of these cottages was built of cut stone and at one end of the building was a large fireplace. The fireplace had a long thick stone mantle placed above it. Wally would often tell of the struggle they had in getting that mantle up and in place. Faulkner's Inn hired many of the local residents to staff the lodge. They also hired some relatives and bought meat, at times, for the lodge from the York Farm.

Lelan York remembers bringing up a large quantity of broilers from his father's farm to the lodge one summer. He stayed at the Inn for three days before heading home.

During his stay, he would help out wherever he could. Wally kept a Model "T" Ford pick-up truck on hand at the Inn. It seemed that whenever the commercial boats on Blue Mountain Lake would made their run down the Eckford Chain of lakes to the Marion River Railroad terminus to pick up the incoming freight, that they would almost always make a stop at Faulkner's Landing to drop something off on the return trip. Lelan would take the pick-up and run down to the landing and return with new guests and luggage or supplies of one nature or another.

Louisa Faulkner, "Aunt Lou," died in 1929. After her death, Wally's nephew, Faulkner Rogers, who had worked at the Inn for several years, helped him manage the business. Wally remarried a year or two after Louisa died. Wally died in 1943. Title and operation of the Inn changed twice in the next several years. In the mid-1950s, the old Inn suffered two separate fires. New State regulations concerning fire safety and sanitary codes made the building too expensive for repair. In 1957, the building was deliberately destroyed by fire in a controlled burn by the Blue Mountain Lake Fire Department.

ERNIE BLANCHARD

Thursday evening, Ernie Blanchard came home from guiding out of his remote hunting camps. Ernest Clarence Blanchard was the youngest son of Charles and Harriet Blanchard. He was born at Raquette Lake on January 7, 1877, and was introduced to the Adirondack wilderness at a very early age. At the age of 10, he killed his first buck, and by the age of 12, he was guiding fishermen from his father's camps. At age 16, he was an Adirondack hunting guide.

When Ernie was very young, he used to love to listen to stories of his father's hunting and fishing adventures. Now he was living and making his own adventures. In the winter months, he and his father would run extensive trap lines. There were times when Ernie would be gone from home for up to ten days while running trap lines and being holed up in line cabins due to the weather. There were few restrictions on hunting deer in those days and extra money could be picked up by supplying venison to some of the remote logging camps.

REMOTE CABINS

Ernie's favorite hunting and trapping area was the wild Blue Ridge area which lays between the Eckford Chain of lakes and the Cedar River Valley. During his late teens and his twenties, Ernie built an impressive number of small cabins in this area that he would use to guide hunters out of, and also, use for line cabins during the trapping season.

Ernie was a powerful man physically, and he also had a ton of ambition. One of the first cabins he built was on Brady Pond, and he built several more in different locations in about as many years. Many of the structures he put up were at first built on remote privately owned land, which was owned by logging concerns. In later years, when the land was taken over by the State and became part of the forest preserve, these became "illegal cabins" and were destroyed whenever their whereabouts became known to State officials.

In the Blue Ridge area, he had cabins at Cascade Pond, Wilson Pond, Brady Pond, Bear Pond, Bear Brook Swamp, and Aluminum Pond. The Cascade Pond cabin he disliked the most. He described it as being built in a sour spot. The sun never seemed to shine much on that cabin and, for one reason or another, he always wound up doing his hardest work there. He would often refer to it as "camp mortal agony on a miserable pond!" About the only good thing he had to say about it was that it had a good fresh water supply. This was one of the few cabins he sold, and the fellow he sold it to must have had some political pull, because it stood for a long time after most of the other cabins were burnt down. Ernie hated to see the cabins being burnt up by the State, but they were illegal cabins now and there was nothing he could do.

The Bear Pond cabin was one of Ernie's favorites. Early one fall he hiked into it in order to check on its condition for the upcoming hunting season. When he got to it, he found two young men from New York City using the cabin. Normally he wouldn't have thought too much about it if the men had used his property right and things were pretty much in order. It became immediately apparent to Ernie that his cabin was far from "in order." The bedding and a lot of his supplies were outside the cabin and lying on the ground. Ernie had a number of storage tins in the cabin with tight-fitting lids that kept those supplies safe from chewing rodents and moisture. These tins had all been opened up and their contents scattered about with careless disregard.

The Blanchard boys were easy enough to get along with most of the time, but they were known to have a short temper and you didn't ever want to get them really upset. Right about then Ernie was seeing RED! He grabbed right ahold of the two of them and jerked them around sharply tearing their clothing, all the while explaining to them about a code of conduct in the woods that had let that cabin stand undisturbed and serviceable to anyone for years and years, until now! He sent both of the men packing for the road with a new respect for the Bear Pond cabin, and its apparent owner.

This incident really bothered Ernie. He no longer had that warm, secure feeling that the Bear Pond cabin would be there for him whenever he had need of it. Ironically, when the illegal forest preserve cabins were searched out and destroyed, the Bear Pond cabin was one of the first to go.

Ernie continued to guide the same areas even after most of his cabins had been destroyed. He disliked canvas tents. He would instead build a pole-framed structure and cover it with tar paper. When the hunting season was over with, he would strip off and burn the tar paper and disassemble the frame and store it off the ground.

Ernie's most remote cabin was located just north of and not far from Aluminum Pond. He would normally get into it from the Bear Pond cabin by heading southeast over the lower elevations of the west end of Blue Ridge. Because of its remote location, the cabin was used more for trapping than for hunting. This was one cabin that was never found by the State and destroyed.

MAPLE LODGE

In 1915, Ernie married Maude Myrtle Gray. The couple moved to the village of Blue Mountain Lake where Ernie had purchased Maple Lodge from Mrs. Charles E. Van Barr. Mr. Van Barr was band master for a while at the old Prospect House. He originally started building Maple Lodge as a private camp, but he began running out of money. He then made it over as a summer hotel. He died before it opened, however, and that's when Mrs. Van Barr sold it to Ernie. This was Ernie's first experience as a hotel proprietor. The first year was the hardest, and Ernie found himself borrowing three thousand dollars, just to pay the help! After that, Ernie and Maude made good money at it.

The Lodge and three rental cottages would accommodate up to fifty guests. They were built upon the eastern shore of Blue Mountain Lake, and the view to the west over the lake was very picturesque. Maple Lodge immediately enjoyed the benefit of the growing numbers of automobile tourists. In addition, the woods were full of game, and the lakes and streams were full of fish. It was fairly easy to keep your sporting guests happy.

During the deer season, Ernie handled a large deer hunting clientele. He employed guides from all over the area, including Indian Lake, Long Lake and Raquette Lake to help guide guests. In 1923, Ernie sold Maple Lodge to John S. Kathan. John ran the Lodge until 1926 when it was destroyed by fire. When Ernie sold to Kathan, he bought a white frame house on Blue Mountain. The house was located just below where the Adirondack Museum entrance is, and right in the middle of where the road now runs. When Ernie and Maude moved into their new residence they had three children with them: Nancy, Mary and Ernest; and these were the children Glade was introduced to. Ernie's wife, Maude, had died earlier in the year.

Glade's first impression of Ernie Blanchard was that he was a quiet man. At first he was reluctant to tell Glade anything, but once he got to know you, and you caught him in the right mood, then he would tell you "quite a lot." In appreciation for his stay at the Blanchard home, Glade gave Ernie a Model 94 Winchester, lever action, 30-30 rifle. It had an octagon barrel, pistol grip stock, checkered fore end, and engraving on the receiver. It was in excellent condition and Ernie was very appreciative of it.

That winter, Glade was telling his own Adirondack stories, of visits with Carlton King, Charlie Blanchard, Ernie Blanchard and Louisa and Wally Faulkner. He had stories of hunting up spruce-topped mountains and through vast hardwood forests, as well as hunting the spruce and alder-lined beaver meadows, some of them several hundred yards long.

In the 1920s, young Glade Keith was ready for the "Adirondacks"!
Photo donated by Jean Swartz.

Gene Perkins was an excellent, and very popular fishing guide around Blue Mt. Lake.
Photo donated by Charolette Waterman.

*Ernest C. Blanchard home on Blue Mt. Lake, 1925. Ernie's new home after
Maple Lodge. Blanchard family photo.*

*Early picture of Ernie Blanchard (center) with 2 clients at Blue Mt. Lake.
Blanchard family photo.*

Wally and Louisa Faulkner. Photo donated by Charolette Waterman.

Wally Faulkner's Inn, Blue Mt. Lake (early 1920s). Charolette Waterman photo.

Guests at Maple Lodge feeding a fawn. Blanchard family photo.

Before the new state road was built, this was the road between Blue Mt. Lake and Long Lake, early 1920s. Blanchard family photo.

GLADE'S 1927 HUNT

In 1927, Glade made plans for returning to Blue Mountain Lake. In talking with his cousin, Gene, Glade learned of a small shelter on the south side of Utowana Lake near the mouth of Loon Brook. It was just a tiny wooden structure that fishermen sometimes used to escape a summer storm or to get out of the weather for a short while. It wasn't very big, but it would provide some shelter for a week of hunting. In early November, Glade and an older friend of his, Joe Mickle, headed north in Glade's Model "T" Ford.

Joe was from East Hamilton, and worked at the local feed mill. A change of scene for a week or so and a chance for some venison had sounded real good to him when Glade made the offer. They were cruising along as good as could be expected on the narrow sandy road between Speculator and Indian Lake. It had been a good trip so far and they had seen a fair number of deer along the roads on the way up raising their expectations for a good hunt. Suddenly, the old Ford let out a loud, "KER-KLANG!" Joe said, "Jee-sus, does your car do that very often?" Glade said, "I guess it will when it wants to." They drove for a long ways farther and "CLANG," it sang out again. More noises followed at much closer intervals, some with very dramatic sound variations like DRA DA DA DA DUP, CLANG! By the time they got into Blue Mountain Lake, Glade had his left foot holding the car in low gear for the last few miles. He drove through town and along the side of the lake to where the swing bridge crossed the channel between Eagle and Blue Mountain Lake. The swing bridge was built to let the large steam boats pass through the canal on their way up and down the Eckford chain of lakes. They had a small shelter for the bridgetender to stay in when the weather was bad during his shift. There was no one around at this hour and since it was quite frosty out, they lay out their bedding in the bridgetender's shelter, and spent the night.

The next morning after breakfast, they each shouldered a load of supplies and headed down the southern shore line of Eagle Lake, heading for Utowana Lake and the mouth of Loon Brook. On the way down they spotted a small flock of ducks swimming nearby in the lake. They didn't know much about ducks, but they figured one might be pretty tasty for one of their evening meals. Glade shot one in the head and then waited for it to float into shore. After a lengthy hike they made it down to where Loon Brook flows into Utowana Lake and they found the shelter that Gene had described to Glade earlier in the year. Gene said it was small, and indeed it was. Glade described it as being about the size of a box one might ship a piano in. In fact, he later referred to this camp as being the "Piano Box Camp." One of its former occupants had painted a crude sign which hung over the front opening that read, "The Woolworth Building." At any rate, the rent was cheap enough and it would be "Home" for at least a week. They made one last trip out to the car for the balance of their supplies before calling it a day.

The next morning they spent a little more time fixing up the shelter and gathering a supply of firewood that would last them through the week. Joe had the duck that Glade shot on the first trip down, all cleaned and dressed and began boiling it at an early hour. Glade went out hunting for the first time in the Loon Brook area that afternoon, but Joe, who was much older than Glade, remained in camp boiling the duck and resting his muscles. Glade was back by nightfall without seeing a buck, and the duck, which had boiled all day, was just as tough by evening as it was when they started cooking it in the morning. Joe couldn't even stick his fork into it to get it out of the pot. They threw it off into the woods and would never shoot another Merganser duck again!

Joe and Glade hunted the next two days, and although they were seeing deer, they weren't seeing any with horns. Glade decided to hike into town the next day and see if he could hunt up some parts for his car and maybe use one of Wally Faulkner's garage stalls. He had determined that the rear end was shot on the Model "T" so after getting into town, he headed right for Frank Fuller's garage. He told Frank what he needed and at first it didn't seem like he was going to get any parts for a while, then Frank remembered that his father had put an old Ford out on the town dump the year before and that the rear end in it would probably fit. They went over to the dump and took out the rear end and Frank charged Glade $15.00 for it. It was kind of an unusual place to do business, but Glade didn't care, he was just darn glad to get the parts.

FRANK FULLER

Frank Fuller was originally from the Herkimer, New York, area. He had come into a sizable amount of money at an early age and was advised to invest it in a Herkimer bank. A short while later, the bank went "Belly Up" and Frank lost just about all of his money. After that, Frank would never trust any bank, so he never used them. He was a very energetic person and was always into anything he could make money at. During his lifetime, he was involved as a garage repair shop operator, car and truck dealer, trucker and fuel oil distributor, taxi operator, farmer, Bookie for horse wagers, cabin rentals, and Adirondack Deer Guide. Ernie Blanchard taught him how to trap beaver and make good money at it, so we'll add Beaver Trapper. Frank had a huge safe in the back of his garage and only he knew the combination to it. He had a cardboard box in the back of it, and whenever he had an extra twenty dollar bill, he would throw it into the box. He considered that box his retirement fund. Well, Frank died unexpectedly and a little bit short of his anticipated retirement date. When his widow tried to settle his affairs, she couldn't get into the safe, so she had to hire a locksmith to get into it. When the safe was finally opened, she found over $50,000 in cash in the cardboard box.

Glade got the use of one of Wally's garage stalls and put his car and the parts into it. He bumped into Ernie Blanchard before leaving town, so he got caught up on the news from him. When Ernie learned that he was hunting from the small camp on Utowana Lake, he invited Glade and Joe to join him for a couple of days at his Wilson Pond camp. Glade agreed and Ernie gave him a ride back as far as the Grassy Pond trail in a brand new, super six Buick. The next day, Joe and Glade hiked over to Wilson Pond and then located Ernie and the cabin. They hunted with Ernie for two and a half days, with Glade missing a nice buck. They had to leave on the third day because Ernie had a hunting party coming in for the last weekend of the season.

The season closed without Glade or Joe filling their tags. However, before packing up their camp and heading out to their car, they decided to give it one more try. On the morning after the season had closed, "Lady Luck" smiled on Glade and Joe. They were only out hunting for a little while when Glade dropped an eight-point and Joe got a four-point. It was a great way to finish up the deer hunt and have something to show for their effort when they got home even though they had lengthened the season a tad! They spent the remainder of the day getting their deer down to the lake shore and hung up.

Early the next morning, Glade hiked the four miles back into town and went to the Collin's Hotel, "The Hedges," and rented a row boat. He rowed the boat all the way back to Utowana Lake, and then they put in all their camping equipment and the two deer. When all was packed, they could plainly see that there was only room left for the oarsman. It was decided that Joe would row the boat back to the Collin's dock and Glade would hike back into town and wait for him there.

Glade waited at the dock until well after dark, and then hiked back through the darkened woods to Loon Brook. When he got near the Woolworth Building, he hollered for Joe and he got an answer. Joe said he started out into the lake after Glade left, but there was a good breeze blowing and he was afraid the waves would swamp the boat and all would be lost, so with a great deal of difficulty he turned the boat around and came back. The two men spent another night in the shelter and in the morning Joe said, "Do you want to try the same again today?" Glade returned with, "No, today I'll row the boat and you walk into town!" This time everything went smoothly.

GLADE'S 1928 HUNT

In the fall of 1928, Glade came up to hunt the area again. He would be hunting with his cousin, Gene Perkins, and three of his Brookfield area friends, Charlie Yale, Don Cross, and A. I. Alderman. They went to Doty's boat rentals and rented one of his cottages to hunt out of. They hunted the areas of Crystal Lake, Grassy Pond, Brady Pond and Wilson Pond. All the while they were hunting they could hear the road construction crews, blasting away the rock from the new State road right of way.

There was quite a bit of blasting that was done right in the village itself. In the process they managed to put holes in all the nearby roofs and a few windows. Each blast sequence had two parts. A first blast would put deep fractures into the rock. The second blast would hopefully loosen it all up. The rock would be covered by a heavy rope mat to keep rocks from flying. This usually worked good for the first blast, but the second blast would always find a few holes, and the rocks would be flying!

Glade's group put on a drive over near Crystal Lake and Glade, who was one of the drivers, shot a spike horn as it ran past him during the drive. It was the only buck they would take on the trip. Glade got way off beyond Wilson Pond by himself one day and hiked up onto the lower elevations of Blue Ridge. He was beginning to learn the country, and feel much more at ease within it. When the week's hunt was over, he was already making plans for next year's hunt. The new State highway would be open by then and traveling up by way of Old Forge and Raquette Lake should be much easier and shorter.

UNCLE JOHN

After the death of his wife, "Maude," in 1925, Ernie Blanchard could see that raising his three children at home and pursuing his outdoor career as a guide and trapper would be very difficult. He made arrangements for his children, Nancy, Mary and Ernest, to live with his brother, John, and his wife, Nancy, until he could get his life back in order. John and Nancy Blanchard ran a tourist home at Raquette Lake during the summertime. John was also a well known and highly respected boat builder. The entire winter was devoted to building or repairing boats. Young Ernest remembers his Uncle John well, and he learned a great deal about the boat building trade during his close to three-year stay with him. Uncle John could build a beautiful guide boat. There were guide boat races held every summer on Blue Mountain Lake, and every summer Uncle John would send up a new guide boat for Ernest's father to "try out." Ernie would win the race every year and eventually they discontinued the races because Ernie was winning them all.

Ernest really liked his Uncle John, but said, "He had the Blanchard temper." When things were going well, he was the nicest person in the world to be around, but when things started going bad, watch out, and get right out of his way!

THE NEW STATE HIGHWAY

In the early spring of 1928, Ernest was hiking through the woods around Raquette Lake in the vicinity of South Inlet. He came across a number of bright red steamers that were hung on the smaller trees. He followed them a short way and came upon two men who were placing them. He asked them what they were doing and they said they were going to build a road through there. Ernest thought they were kidding him until a couple of weeks later when they began cutting trees and blasting rocks.

It was a new state highway that was to connect Raquette Lake with Blue Mountain Lake. Before this road went in, all the freight and passengers heading for Blue Mountain would have to cross Raquette Lake by steamer and go up the Marion River as far as navigable, to the Marion River Railroad. The Railroad, which began service in 1900, would haul passengers and freight its whole 3/4-mile length to the head of the Eckford Chain of lakes. There, they would transfer onto another steamer that would take them into Blue Mountain Lake village. The entire trip from Raquette to Blue would take just over two hours, barring complications.

In the winter months, when the lakes and forests were frozen hard, there was a winter haul road connecting the two villages. In ran west from Blue Mountain and through the woods just south of the Eckford Chain and Marion River. It came out on Raquette Lake at Silver Beach. Silver Beach is just north of the golden sands of Golden Beach campground on Raquette Lake. From Silver Beach, the haul road would continue on across the lake ice to Raquette Lake village. In the winter when the road got packed hard, people would occasionally drive their Model "T's" over its entire length with no problem at all.

The new state road from Blue Mountain to Long Lake was also surveyed in 1928. Ernie's white frame house was located just below the stone mill dam and right in the middle of the new road right of way. Ernie had been talking to an insurance man in an effort to get his house insured just before the surveyors began their work. His policy hadn't been written when Mother Nature dealt Ernie a losing hand. Lightening struck the building and it burned to the ground. He never got a nickel for the building, only the property it was built upon.

GROWING UP WITH A FAMOUS GUIDE

In 1928, Ernie married Lavina Gates of Blue Mountain Lake. Lavina provided a warm and loving environment for the Blanchard children, and in the coming years she would bear six more children for Ernie. They are Ann, Evelyn, Albert, Paul, Irene, and Ron.

Ernest was the oldest boy in the family, born of Ernie's first marriage with Maude. He grew up with his eyes wide open, and his hands on everything! Being the oldest boy in a large family, he was soon handed a full share of chores and responsibilities. He learned to guide from the "best," and he learned to build and repair boats from the "best." He has mastered many hands-on skills along life's path. He is a skilled machinist, carpenter, plumber, electrician, mason, equipment operator, and lately, he builds high quality golf clubs.

Ernest is well into his 70's now, and is in great physical shape. He and his wife Carol are avid golfers, and very active members of their community. Carol is tax collector for the town of Indian Lake and also works part time at the Cedar River Golf Club. Ernest is always busy at something. In his spare time, he is building a 28-foot sailboat in his back yard, complete with auxiliary 10 hp inboard motor. Launch date is in spring of '98!

SIDE TRACKED

Ernest's boyhood days weren't always easy. The children were expected to do whatever they could to help out. One time, Ernie had a party to guide for lake trout, and he needed some of the large golden shiners that could be found in one of the local streams. On this day, he told Ernest to take the boat and go over to a certain inlet brook on Blue Mountain Lake, and catch a quantity of these shiners, and be back as soon as possible.

Ernest went right over and began fishing all the holes with a small hook that was baited with a tiny piece of worm. Ernest really loved his fishing, and he began to get some action right away. However, instead of catching the golden shiners that his father was in need of, he began catching nice fat brook trout! Nobody had fished that brook in quite a long time because they had considered it all fished out. Ernest had a ball catching trout during the next two hours, and returned with a fine mess of brook trout and no shiners. Old Ernie was a little "put out" when he didn't get his shiners and had waited half a day for them to come, but young Ernest will never forget the two-hour session of fishing that inlet brook!

When Ernest was attending school, he would always look forward to the spring warm-up, when the fishing started to get good. Quite often, on Friday afternoons, when school got out, he would head for Salmon Pond, and do some trout fishing. Ernest would have everything packed and ready to go as soon as he got home. He would ride his bike north on Route 30, and when he got as close as the road would bring him, he would hide his bike off the road, and then hike in to the pond.

At Salmon Pond, he used to catch those big, deep-bodied Brookies. They were beautiful fish, and they tasted just as good as they looked! If the weather turned stormy, Maynard Forton always had an army tent set up by the pond. Those were memorable trips!

OLD ERNIE
COULD SHOOT!

Ernie was an excellent rifleman and loved to shoot. Ernest can remember throwing bottles into the air for his father to shoot with a 22 rifle. Ernie would break the bottle with his first shot and then break the next biggest piece on the way down with his second shot, and he would do it almost every time.

Out behind his home on Blue Mountain, he had a white target on a dirt bank that was about 14 inches around and 500 or more yards away. He used to hit it regularly, just to stay in shape. Ernie hunted with a lot of different rifles over the years, but the one he carried the most was a Model 54 Winchester, in 30-06 cal.

He had an old Marlin 32-20 cal. that he carried for a while, just to see if he could kill a deer with it. It wasn't much of a deer cartridge since the standard load was a 115 gr. bullet with a muzzle velocity of 1280 f.p.s. A high-velocity load would bring the muzzle velocity up to around 1600 f.p.s. — still not very impressive. When Ernie finally put it back on the rack and went back to his 30-06, he had taken ten deer and one bear with it.

ERNIE'S FRIEND MOSSY

Ernest remembers his father leaving for New York City one day with the trunk of his Buick loaded with furs. When he returned, his trunk was loaded with World War I Mausers. He had nine or ten of them sporterized and kept one of them for himself. He took one of the sporterized Mausers and gave it to his best friend, Fred "Mossy" Maxim. Mossy was originally a mason by trade, but worked his way into full-time guiding and trapping. Eventually, he became "house guide" for some of the "Great Camps" just east of Raquette Lake. He worked at Camp Unca's for J.P. Morgan, at first, and then for ex-Governor Woodruff at Kill-Kare, and still later, for F.P. Garvan at Kill-Kare. Camp Sagamore, which at this time was owned by the Vanderbuilts, also employed Mossy from time to time. All three of these properties are located just off the western limits of Blue Ridge.

Mossy also ran extensive trap lines on and around these wilderness retreats. Two of his trap line cabins were located near the western end of Blue Ridge. His "Pine Stump" camp was on Squirrel Top Mountain and Silver Run Camp was in the upper reaches of Lost Brook. Mossy and Ernie had a lot in common and whenever conditions were right, they would get together to drink, visit, or hunt. When F.P. Garvin owned Kill-Kare, he would hold a Bazaar almost every year, and he would invite many of his well-to-do friends up to participate. Old Mossy would sell most of his fur at these affairs for excellent prices. He would also sell a lot of Ernie's fur for the same prices.

SHOT BY HIS BEST FRIEND?

One winter Ernie and Mossy were snowshoeing the deep woods, looking for active beaver colonies. For the evening, they decided to stay at Mossy's Silver Run cabin. Sometime during Mossy's absence, a spruce stub had fallen against the cabin wall and it had opened up a good-sized hole in the bark covering, under the gable end. The cabin itself was pretty rough and crude, but it would be comfortable enough for a couple of old woodsmen, such as themselves.

The spruce stub was left in place that evening, providing some cool ventilation for their sleeping area, which was up over the living area. There wasn't a lot of room under the rafters and pearling beam. To make matters worse, when Mossy built the cabin, he didn't take pains to trim the spruce poles flush, so there were quite a number of hard limb stubs sticking a short way out of the rafter poles. One had to be careful about climbing in and out of the cramped sleeping quarters. The Porky Pines had been doing a lot of chewing on all the line cabins that year, so Ernie kept his 30-06 handy in case he heard one working that evening.

The evening turned out to be one of those brilliant, full-moon nights and you could see pretty darn good outside without a light. When the two tired woodsmen turned in that evening, it wasn't long before old Mossy was "sawing wood." The moonlight was streaming in through the hole above the spruce stub, giving some illumination to their quarters. Ernie had been rethinking the day's events and pondering some commitments he had to fill later in the week, when he became vaguely aware of a scratching noise and some movement from the spruce stub.

He rolled on his belly and crawled far enough forward to look down the length of the spruce stub. In the bright moonlight he could make out the forms of three porcupines climbing up the spruce stub toward the hole Ernie was looking out of. Ernie reached back and grabbed his "06," thinking, "if I shoot the rear one first, I should have time to get the other two as well."

When the first shot shattered the stillness of the night, old Mossy sat right up in bed, smacking his forehead on one of those hard spruce stubs. Ernie immediately realized what had happened, and cried out, "Oh, my God!" Mossy felt his forehead with his hand and could feel warm blood streaming down his face. He cried out, "Ernie, you shot your best friend! What the hell did you do that for?"

DON'T LOSE YOUR TEMPER!

On another occasion, Mossy was guiding for the Vanderbuilts over at Sagamore Lodge. He was asked to take young Anne Vanderbuilt out and try to get her a shot at a buck. Now Mossy was a rather coarse person, short on patience, and well-known for cutting loose a string of four letter adjectives that were far from being socially acceptable. He was warned before hand to be careful, patient, and on his best behavior, because we don't want to embarrass Anne.

Mossy got out his rifle and picked up Anne with her rifle, and the two of them headed off into the woods together. They would walk along slowly and quietly, stopping often to search the woods ahead for deer. Mossy was in the lead, and after a while of this, he spotted a deer in the distance, head down, feeding, and broadside. A closer inspection proved it to be a nice buck and in its present position, it would be easy to hit it with a killing shot.

Mossy, not wanting to spook the buck, raised his arm and pointed at the buck. Anne was looking, but couldn't see the buck. She said softly, "I can't see it Mossy." Mossy was a little hard of hearing and returned with, "What d'you say Anne?" Anne a little louder, "I can't see it, Mossy." Mossy kept pointing at the buck and Anne realized that he wasn't hearing her, so she repeated out loud, "I can't see it, Mossy!" With that, the buck spotted the two hunters, turned and started heading away. Anne spotted the movement, eyed the buck, and brought her rifle up for a shot, excitedly asking, "Mossy, where do I shoot him?" Old Mossy, all frustrated now with her talking out loud and losing a good opportunity for an easy kill, hollers out sarcastically, "Shoot him in the ass, Anne, it's the only shot you've got now!"

THE MASTERPIECE

Mossy was never a person that would acknowledge anyone's social rank or gift of talent. On one occasion a group of high-ranking politicians were visiting Camp Kill-Kare. The gathering also included a well-known artist (thought to be McClellan Barclay). Old Mossy was cooking eggs, bacon, trout and coffee on the stove. It was a classic Adirondack scene of a weathered guide in rustic surroundings, putting out the morning meal. The artist was inspired to paint a picture of it, which he did, and the work was a real masterpiece. It hung for a while in one of the big New York City art galleries. One of the regular visitors took a picture of it and brought it up to show Mossy. When Mossy picked up the picture, he looked at it briefly, and then tossed it down on the table. "Oh, yes," he says, "I remember it. Those eggs was cold storage, ya know."

"THE OLD RED HORSE"

When the main lodge at Camp Kill-Kare burned to the ground in 1915, history recorded it as a lightning strike or accidental fire. However, in later years, another story surfaced concerning the fire, that was told by the locals. The following account was told to Ernie, by Mossy, and then to Ernest by his father.

When F.P. Garvan took over Camp Kill-Kare in 1914, Mossy Maxim was the head guide. Mossy had been on the property for years and knew all the buildings and every inch of the property. Garvan did a lot of entertaining, and he thought the main lodge was starting to show its age. He had lots of money to rebuild or improve with, but he couldn't see passing up an opportunity to collect come insurance money. He talked to Mossy and arranged to have the main lodge burned down as if it were an accidental fire. Mossy did, and no one ever caught on to what had happened. A grand new lodge was built in its place.

Mossy and Garvan didn't always hit it off real good though. Garvan would sometimes hunt out of Mossy's woodland camps, but Mossy would never show him any respect that a man of his money and power could command. Furthermore, Mossy was getting on in years, and Garvan thought some younger blood might be good for the place.

Garvan made up his mind to retire Mossy, and one day, when it was just the two of them at one of Mossy's camps, he tried. "Moss," he said, "I'm thinking of letting you go. We've got a new camp now, and I'm going to be getting all new blood." "Oh, you're not thinking about letting Old Moss go, are ya? You're not going to fire me!" "Well," Garvan said, "We're going to terminate you, but we're going to give you a nice going away present!" "Well," Moss says, "as far as I'm concerned, presents are for Christmas time, and if you let Old Moss go, 'The Old Red Horse' (meaning another building fire) is liable to come over the mountain again!" Garvan didn't dare fire him, because he was afraid he would burn the new lodge down. Mossy spent his remaining years there. Several years later, Mossy got a bad infection on one of his feet due to a snowshoe harness chaff. It eventually led to his death in 1930.

MARY'S BUCK

After Ernie's home had burned down on Blue Mountain due to the lightning strike, he had a new home built for him a few years later that was just below the original home site. He had hired a contractor from Glens Falls to build it for him. One of the carpenters that had worked on the house had developed a close relationship with Ernie, and also his three children, Nancy, Mary, and Ernest. Mary, in particular, was especially fond of visiting with him and was sad to see him leave when the house was completed.

The following November, twelve-year-old Mary awoke early one morning to the smell of fresh coffee and the sound of men talking downstairs in the kitchen. She immediately recognized one of the voices. It belonged to the carpenter she had enjoyed visiting with so much the previous summer. She got dressed right away and hurried downstairs to say hello and see his friendly face again. They were both happy to see each other again, but at the end of a very short visit, breakfast was over and it was time to go deer hunting. Seeing this, Mary cried out, "Oh, I wish I could go hunting today too!" The carpenter looked at Ernie and said, "Well, why don't you take her?" Ernie replied, "If it's alright with you, she can come along!" Mary raced back upstairs and put her woolen pants and shirt on and got her rubber packs also.

All the Blanchard children learned gun safety and how to shoot at an early age so Mary would do alright in the woods. Ernie, meanwhile, was looking over the gun rack and wondering if he had a weapon suitable for Mary. He finally selected a little 20-gauge shotgun and put it by the doorway. He had no slugs for it though, so he took three shots shells and emptied, just the shot, into a small bowl. He then softened up a small amount of hand soap and worked it into the shot. Then he reloaded the soaped shot into the shells and folded the end back over the shot. Ernie reasoned that the "soaped shot" would solidify in the cold mountain air and fly as a single projectile, should his daughter get a shot. Now that Mary was ready, they all piled into the car and headed out to their first hunting location.

Mary was to help with driving the deer. They hunted all morning and into the afternoon, trying one location after another, and all the while the carpenter would be on watch. The carpenter might have been tiring of the wait and watch routine when he suggested that Ernie put Mary on watch and he would drive for a change. Ernie agreed, so he put Mary on a watch and the men left.

About 20 minutes later, she could faintly hear the drivers start her way. They would occasionally bark like a dog so she could mark their progress. A few minutes later she heard a noise, and in the distance, she could see this nice, beautiful buck walking her way. Mary turned slightly and raised the shotgun, keeping the bead on the animal's chest. She waited until the buck was only 30 yards away and then she shot. The buck stumbled and then ran off a short distance and fell down dead. The load of soaped shot had struck the deer right in the center of its chest, destroying the buck's heart.

When Ernie and the carpenter showed up and learned what had happened, they just couldn't believe it! Ernie was jumping up and down and laughing so hard. Mary had never seen her father quite so happy before this. Mary was as proud as a peacock and it would forever be her most memorable hunt. The buck sported a nice 7-point rack and the next morning Mary posed for pictures in her school clothes beside the buck before heading off to school. It was the carpenter's hunt though, and the rules were that he keeps the buck, so shortly afterwards, he headed for Glens Falls with his buck.

Ernie lost the new house to the bank during the depression years. Ernest didn't always know what to think about his father's activities. His father had always made home brew for his own personal use at home. However, during Prohibition and the depression years, his father ran a "Speak Easy" at their home to help provide money during those times. Ernie would make home brew to sell and also order grain alcohol. He would get the alcohol from a druggist down near Hastings, on the Hudson. He would color it with burnt sugar and then sell it by the tumbler. Ernest was just a kid when all this was going on, and he had the idea that his Dad was the only one who was doing it. When he got older and began to circulate, he found out that an awful lot of other people were doing the same thing!

THE BEGINNING OF A TRADITION

In the fall of 1929, Glade and his neighbor, Gary Gray, drove up along the Fulton Chain of lakes, and then on to Raquette Lake. At Raquette Lake they continued on towards Blue Mountain over the brand new State road. They parked their car just a few hundred yards west of where Loon Brook flows under State Route 28. An old logging road came out to the highway there, and it provided easy access to an old lumber camp clearing on Loon Brook that was only one quarter of a mile south of the State road.

They pitched their tent in the lumber camp clearing. At that time you could plainly see where three or four of the old buildings stood. The camp cook house was still partially up and had most of its roof on. There was a considerable amount of equipment left laying around, some broken and some just abandoned.

Ernie Blanchard told Glade that there were eight separate logging camps located on our side of Blue Ridge, and he had been to every one of them. Signs of the early logging operations were very much in evidence at this time. The old logging roads were still in pretty good shape, including those sections that had been corduroyed through the wet areas. There were also some good-sized piles of logs laying at loading areas back in the woods, that for reasons unknown, were never hauled out to market. These log piles could still be found as late as the mid-1960's.

A beautiful set of iron snow plows remain far back in the unbroken woodland. They are much too heavy to be brought out and I personally hope that they never will be brought out. For those who are adventurous and lucky enough to find them, they will be a fine monument to the memory of the early loggers. Most of Township 34 became part of the Forest Preserve in 1906.

Glade and Gary hunted this region for a week and when it was over with, they had two Loon Brook bucks, riding on the car fenders for the trip home. Glade got a big 10-pointer, and Gary a fat spike horn.

During the 1929 trip, Glade realized just how much he enjoyed hunting this country. He was going to come up and hunt it every fall that he was able to. When he got home with his buck, he convinced his brother, Parks, and his friend, Fred Hodges, to invest some money with him into a good wall tent, wood stove and lamp, so they could hunt the area every fall with their own outfit. The annual fall hunt in the Blue Ridge area for Glade would last for close to 70 years!

Glade and his brother worked the farm as a partnership. When the fall hunting season rolled around, only one of them could be away from the milk herd at one time. Parks and his hunting friends would go up in the early part of the hunting season, set up the tent and hunt out of it for a week or so. Later in the season, Glade would go up with his hunting friends and hunt for a week or so, and then bring back the camping outfit. Glade always preferred the second week in November for his hunt and he commonly referred to it as "buck week." There were very few "buck weeks" where Glade didn't get a buck! The boys were very generous with the use of their tent and they wouldn't hesitate to let their friends use it in their absence, provided they were responsible people.

When the new outfit was set up at the lumber camp clearing in 1930, there were three other parties camped there also. Ray Burke, from Raquette Lake, was the game protector at that time. They had only been camped there for a short while when Ray came in and caught one of the parties from Oneonta with an illegal deer and an illegally taken mink. He hauled them all off to court where the judge fined them and then ordered them out of the woods for five years!

Glade didn't know why, but somehow, Burke thought Glade's outfit and the Oneonta party were somehow connected. Glade and his friends would get back from hunting just before dark and there, in their own tent, would be Ray Burke waiting to see if they brought in anything illegal. Glade and his party thought it was all very uncalled for. For the next three years he was around them pretty regular, but he never found anything illegal.

LESTER TURNER

Lester Turner was born at Blue Mountain Lake, just after the turn of the century in 1905. He was the oldest son of Art and Bessie Turner who had seven children in all. They were Elsie, Lester, Tom, Herb, Florence, Julia, and Maude. Art was a caretaker and a carpenter in the area and later moved his residence to North Creek. Lester was raised in the Blue Mountain Lake area and worked his late teens, twenties, and early thirties there in a variety of jobs. He spent a good deal of this time working for Ernie Blanchard, and spent a couple of summers living behind the Blanchard home in a small cabin. He shared the cabin with Ernest, Ernie's oldest son.

Lester was physically very powerful and a good man in the woods. Ernest remembers his Dad talking about Lester's strength. There was an old woods road heading into the area of Cascade Pond, from the east end of Lake Durrant. It began by an old cabin that was located where the campsite is now. For a while Matt Johnson lived in this cabin, and he owned a team of horses with a wagon. He used to haul in supplies to some of Ernie's camps that were located near Cascade and Brady Ponds. One fall, Les, Matt, and Ernie were cutting out a considerable number of new windfalls that had come down across the road. Ernie said they would cut down through some darn good big ones, and when the cut was through, Les would grab hold of them and then toss them aside, "Like they was nothing!"

MOLLY

Les had his own horse, "Molly," that he used for skidding firewood, hauling supplies, and when he was available, for bringing deer out of the woods. He used to keep it at his Uncle Walt and Aunt Alice's house up on Blue Mountain. Molly was a good horse, but she had one bad fault. She hated to cross the mountain streams with their slippery rock-covered bottoms.

In the fall of 1930, Parks Keith was camped in the first lumber camp clearing on Loon Brook, along with Fred Hodges, and Emmit and Gene Perkins. There were two other tents pitched in the clearing as well. Early in the evening Les came down the trail with a lantern in one hand and leading Molly with the other. He was heading into a cabin that he and his Uncle Walt had built several years ago. It was located fairly high on Blue Ridge's northern slope. Molly had a load of supplies on and Les was intending to head in for a few days of hunting.

The crossing at the end of the meadow was one that "Old Molly" particularly hated, since it had more than its share of the slippery round stones on its bottom. Les gave her the usual amount of coaxing and encouragement and finally the old horse began moving out into the brook, carefully feeling for each hoof-hold on the bottom. About half way across, Molly slipped in the knee-deep water and went down hard. He tried to get her up right away but Molly refused to move. He worked with her for the next half hour and still she wouldn't get up.

Les then went to all three of the tents in the clearing to see if he could get some help. Parks Keith was the only one to come out though. Parks was a good man with horses. The two men tried everything they knew and still it was a futile effort. They stayed with her all night and by morning things didn't look good for Molly. Several of the hunters came out of their tents and they tried to physically drag her to shore, but she was just too heavy. Finally, Les asked Fred Hodges to end it all for Molly, which he did. It was quite sad and ironic that "Old Molly" died a victim of the very rocks she had feared all her life. Her old bones were quite visible for the next several years around the rocks at the Loon Brook crossing.

THE ILLEGAL CABINS

In the winter of 1930, during the Christmas vacation from school, three young boys from Raquette Lake decided to take an overnight snowshoe hike into Bear Pond and spend the night at Ernie Blanchard's cabin. The boys were the children of Orrin and Hazel Lanphear and their home was on Poplar Point. The boys were Edgar, Stanley, and Jerry Lanphear and their ages were 17, 14, and 12 respectively. They had all been into the pond at various times during the spring and summer months so they knew the trail in well. They had permission from their parents to stay one evening, but were to be home by dark on the following day. They started off snowshoeing over the frozen lake for a little over a mile and then entered the woods in the vicinity of Golden Beach. It was about two and a half miles up through the woods to the Bear Pond cabin. Snowshoeing conditions were good and it didn't take the boys a great deal of time to get in. They got a fire going to take the frost out of the walls, and began gathering in some extra firewood.

These boys had been taught to respect other people's property. They had brought in their own food and would leave the cabin neat and with as much firewood as when they arrived. They also knew that it was an "illegal cabin," one of many that existed during that time frame of the park's history.

That evening at the cabin, the boys talked about other "illegal cabins" that they had either been to or heard about. Edgar and his brother, Stanley, had stumbled onto one last summer while fishing Bear Brook along the foot of Blue Ridge. They had found some skid marks on the ground where a horse had dragged a small log or good-sized pole up the slope of the ridge. They had followed the skid trail out of curiosity and well up the slope; they came onto a real nice cabin. The boys decided that if the weather held good, they would snowshoe off along the foot of Blue Ridge and try to find that cabin tomorrow.

In the morning, with the weather looking good, the three boys set out bush whacking since there was no trail from there to the ridge. It was a good four mile-plus hike to where the boys found some faint blaze marks showing the way up the ridge to the cabin. It seemed like a lot longer hike up the ridge on snowshoes than it had been on the ground from the summer before, but eventually they made it.

The cabin was in excellent condition and was very comfortable when the cast iron "General Scott" wood stove was fired up. Edgar and Stanley wanted to spend the night, but they had told their parents that they would be home by dark. Twelve-year-old Jerry volunteered to return home alone and tell them that Edgar and Stanley would head for home early the next morning. Young Jerry had already put in over four miles of snowshoeing and now he headed off on the eight-mile trip back to Raquette Lake where home was. He snowshoed into the front yard just after dark, ending a full day on the "webbs."

Meanwhile, back at the cabin, his two brothers were having another adventure. Just before dark, Edgar was looking down the ridge from the cabin window when he spotted the form of a large man heading up the ridge towards the cabin. Almost no one goes into these camps during the dead of winter! The boys were thinking of all the bad things that might happen to them if the owner was mad and had a real bad temper! They were reaching a high point of nervous anxiety when the door opened and in walked big Les Turner.

As soon as Les began talking, they knew they had nothing to fear from him. "How are you boys doing? I'm sure glad you got the fire going!" They introduced themselves and visited for a while. Then Les said, "I'll bet you boys are hungry, too!" And with that he got up and went outside to a nearby tree. It had a hollow cavity in it that opened up just above the level of his head. He reached down into it and pulled out a big chunk of frozen venison. The boys had only a few mouthfuls of food left in their packs that they were saving for breakfast. A short while later, they sat down to a big supper of venison steak and pancakes, much to their delight!

The boys turned in early after supper. The big meal and all the outdoor activity had made them very sleepy. Edgar woke up three or four times during the night, and every time he awoke, Les would be sitting by the stove with the boys' Cocker Spaniel on his lap and a hot cup of tea nearby. In the morning after breakfast, they reassured Les that they wouldn't tell anyone of the location of his cabin. Then it was back on the trail out and home. When they got back, they told their parents that they had never been treated so good in all their lives!

It's hard to tell what Les may have been thinking about that evening by the stove with the dog on his lap. Maybe he was worried that his cabin would be visited often and then found and burned by the rangers. Or maybe he was thinking of a time when he would have his own dog on his lap and his own kids in the bunks!

WILD MAN
OF THE ADIRONDACKS

It was early March in 1932. Les Turner and Ernie Blanchard were heading out of the winter woods, east of Blue Mountain, after running a long line of beaver traps. Les was quite a lot younger than Ernie, so he was in the lead when he came upon a huge set of tracks. Les couldn't get over the size of the tracks, and before he examined them closely, he said, "They must be bear tracks." Ernie fired right back, "Hell no—bear tracks toe in, these toe out!" They both studied the tracks, but there was no real definition to them. They had no guess as to what it might be. Ernie said, "Let's head for home, we've had a long day."

They had only traveled a short distance when they smelled the smoke of a near-by fire. The big tracks were still in sight so they followed them in the direction of the smoke. Suddenly, a big guy jumped out from some spruce cover. He was a Negro man with huge foot coverings on and he had a double-barreled shotgun pointing right at Ernie's chest. He shouted something like, "I don't mind the Americans, but God damn the Canadians! Now beat it out of here. Get the hell away from me!" Well, when you've got a shotgun pointed right at your chest by some big guy that is acting like he'd had a really bad day, you don't want to irritate him further! Old Ernie and Les turned their snowshoes around and headed for home.

The incident really shook up both men, but by the time they got back out to the road, Ernie had thought things over and asked Les not to report it. Ernie had a lot of equipment stashed around the woodlands, not to mention a few illegal cabins. The last thing he wanted was a large number of men searching through his hunting and trapping country for this "wild man." Les was worried that this might not be the end of it, and maybe someone would get hurt before it was all over with. That evening, Les drove into Long Lake and reported it to the State Police.

THE POSSE

A posse was formed with Les and Ernie being deputized. They would help track down the man for threatening with a shotgun. The posse was led by Lieutenant McCann from Troop "R" in Malone. It had four State Troopers, two forest rangers, and the trackers, Les and Ernie.

The search started in Hamilton County, just east of Blue Mountain and north of Route 30. It was in the fourth day of the search that they finally caught up with the "wild man." The tracks led them to a deserted logging camp that was northeast of Dunn Brook, and just into Essex County. He had fixed up what was left of the horse grainery building for a shelter, and that's where they found him.

Lt. McCann hollered in to the man to come out peaceably and give himself up. He was answered by a blast from the Negro's gun. The posse returned fire and the Negro was slightly wounded in the leg. He escaped out through a rear window. The posse gave chase and finally surrounded the man. He was again ordered to surrender peaceably and in reply he began firing at the posse. Les was struck in the ass by one of the projectiles, but fortunately it hit him in his wallet, which had a silver dollar in it. This prevented him from getting a serious wound. Ernie, who hadn't brought a rifle along on the search said, "You could hear the loads bounce off the near trees and whistle by you."

After Les got hit, they opened up on him again and this time he fell dead. Les was acknowledged for having delivered the killing shot. When they closed in to have a look at the strange hermit, they found a large Negro man around 25 years of age. They could only guess how long he had been living in the woods, but by the tattered condition of his clothing and the shaggy hair and beard, it must have been quite a long time.

It was assumed that he had been living almost entirely on venison. He wore no shoes and on his feet were some old woolen socks. Over these, he had wrapped pieces of an old woolen sweater, and over this he had pieces of untanned deer hide. In this manner, his feet appeared huge, and amazingly he was able to travel quite fast over the deep snow.

When they looked over his double barrel shotgun, they got another surprise. It was a 20-gauge, but he had no 20-gauge shells in it. He had been using modified 303 British rifle shells in it. He had wrapped each shell so that it could be forced into the chamber with the primer centered for the shotgun firing pin. He had removed the bullets from some of the shells and then cut and bent the brass so that the wadding and then nail heads and various projectiles could be used. It couldn't have been very effective, but that's all he had! When Ernie saw the shells, he suspected that they may have come from his Bear Pond cabin. He used to keep a couple of tins of 303 ammo stored in there for a spare rifle that he would bring in during deer season. Last summer, he noticed that some were missing, and last fall, he saw that they were almost all gone.

They couldn't bring the body out that day since they would need a toboggan to transport him over the deep snow. Les helped in bringing the body out of the woods. He didn't care much for being around any dead body, and much less for a man that he had killed. On one of the downhill grades, while bringing the body out, the toboggan suddenly shot forward, striking Les in the calves and knocking him down on top of the corpse. All Les could think of was, "Now he's got me!" He couldn't get off that corpse fast enough, and everyone had a good laugh at his expense.

They never were able to identify the man after the investigation was over with. Acting the way he did, it was a good guess he was probably running from the law, but we'll never know for sure. It must have been a very hard existence for the hermit, no matter what the reason for his exile.

A TIME TO SETTLE DOWN

By the mid 1930's, Les had made some major changes in his life. He had met and married the woman of his dreams, Charlotte Kegle, and they made their residence in the Schenectady area. He got a full-time position with American Locomotive, also in Schenectady, and in 1936, he became the proud father of a son, James Turner.

The regimentation of a permanent job didn't keep Les out of the woods permanently though. He was up almost every weekend he could get away. In 1942 during the hunting season, he brought his wife and son into his cabin up on Blue Ridge for a weekend hunt. Jim can remember warming himself by the big "General Scott" wood stove, and that his dad got a buck.

The snow was deep enough so that the only place six year-old Jim could walk was in the deer's skid trail. It was after this hunt that the cabin was found and destroyed by the State. Les turned to using a large wall tent and a wood stove for his annual fall hunts at the ridge. He used several different campsites over the years. He camped at Potter Pond for a number of years, and then along the foot of Blue Ridge in the area of Loon Brook. He took some really fine bucks while hunting out of these camps every fall.

Lester's son, James, began hunting the ridge at an early age. Jim's cousin, Ed Edwards, lived with the Turners for a while, and Ed was more like a brother to Jim than a cousin. They both started hunting the Blue Ridge area at about the same time. Ed was about eight years older than Jim was, and Jim was under the legal age for hunting when he started, so they were always very careful when they approached the road and their car. Les, Jim, and Ed used to hunt together regularly.

Jim remembers one hunt with his father when he was still quite young. Les would get out of work from American Locomotive at midnight, and shortly after he got home, they would leave on the two-and-a-half-hour ride to the trail head at Loon Brook. Then they would make the three-mile hike into the tent with their flashlights. After a big breakfast, they would be heading off into the woods just before dawn. Les was always a hard hunter. He would be out of the tent before dawn and wouldn't get back until after dark.

On this Saturday, they hunted all day in a heavy snow, and it was still coming down just as hard when they returned to the tent at dark. After supper, Les asked Jim if he wanted to stay the night at the tent, or head out to grandma's house in North Creek. Jim said, "Grandma's," so after closing up the tent, the two of them headed off into the snow-laden woods.

The snow was deep and it clung to the tree limbs, bending them over so they obstructed both view and progress. Les lost the trail and had to resort to using his compass, something he rarely had to do. It took over three hours to make their way out to the road and back to where the car was parked. The car was buried behind a huge snow-plow berm. It was early in the morning on Sunday when they finally pulled into the driveway at grandma's house in North Creek!

A CHANGE OF HEART

Jim went into the service in the mid '50s, and after his tour was over, he went back to the ridge for a hunt. During the hunt, he got a chance for a buck, and bringing his rifle up, he aligned his sights for the shot. He never did shoot. Somewhere along life's path, he had lost his enthusiasm for the hunt. He never again returned to the "Ridge" to hunt, and he never told his father why.

Les retired from American Locomotive after 30 years of service. He worked at the Albany County Airport for supplemental income after that. During retirement, Les would spend most of the deer season back in the "Ridge Country" hunting out of the tent. He would always come out for Election Day though. Most of the time, he would be alone between the weekends.

A REAL DREAM

One evening while he was alone, Les was dozing off on his bed after supper before doing up the dishes and banking the fire for the night. He had put in a long day in the woods and sleep came easy. He began to dream, and he dreamed that somehow he was caught up in a building fire. He could hear the roar and crackle of the flames, but above that, he could hear the rattle and clatter of dishes and silverware. He began to rise from the subconscious state of sleep and became aware that he was only dreaming. However, he could still hear plates and silverware rattling around. He jerked himself up into the sitting position, and there on the table at the end of his bunk was a black bear licking up the remains of his evening meal! Their eyes met simultaneously and Les let out one hell of a yell and reached for his rifle. The bear leaped off the table, tore a hole in the wall of the tent, and was gone in a flash!

Les hunted right up into his eighties. After his father became too hold to hunt, Jim flew up over the Blue Mountain Lake and Blue Ridge area with his light airplane. He took video pictures of the Ridge, the Loon Brook drainage, Potter, Wilson, and Cascade Ponds. When he got home, he brought the video over for his father to see. While watching it, the beautiful memories of a lifetime must have come flooding back to him. Les broke down and cried. It was the first time Jim had ever seen his father cry. Old Les died on January 1, 1989.

VERNE TURNER

Verne Turner was born at Blue Mountain Lake in 1924. His father and mother were Walter and Alice Turner. He was the youngest of three children and the only boy in the family. His sisters were Alice and Nina. Walt and Lester's father, Art, were brothers, and Walt was also a carpenter by trade. He worked for Hemlock Hall and also did quite a bit of work for a Mr. Storrs. He also built and repaired guide boats.

In 1905, Walt and Alice built their own home on Blue Mountain, and Alice worked right alongside her husband in the building of it, as well as helped shingle the roof! It was a good, solid, comfortable home, and in the coming years they would begin to raise their children under its roof. Alice was a woman who loved to hunt. Every fall, Walt and Alice would put a camping outfit into their guide boat and then row down the Eckford Chain into Utowanna Lake. They would set a camp and then hunt the Loon and Bear Brook drainages. In the early 1920's, Walt and young Lester built a cabin up on the side of Blue Ridge above Bear Brook. It was one of those "illegal cabins," and they hoped to use it primarily in the fall for many a hunting season!

In 1930, disaster struck the Turner family when Walt was stricken with cancer. It was a heart-breaking convalescence for the whole family. Les stayed at his uncle's home in order to help out in any way he could, until Walt died in 1931. Alice and her children were to live through some hard times. Alice would work whenever she could, and quite often it would be at Faulkner's Inn. She also did washing and ironing for extra money. The children would pick berries in season and Alice would sell pies and homemade bread in town. The family kept a good-sized garden, and Alice would can whatever she could to help them through the winter months. They heated their home with wood, and many a day Alice and her three children would head into the woods to cut wood for the coming winter. Verne still has the old buck saw as a reminder of some very tough times.

MEAT FOR THE POT

Alice had her own 32 Winchester and she was a darn good shot. She also kept a salt lick out behind her house for the purpose of attracting deer. On one occasion in late spring, they were all out of meat, and there was little money to procure it with the legal way. Les was staying with them at the time, and he knew what the situation was. When the morning was still quite young, he told Alice, "I'm going to take a walk with my rifle and see if I can't get some meat to go with our vegetables tonight." Shortly afterwards, he disappeared into the woods out behind their home.

About an hour later, Alice spotted a fat doe feeding under the apple tree by her barn. She grabbed her rifle and walked out on the front porch where she could get a shot at it. Verne was right beside her. She brought the rifle up to make the shot and as she did, the school bus was coming up the hill and almost in view. Verne whispered, "Don't shoot, ma, the school bus is coming!" Alice told him, "It's now or never," then her rifled roared! The doe dropped instantly, then got up and ran off. She quickly brought down the gun and entered the house.

Later in the morning Lester came back and said, "Well, if you want any pluck for supper tonight, you're going to have to get it yourself." (Pluck is slang for the heart and liver.) Alice returned with, "Why don't you go up behind the barn and get the one that's up there?" Lester started laughing, "What one?" "The one I shot, but you'll have to dress it out!" "Go on, you didn't shoot one and I didn't hear any shot!" Alice replied, "That's because you went up on the mountain and took yourself a nap!" Les walked up behind the barn, feeling a little foolish for even looking, but when he returned, he was all smiles, saying, "By God, you did get one!" Deer were plentiful during the depression years, and a great blessing to many a needy family, legal or not!

PANIC ATTACK

Alice used to make home brew to sell during Prohibition for extra money. On one occasion, Les brought Alice a large number of glass bottles that would be perfect for filling with her "brew." She had them all washed up and stacked in boxes near the rear door of her home. A short while later, she got word that the revenuers were about to raid Ernie Blanchard's home. Ernie ran a Speak Easy there and sold beer and liquor to the "trusted" public.

Alice began thinking about the oncoming raid. Her house was only a short distance from Ernie's. What if they come to my house as well? Her eyes locked onto the stack of clean, recapable bottles and she began to panic! She called Verne to her and the two of them began tossing the bottles, one by one, out into the field behind the house. Verne said it took them a half hour or more to throw them all out and away! The revenuers didn't show up and next spring Verne spent quite a bit of time recovering whatever bottles were still usable!

Alice and her family lost their home to the bank in 1941 on Verne's 16th birthday. It was a very bad day for all of them and the only good thing to happen was Alice giving Verne his father's 32 Winchester rifle for a birthday present. They moved into a large old frame house a short distance away for two years, and then up the mountain and into a smaller home.

A good friend of the family was the area Forest Ranger, Ralph Spring. Verne hunted for deer and white rabbits with Ralph quite a lot. Ralph was a good role model and Verne always had a great deal of respect for the man. As Forest Ranger, whenever he had a job that Verne could handle, he would be sure to offer him the job. Verne entered the Army in the spring of 1943, and whenever he came home on leave, Ralph would drive down to Thendera and bring him back up to Blue Mountain. Ralph was always there for him and was more like family than a friend.

After discharge from the Army in 1945, Verne was hired as Assistant Ranger at Golden Beach, Raquette Lake. Later on, he became Ranger at Lake Durrant and then back to Golden Beach. It was at Golden Beach that he met Wilma Day. Wilma's parents would camp every summer at Golden Beach, and in 1952, Verne and Wilma were married. They made their home in Fort Plain near Wilma's parents. Verne worked for Remington Rand, Sperry Univac, and then for a short period at Nabisco and Beechnut before retiring in 1987.

Spiritually, Verne never left the central Adirondack Mountains of his youth, and he returned every chance he could to visit, especially in the fall to hunt. On these fall hunts he would always stay with his sister, Nina, in North River and make the daily drive to and from Blue Mountain.

Verne has hunted those mountains now for over 50 years, and has taken some real fine trophies during that time. He has been a member of the Blue Mountain Lake Hunting Club for over 40 years and enjoys hunting the areas of Minnow Pond, Terrill Pond, Salmon River, Mud Pond, and Buck Mountain.

TEMPTATION

Verne is a very conscientious hunter and always tries to obey the law. A good example is when he came out on Route 30 one November afternoon in the area of Salmon River. He had unloaded his rifle and was about to start hiking back to where he had parked his truck, when he saw movement up and across the highway. There, coming out of the woods and slowly heading for the road, was a big buck with a grand set of antlers. He stood there looking at that big fellow with his massive headgear, and all the while thinking, should I or shouldn't I? He knew it was illegal to shoot across a highway and he also figured that if he did, the deer would most likely die in the middle of the road; and before he could get it off the road, the next damn car would be the Game Warden's. Yet, here was this truly fine buck and no cars to be heard or seen.

Verne decided to try his luck. He pulled a cartridge from his pocket and had the round almost chambered when he could hear a car coming. Back in the pocket went the shell. The buck came up on the shoulder of the road, walked across, and was just entering the woods when the car came into sight. As the car approached Verne, it slowed and then stopped beside him. The two passengers were two of his former neighbors up on Blue Mountain. Verne visited briefly and then told them of his experience just before with the buck. "Why the hell didn't you shoot!" they said. Verne replied, "If I did shoot, chances are I'd be talking to the Game Warden now instead of you."

A SURE SHOT

Verne enjoys hunting alone and prefers to track his deer. He's an excellent shot and won't let a bullet fly until he's got a fairly sure shot. He has taken close to 40 bucks, and he has never lost a buck that he has hit. That's a record few of us can boast of! He hunts from first light to last light, and when an opportunity develops, he patiently waits to make the shot that counts.

One season, Verne was looking down a steep hardwood slope when he spotted a doe bedded about 60 yards below him. He was in plain sight of the deer, but she was facing down the slope, away from him. He stayed still and watched her for a while. About 20 minutes later, he made out some movement, and then spotted a large rack of horns as a buck made his way uphill towards the doe. The buck was screened by a large windfall so he couldn't get a clear shot. The big buck got to within 20 feet of the doe, but never stepped clear of the windfall. Then, he turned and slowly went back down the slope.

Another movement was spotted on the other side of the doe, and this proved to be a spike-horned buck approaching the doe. As the spike-horn closed with the doe, the big buck moved back up the hill towards the doe also. This would turn the spike around and he would move away. As soon as the spike-horn left the doe, the big buck would go back down the hill. Several times the spike would try to get near the doe and Mr. Big would head up the hill threatening and driving him away, but never giving Verne a clear shot. This went on for well over an hour until Mr. Big took one step too many. He fell instantly at the shot and stayed down. The doe damn near ran Verne over in her attempt to get out of there. Patience put another beautiful buck on the meat pole.

A DEER PREDICAMENT

Verne's mother, Alice, would hunt every fall with her 32 Winchester rifle. She took several nice bucks, but one kill was most unusual. It was on a warm and sunny October day when she took her rifle and hiked quite a long way off into the woods on Blue Mountain. She located a good place to sit where she could watch one of her favorite deer runs. She had been sitting there for perhaps 20 minutes when she noticed a tree down the slope from her that came out of the ground in two places before forming one trunk about two feet off the ground. It formed a triangular opening under it, and on the other side of it, she could see deer hide on what must be a bedded deer. The tree and deer were about 60 or 70 yards away, and after watching carefully, she could see the antler beam of a nice buck as the deer occasionally turned its head.

Conditions were too noisy to risk circling around for a shot so she decided to wait him out. Alice waited for a considerable length of time, but still the buck was content to lay. It was getting late in the day when the thought came to her that if she put a bullet into the tree behind the buck, it might confuse the deer enough so that she could get a shot into it. This she did, and at the shot, the buck jumped to its feet. Then he turned and stood on his hind legs while putting his two front hooves against the tree Alice had just shot into. She couldn't believe her eyes, but she sure didn't forget what she was out there for, and she dropped the buck with her next shot. She told of that experience to many people and nobody ever gave her a plausible explanation for the buck's behavior. Alice hunted well up into her old age. She got her last buck at the age of 81. She died at the age of 87 in Glens Falls Hospital.

FISHER CAT

A hunter accumulates many small, but memorable experiences during his time afield. Each one adds to his appreciation of the uniqueness and beauty of the Adirondack environment. One of these happened to Verne on a November morning while he was on the slopes of Blue Mountain. He stopped to look around near the stump end of a large yellow birch windfall. He had only paused a minute when a beautiful fisher cat jumped up on the far end of the trunk and then came running towards him. Verne stood very still and the fisher got alarmingly close to him. They both eyed each other and Verne couldn't help but admire the beauty and healthy appearance of the animal. The fisher turned and retraced his steps back down the log, then he turned around and came all the way back and closer still! The fisher evidently had never seen a stump quite like Verne before and wasn't able to get a whiff of man scent because of the direction of air drift. He finally jumped down off the log and ran up the slope, pausing twice more to look back down at the strange looking "stump" he had encountered.

MAX FREEMAN AND GERRY MINOR

Max and Gerry were best friends, as well as life-long hunting partners. They both lived in the Sherburne, New York area and were regular visitors to the Loon Brook watershed for hunting from 1929 through the early 1960's. They were first introduced to Blue Mountain in 1928 when they contracted to paint Wally Faulkner's Inn. They drove up to Raquette Lake and then took the ferry system across the lake and used the Marion River Railroad over the portage into the Eckford Chain. While they were painting the Inn, they could hear the construction crews blasting away the rocks from the new State highway being built between Raquette and Blue Mountain and on to Long Lake.

Their first hunt in the area wasn't until the following year. They came up to hunt the vicinity of Loon Brook on a day trip, using the newly opened state highway. They parked their Cadillac truck near the Loon Brook Bridge. Max hunted upstream, or south of the road, and Gerry hunted down stream and in the woods above Utowanna Lake. Gerry killed a buck in the early afternoon and had it back to the car by dark for the trip home. Later in the season, Ralph, Max's brother, came up and hunted the same area with a party of four people. He killed a huge buck about a mile south of the state road. The four hunters had a major struggle in getting the buck out of the woods. When they got the buck back to Sherburne, they had it weighed on a dependable set of scales. It weighed 310 pounds and was the heaviest buck ever known to come out of that area. The buck had a heavy-beamed rack, but it was deformed and carried few points.

Gerry and Max first began hunting big game in 1925, with a weekend trip into Round Pond, which lies just a short distance north of Otter Lake on Route 28. Max began to keep a brief diary of their annual fall hunts, beginning with this first adventure. If any trip could have discouraged the boys from hunting, then this one should have done the trick. The following notes were entered in Max's diary in 1925.

> First year of hunting. Baby Grand car arrived at Round Pond around dusk. Raining and roads muddy. No fly for tent (loaned out)! Rain and snow for most of two-day stay. Rain soaked firewood, smoky fire, wet pancakes! Max carried 45-70 and Gerry a 32 Winchester Special. Max saw two deer and Gerry got a shot at one of them. Max wearing short pants (knickers), and low cut shoes, gets lost, comes out on Moose River. On way home to Sherburne, had smash up in Utica. Car hurt bad, got home late.

The boys hunted that area during the next four years and had some luck there while sharpening their hunting and woodsmanship skills.

HUNTING AT LOON BROOK

After 1929, hunting at Loon Brook became the annual fall tradition. Max and his brother, Ralph, and Gerry and his son, Frank, made up the bulk of the early hunting parties. They enjoyed excellent hunting during the decade of the '30s and took 26 bucks out of the area in that time. The best head was an 11-pointer taken by Gerry in 1938.

They didn't always pitch a tent or haul a trailer for their weekend hunts. Quite often they would stay at Faulkner's Inn and then drive to and from Loon Brook. It was while staying at Faulkner's one weekend that their hunting luck took a brief, but sharp, nosedive. Gerry had driven his car up with a full load of hunters one weekend, when the weather turned bitterly cold. The next morning, he parked the car as usual near the Loon Brook Bridge. He was one of the last men to enter the woods that morning, and he was wondering if his car would be able to start at the end of the day's hunt. He had a big old buffalo robe in the back of the car, so before leaving he threw it over the hood and front grill in an effort to keep some of the chill out of the motor. Later in the day, one of his own hunting party was hunting his way back out towards the road, when he spotted a large, black, fur-covered object down through a small opening in the forest. He was sure it was a bear, and fearing that it might move and be lost to sight, he took his best shot. It was an excellent shot, right through the buffalo robe and the radiator, and it bounced off the engine block! Gerry wasn't a happy camper when he got out to the road that afternoon!

In the 40's, Ned Welch, Gerry's nephew, and Dick Marsters, Gerry's son-in-law, began to hunt with them. Ned was still in high school when he began to hunt there. He thought the North Woods were really awesome and he felt very small within them. He said, "It really made you listen carefully to all the advice the older guys were giving you."

Ned recalled one weekend at Faulkner's Inn when a couple of fellows stopped in and asked for lodgings. They had been out hunting for pheasants near where they lived in the Buffalo area. Afterwards, they stopped for a sandwich and a few drinks. They were having a real good time when one of them suggested that they head for Blue Mountain in the Adirondacks and some deer hunting. It seemed like a great idea so they headed right out without informing their wives of their travel plans. At the end of the second day in their hunt, one of the men decided to call home and check on things. Ed was seated near the phone and he could plainly hear the conversation. It went something like this: "Hi..........Blue Mountain Lake..........Deer hunting..........Yes, dear........... Yes, dear........Well, I didn't............. They were!"

It turned out that their wives had reported them missing after the pheasant hunt. The local sheriff and the State Police had a major search on for the two hunters. The two men headed back to Buffalo the next morning, stone sober!

DEER THIEVES

On a November weekend during the early '50s, Dick Marstars was hunting a hardwood hillside that was about a mile in from the road. A crotch horn buck came running down the slope towards him, and he quickly dropped it with a shot from his .32 W.S. While Dick was still admiring his kill, four men came walking by. They gave a brief greeting, looked over the buck, and then moved on. He noticed that all four hunters were wearing a feather in their hats. Dick dressed out the buck and then attached a pulling rope and stick. He pulled him a short distance from the gut pile, then rolled him on his back and propped open the cavity so the buck would cool down quickly. He left for the road, intending to return the next morning and drag out the buck.

Dick had driven his own car down to Loon Brook in the morning, so when he got out to the road, he headed back to Faulkner's. Max got back to the Inn about dark, so Dick told him the whole story about getting the buck, which included the part where the four feathered-cap hunters walked by. After hearing Dick's story, Max said that he had seen the same four hunters out at the road near dark and they were looking mighty guilty about something.

After cleaning up and having dinner, Dick and Max went into the barroom for a drink or two. The four hunters that had walked by Dick and his kill were also at the bar having a few drinks. After hearing what Max had said, Dick was feeling a little uneasy about his buck, so he wrote some of their back tag numbers down, just in case. At that time, you had to display your hunting license tag for big game outside on the middle of your back, and they were all wearing their hunting jackets.

The following morning when he got back in to where he had left his buck, all he found was the pull rope. When he returned home from the hunt, he turned the back tag numbers into his local conservation officer. Dick didn't get his buck, but he did learn the names of the hunters involved. He found out that some of the hunters involved didn't want anything to do with the taking of the buck, and that the group broke up permanently after the investigation. You've got to be a pretty small man to even think about taking another man's buck!

Max and Dick came up to hunt after a heavy snow had fallen. There was snow hanging all over the trees and bending the branches right down to the ground. After parking their car, the two men headed up the old bridle trail, which parallels Route 28 on its south side. The bridle trail has its own bridge across Loon Brook, and the two men were crossing this bridge when they happened to look upstream. There is a small section of still water above the bridge, and standing in the middle of it, was a large, graceful doe deer. She was framed by a beautiful arrangement of snow-draped spruce and alders. They watched silently until the doe walked slowly across the brook and disappeared into the snow-covered woodland. They both had to agree, it was one of the most beautiful scenes they had ever witnessed, and isn't that a big part of what it's all about?

HUNTING FROM GLADE'S TENT

Hunting out of their tent during the deer season became an annual tradition for Glade, Parks Keith, and Fred Hodges. The men had learned the country quickly, and each man looked forward to whatever time he could spend in hunting the area every fall. Their normal range of hunting from the tent would be out to Bear Brook Swamp on the west, to Wilson Pond and Cascade Brook on the east, and up to the top of Blue Ridge on the south.

Glade said that in those early days of hunting, it wasn't unusual to see three or four groups of deer just in walking out to the area you chose to hunt that day. Early in the hunt, or when the deer didn't seem to be in their normal haunts, Glade would go "touring." Touring is nothing more than taking one hell of a long hike around the area to locate the best concentrations of fresh deer sign. Once a good area was found, he would then concentrate his hunting effort in that locale.

Glade has a unique way of looking for deer among the spruce cover. Once he's looked the cover over in a normal manner, he then bends way over at the waist, and looks under the lower branches of the spruce trees, looking for deer legs. The technique has paid off for him several times over the years. He also likes to use military ammo to hunt with. Ernie Blanchard used it regularly and thought it was quite effective as well as economical. It's worked out real good for Glade also.

Glade's favorite method of hunting is tracking. There are few things Glade enjoys more than cutting a big track first thing in the morning, and then having the rest of the day to follow him around and figure him out.

Map of our hunting area.

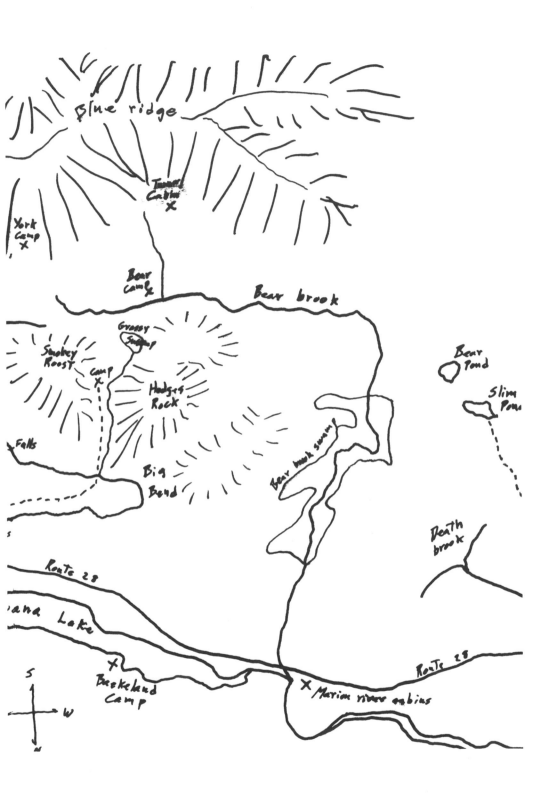

Les Turner and "Molly."

*The "General Scott" wood stove is the only monument left to mark the site
of Turner's cabin. Photo by Bob Elinskas.*

Walt Turner.
Turner family photo.

Walter and Alice Turner built
their home on Blue Mt.
Turner family photo.

Alice Turner, a women who loved to hunt. Turner family photo,

Verne Turner and a nice Blue Mountain buck. Turner family photo,

Gerry Miner (left) and Max Freeman with a nice Loon Brook buck. The new state road (Route 28) is right behind them. Ed Welsh photo.

A 1930s camping outfit, about to leave for the Adks. Ed Welsh photo.

Iron snow plow used by the old loggers remains as a monument to their activities.
Photo by Bob Elinskas.

Tents and hunters in the first lumber camp clearing on Loon Brook 1929.
Keith family photo.

A SOUR ENDING

A buck led Glade on a grand tour of his hunting area one day, and eventually went over the top of Blue Ridge and into some unfamiliar country. Glade stayed right on his track and managed to kill him over on the south side. The buck was one of those oversized critters, and the rack carried 13 points. Glade had no appetite for dragging him back up the ridge, and then all the way out to the road, so he decided to cut him up into pieces that he could handle. Lester York was hunting with him that week, so they came back for him the following day and packed him out to the tent. On the way home, they pulled into the game check station to report their deer. All the parts for Glade's deer were there, and the head was properly tagged, but the conservation officials took away the hindquarters from him.

When he got home and told his story, some of his friends didn't think he had been treated fairly. They encouraged him to write to the Conservation Department about it. Glade wrote the letter, and about two weeks later, two officials got a hold of Glade and Les. They hauled them off to the Town Justice and paid a fine of $12.50 each for cutting up the deer.

DON'T CURSE YOUR LUCK

Glade was hunting across a large hardwood hillside one day when there was about three inches of wet snow on the ground. The going was a little slippery, but the woods were fairly open and you could see a fair distance in some directions. He stopped when spotting a movement in some thick slashings, about 100 yards up the hill. What he saw was a young maple tree being whipped about as a buck rubbed his antlers against its trunk. Glade knew just what was going on, but the buck was in some pretty thick stuff and he could just barely make out its form. It was way too thick to risk a shot, so he brought up his rifle and got ready to take the first decent opportunity for a shot when the buck began to move. He had his sights on the buck with his safety off when his right foot suddenly slipped and the gun went off. The slip was quite a surprise to Glade, and when he regained his composure he thought, "Damn, now that was a hell of a thing to do!" The buck was gone, so cursing his luck, he went up to see the tracks and find out where he went. When he got into the slashings, he found the buck dead in his tracks! Glade's wild shot had hit the buck right behind the ear, killing it instantly.

SOME HUNTERS JUST CAN'T SEE

One season Glade killed a big-racked buck way off to the southwest of his tent. He killed the buck just before noon, so he spent most of the afternoon pulling on him. He managed to get him just west of what we call the Big Bend on Loon Brook when he stopped pulling for the day. There were a number of good-sized rocks or boulders lying on top of the ground in that area, so Glade left the buck lying on top of one of these. When he left the buck, he turned and looked back a couple of times to make sure he had its location marked mentally. Each time he looked back, he couldn't help but think, "Boy, that rack of horns sticks out like a sore thumb!"

The next morning there was an inch or so of fresh snow on the ground. When Glade hiked into the area of the buck, he noticed the fresh tracks of a hunter heading up the hillside towards the buck.

He followed the tracks up the hill and they passed within ten feet of the dead buck, which still stood out like a sore thumb! It didn't appear that the hunter even saw the buck laying on the rock. Glade got his buck back to the tent, and later that day he met the fellow coming up the trail. His name was Hayden and he was from the Oswego area. He remembered hunting up through that hillside, but he never saw the dead buck. Glade said, "If he passed any closer, the horns would have hooked his jacket!"

EDGAR DYMOND

During one "buck week" at Loon Brook, Glade found himself tracking a buck he had wounded in the neighborhood of Potter Pond. It was one of those dark, gloomy, rainy afternoons and Glade was having trouble following the buck's trail. Darkness came early that day due to all the cloud cover, and when Glade finally quit the track it was almost dark. He had no light with him and he had a lot of trouble just finding the trail. A short while later, he couldn't see well enough to stay on it. He fired a signal shot, and a short while later he got an answer. He worked his way along the beaver meadows of Loon Brook and 30 or 40 minutes later, he fired another signal shot. This time he could hear someone holler an answer.

He went on for a while longer, and in the distance he could see the light of a fire. After getting closer yet, he could see a good-sized fire burning against a bank. He had to cross Loon Brook twice in order to get over to it, but when he did, this fellow dashes over to him and said, "Oh gosh, I'm awful glad you've come!" His name was Edgar Dymond and he lived on the Cedar River Road.

Ed had started hunting up on Blue Ridge early in the morning and had gotten up into the spruce trees on top when the weather turned foggy. When he went to come down, he thought he was going down the Cedar River side, but in fact, he was on the Loon Brook side of the ridge. When darkness overtook him, he built this big fire to spend the night by. Glade explained to him where he was and what must have happened. The boys at Glade's tent did some more shooting, but Glade decided to keep Edgar company that night.

It rained lightly off and on during the night, but it wasn't all that uncomfortable. The two men visited the night away. At first light, it only took 25 minutes to get back to Glade's tent and the road. He gave Edgar a ride back to his home on the Cedar River Road. Years later, Glade bumped into Edgar at a gun sale. As soon as Edgar realized who Glade was, he got right away from him, like he didn't want to be embarrassed or whatever.

When I was interviewing Ed Mitchel, I asked him if he knew Edgar Dymond, but I hadn't told him Glade's story. Ed told me he used to hunt with Edgar when they were teenagers. Ed used to go over to Edgar's house on weekends during the deer season, and the two boys would hunt Blue Ridge together. Later on, they ran a trap line for beaver, fisher, bobcat, or whatever.

Ed told me of one particular hunt on Blue Ridge where they got way up into the spruce trees towards the top. They were jumping quite a few deer in that area but were having trouble getting a good look at them. They split up hoping to drive deer into each other, but a short while later, a thick fog rolled in to cover the ridge top. About 45 minutes later, they met up again. Edgar said, "Well, I've had enough of this, we better head for home." Ed answered, "All right," so he started following Edgar. They hadn't gone very far when Ed said, "Whoa! You're going right off the back side of the mountain, aren't you?" "No!" "Well, by God, you are!" "No, I'm not!" "Well, I'm not going any farther that way!" "Where are you going?" "I'm going down to see your father." "Well, by jeez, you won't see him tonight!" "Maybe not, but I'm going to take a chance." Ed went one way and Edgar went the other way.

Ed got back to the Dymond house just before dark. He went in and hung his rifle up and took off his jacket and boots. He told Edgar's father about their dispute and he was hoping Edgar would be walking up the road in the dark shortly. Along about nine o'clock, Edgar's father said, "We better call it a night and turn in." "Well, what about Edgar?" "Oh, hell, he'll be all right, we'll go get him in the morning."

Edgar's father had an old Star car. After breakfast, they got into the car with Ed driving. They drove over to Blue Mountain Lake and started south on 28. They only got as far as John Collin's place and there sat Edgar on the road bank. His father later told Ed that every once in a while, Edgar would go up on that ridge and get turned around. The next morning he would find him sitting along the road in the Blue Mountain region. Edgar worked in the area all his life as a carpenter. He was a good hunter and a good trapper, but there was something about the top of Blue Ridge that turned his mental compass around!

FRED HODGES

Fred Hodges hunted out of the tent for a good many years. Fred was an excellent rifleman, and took his share of the bucks from the region. Fred used to enjoy watching a good run during the rut, as one method of taking his bucks. On a hill top, immediately south of the Big Bend on Loon Brook is a huge boulder. The boulder is about 10 feet high and 14 feet in length, and it can be climbed on its west side by a diagonal ledge that runs part way up that side. There is a good deer run that passes close by its southeast side and it offers a commanding view of the woods on its north side. A small tree and some light brush grow from the soil on its flat top, providing cover for a watchful hunter.

This huge rock was one of Fred's favorite stands. Over the years he had taken several fine bucks while watching from its top, including one dandy 10-pointer. In time, the rock became known as "Hodge's Rock," and the hill as "Hodge's Rock Hill." Many people have sat upon the rock, waiting for their chance at a passing buck; but to this date, nobody has ever taken a buck while seated on its top except Fred Hodges, and many people have tried!

Fred used to like to try for some Loon Brook trout at least once a year. One summer, when his spirit moved him to try again for the elusive trout, he grabbed his gear and headed for the trail head off Route 28. A five-minute walk put him along the banks of the brook where the meadow of the first lumber camp was. Shortly afterwards, he was working the rifles, runs, and pools with his offerings. All was peaceful and quiet, except for the subtle murmurings of Loon Brook. Twenty or thirty minutes had passed by when a movement downstream caught his eye. He moved his attention from the fish line to the movement in time to see a big buck step clear of the evergreens. Their eyes met at the same time and Fred drank in the beauty of a large, healthy, male deer. The rack of antlers was probably two thirds grown and by September when the velvet was shed, they would be a trophy by anyone's standards. The buck lifted his head an inch or two higher and appeared to be thinking, "Now what the hell are you doing here at this time of year?"

A moment or two later, he turned and disappeared into the spruce trees. The whole encounter didn't last for more than 30 seconds, but it was the highlight of the trip. Fred would never again pass by that stretch of brook without seeing that buck in his memory.

Fred was a freelance photographer all his life. He had a deep love for the Adirondacks and enjoyed his nickname, "Adirondack Hodges." Fred worked at the Adirondack Museum for a few years in the '50s. He suffered a fatal heart attack there in 1957.

PARKS KEITH – A LITTLE TOO CLOSE

Glade's older brother, Parks, didn't share the same degree of success in deer hunting that Glade did, but no one enjoyed their trips to the Loon Brook hunting tent more than Parks did. He managed to kill several bucks in his years of hunting there, but his most memorable hunt didn't include a deer. Parks had been hunting in the hardwoods just a little southwest of the falls on Loon Brook. He had been hunting along slowly and looking down towards the alders and spruce growth that lined the brook. While hunting along in this manner, he came upon a tree that had been forced to the ground by some violent force of wind years earlier. The tree had somehow saved enough of its root structure to sustain life, and so the trunk of the tree ran parallel to the ground for about 30 feet before sweeping up to grab some precious sunlight. The broad trunk near the roots provided a comfortable seat and a view of the alders along the brook, as well as the hardwoods up the hill.

Parks got darn good and comfy there, and later admitted he may have even started to doze off a little, when suddenly he became aware that his log was vibrating. He turned to look for the source and that's when he saw a fat black bear walking towards him on the same log! The bear was moving right along and looking off towards Loon Brook, completely unaware that Parks was seated only 10 feet away. Now Parks was an intelligent man, with a nature to be slow and deliberate with most of his actions. Not now though! Parks shot the bear in the head at a distance of less than eight feet. He said it was the fastest move by far that he's ever made with a rifle!

TRYING TO STAY LEGAL

In another season, Parks was seated high up in the hardwoods on Blue Ridge. A movement 80 yards or so down the slope caught his eye, and then a good-sized buck walked through a small opening. He didn't get his rifle up in time for a shot, so he watched the area carefully for several minutes. A while after this, another deer appeared, but he couldn't make out any antlers. The deer hung around the opening and then he observed it whipping the devil out of a sapling. "By God, it must have horns if it's doing a job on that sapling," Parks reasoned. He shot the buck, but the horns were only two inches long! The young buck didn't go to waste, however. It was probably one of the few game law violations that Parks could ever be accused of, since he always tried to stay well within the law.

One year while Parks was up north hunting, the southern tier deer season had opened up down south. His son, Donald, and a family friend, Ralph Burnham, decided to go deer hunting on the Keith farm. They were hunting through a woodlot behind Parks' house when they came upon three freshly killed doe. At that time, bucks only were legal game, so some idiot with a shotgun had wasted three beautiful deer. The deer were still warm, and Don and Ralph hated to see them go to waste. They dressed all three out and then called the warden and related what had happened. He told the boys to hang them in a tree by Parks' house and he would be along Monday to pick them up.

The boys did as they were told and hung all three doe in one of the big maples in Parks' front yard by Saturday afternoon. Sunday afternoon, Parks came back from hunting up north and almost had a heart attack when he saw three illegal deer hanging in his front yard! He didn't calm down until the whole explanation was given to him and the warden picked up the deer on Monday as scheduled.

GEORGE KEITH – HUNTER EDUCATION

In 1932, 17-year-old George Keith came up to hunt with Parks and Fred Hodges. George was the son of George and Bertha Keith. He was Glades' and Parks' cousin. On his first day out, Parks and Fred explained the lay of the land to him, and then left him in the area of Grassy Swamp to begin his hunt. George spent most of the morning in that area and then started to slowly hunt his way back to the area of the falls on Loon Brook. It was moderately warm for hunting and there was a carpet of dry, noisy leaves on the ground. George hadn't seen any deer, but it was very pleasant just being out in the woods. He was hunting down the gentle slope of Smokey Roost Hill, and was nearing Loon Brook when he spotted a large dry maple log that would provide a good seat and a view of the remaining hill. While seated, he thought he could hear the falls. It was then that he heard the rhythmic hoof beats of a heavy animal that was running fast and heading his way. When it came into view, he could see that it was a large buck with a huge rack of antlers. The buck was going to pass about 40 yards off and down the slope from him. When the shot rang out, the buck came to an abrupt halt, and stood there broad side looking at him. George took careful aim and fired again, with the buck leaving as quickly as he'd come. When he went over to look for signs of a hit, no blood or hair could be found anywhere along the buck's line of travel, and George was fit to be tied. He had borrowed a 303 British Enfield rifle and hadn't fired it or checked the sights. It was a tough lesson to learn because in all his years of hunting it was the largest racked buck he can ever remember seeing.

In 1937, George learned another lesson from the big woods. He had come up to hunt with Parks on a week-long hunt. On their first day out, the two men had hiked over the lower trail to the second lumber camp clearing. Parks then left him to hunt in a westerly direction, and George hunted southwest and up the slopes of Hodge's Rock Hill. There was a good stand of beech trees on the top of the hill and beechnuts were plentiful that year. It was rainy and windy that morning in the woods but when he got to the top of the hill, the wind and rain strengthened considerably. The conditions kind of took a lot of the spirit out of the day's hunt, but George thought he would tough it out for a while.

He spotted the huge old stub of a maple tree that had broken off about 12 feet off the ground. The lee side of that stub was half hollowed out, so George backed into it and got some relief from the winds and driving rain. He watched the surrounding hardwoods for a while and then began eating his lunch. He was almost through when a heavy gust of wind knocked a large beach tree to the ground, right beside the stub he was standing against. "God, that was close; better find a quieter section of the woods to watch," he thought. He moved away from the stub and hadn't gone very far when he spotted a large black bear looking through the leaves for beechnuts. He would cuff the leaves around for a while, then lick up the exposed nuts. Every once in a while he would raise his head and look all around, and then go back to cuffing and licking.

George could see that it was a real big bear and he was kind of scared to try for him at first, but then he decided to go for him. He was using a Marlin, lever action 30-30, and his first shot hit him right behind the shoulder. Once hit, the big bear stood right up on his hind legs looking all around. George fired again, this time hitting him in the neck and putting him down. The bear lay still, so George moved in for a closer look. He was still a little scared of him, and when he finally got to the bruin, he couldn't believe how big he was.

He fired some signal shots for Parks, and with the wind blowing so hard, it took him quite a while to zero in on George and meet up with him. Parks was some tickled to see that bear, and he took his time in looking him over real good. George wanted to skin it out so they wouldn't damage the hide in taking it out, but Parks thought they could bring it out whole without hurting it. George went along with this because it sure would be nice to show off his big bear. They cut a couple of skid poles and got the bear so he would ride mostly off the ground, but God, he was heavy! They were about a mile and a half in from the road and it took five, eight-hour days to get him all the way out to the car, and they had help on the weekend.

They had driven up in George's 36 Ford Business Coupe, and they had one hell of a job getting him up and onto the roof. They tied off a leg on each corner of the roof, with the head in the middle of the windshield looking over the hood. It made for quite a sight when they drove down the highway. When they stopped for gas in Old Forge, a woman came out to pump the gas. The boys had been pulling on the beast for five days, sweating heavy, and needing a bath and a shave real bad. She took one look at them and said, "Which one is the bear?" When they got home and weighed him, he went over 375 pounds. George made a rug out of the hide but the meat was course and lacked flavor. After that, George swore he would never bring another bear out whole!

ALBERT L. RAMSDELL

"Bert" Ramsdell also hunted out of Glade's tent. Bert and his wife, Alice, ran a general store and post office in North Brookfield for many years. When I was a teenager and Bert was getting on in years, I would go over to visit with him in his gun collection room above the store. He had a marvelous collection of old Remington rifles and a sizable collection of Colt revolvers. They were all in cases and he would let me look some of them over and then carefully wipe any finger prints off with a lightly oiled cloth before returning them to the case. His wife, Alice, was the nicest, gentlest person. She was always down to earth and easy to visit with. She looked after me like a mother hen. If I was a little short of cash and needed some 22's for chucks or shot shells for grouse, she would always extend me a little credit until payday. When I entered the service, she would always remember me with a little "care" package around the holidays.

Bert used to hunt up north with a Model 8 Remington automatic in .35 caliber. He had two stocks for it—a plain one and a fancy one. In the case it had the fancy one on, but when hunting, it had the plain. Bert took a big old eight-pointer out of the Loon Brook area and he told me how he got it. He was on the lower trail, between the first and second crossings on Loon Brook, and slowly making his way back towards camp. There is a small ridge that runs along the east side of the trail for a good long stretch. Bert was going slow and being watchful when he spotted the buck moving slowly along the top of this ridge. He dropped the buck as it crested the ridge and looked down from its top. It had a large heavy rack with long tines and was perfectly symmetrical. He brought it over to George Lesser in Johnstown and had him mount it up for him. He did a beautiful job of it, and it looks as good today as when he first brought it home, with only some minor restoration work.

GEORGE LESSER – TAXIDERMIST

In the first half of the 20th century, many thousands of trophy whitetails were taken from the game-rich Adirondack Mountains. There were scores of taxidermy shops operating during this period also, and they varied in both size and talent. Every hunter wants their trophy mounted or set-up looking as close to real life as the day it was taken.

George Lesser had his taxidermy shop located at 310 State Street in Johnstown, New York. He owned and operated one of the largest shops in the peripheral Adirondacks. He also had a good reputation for doing quality work. Glade had heard of him early on, and over the years had him mount up three buck and one bear. He was always happy with his work and steered several of his fellow hunters in his direction when it came time to have their trophies mounted.

George was usually in the shop when the heads were turned in and would often provide some interesting conversation. Lesser was a dedicated taxidermist. He was always striving for perfection in his work and seeking out constructive criticism that might turn out a better mount.

Paul Bransom was a very talented wildlife artist and also a close friend of George. The two men were always critiquing each other's work in an effort to become "better." Lesser had a large staff and kept a close eye on technique and detail.

Each year, the business would take in thousands of game heads, not only from the Adirondacks, but also from Canada, the far west, and Africa. Photos displayed in some of his brochures show huge piles of Adirondack deer antlers taken in during the fall and waiting their turn to be mounted. Moose, bear, sheep, goat, caribou, and foreign trophies were also in evidence.

It was interesting to note his price scale over the years. In the 1930s, a full head and shoulder mount for a buck deer was $20; $25 in the 1940s; and $35 in the 1950s. In his heydays, he offered a full-service taxidermy studio, mounting just about anything you might bring in. In addition, he tanned all hides with fur on or off and made fur scarves, gloves, and moccasins. In his later years, he scaled these services way back.

George loved his work and he also enjoyed his hunting. During his lifetime, he hunted the Adirondacks, Canada, Alaska, the western states, and Africa. He was never the bragger, though, and he published several articles to help out the junior hunters. He donated much of his work for public display. A large collection of wild birds and their eggs were donated to the Rodgers Conservation Center in Sherburne, New York, and they can still be seen on display. George H. Lesser was a well respected man with a talent that he generously shared.

A SHOT IN THE DARK

Parks' son, Donald, and Bert's son, Warren, used to hunt from the tent occasionally. Early one season, the two were hunting the area between the falls on Loon Brook and the foot of Blue Ridge. They hunted a little longer than they should have, and then they had trouble in finding the trail down near the falls. They didn't have a flashlight with them and darkness was upon them when they finally got onto the trail. The sky was clear, however, and there was already most of a moon high overhead giving them some good illumination. They had little trouble in following the trail, even in the spruce trees. They had only 1/4 of a mile to go before reaching the first crossing of Loon Brook, when they stopped to take a short break.

While they were standing there, Warren heard something moving through the leaves only a short distance down the hill. A minute later, they could make out the form of a good-sized deer, slowing walking along with its head down. It wasn't very far off, and their night vision was pretty good, but they still couldn't tell for sure if it was a buck or not. Warren whispered to Don, "I'm going to take a chance and shoot." He brought his rifle up, knowing he wouldn't be able to use his sights in the dark, pointed his rifle at the gloomy form and fired. The deer quickly disappeared from sight and sound after that. They had no way of checking to see if he had made a hit, so they returned to camp.

The next morning they returned to the site and looked around in the leaves for any signs of a hit, but it was hard to say exactly where the deer was standing now that it was daylight. The hunt ended without a deer and the boys never told anyone about Warren's shot in the dark.

The following weekend, three of Glade's friends came up to hunt. One of them was Paul Alger, a barber from Leonardsville, New York. While hunting, Paul came across the remains of a large buck that had died only 100 yards from where Warren had taken his shot in the dark. He guessed the buck had been dead for about a week and was real sorry the meat wasn't salvageable. The buck had a beautiful eight-point rack, so he cut it off, and later mounted it on a plaque. He hung the antlers in his shop, and they stayed there for many years. Warren never told him of his shot in the dark, but every time he got his hair cut over at Paul's, he would stare at those antlers!

Fred Hodges (seated) and noted gunsmith Shirley Rizzley at the Keith farm range. Keith family photo.

Parks Keith and his "close encounter" bear. Keith family photo.

*George Keith and his
375 lb. black bear.
Keith family photo.*

"The Falls" on Loon Brook. Photo by Bob Elinskas.

Albert Ramsdell gun collector, postmaster and grocer. Burnham family photo.

George H. Lesser advertisement. Donated by Richard Lesser.

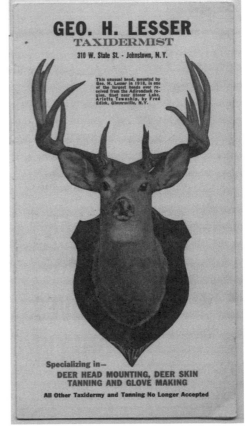

THE BAEKELAND CAMP ON UTOWANNA LAKE

Leo H. Baekeland was born in Ghent, Belgium in 1863. He graduated from the University of Ghent in 1889 and taught chemistry there. In 1889, he and his wife, Ce'line, immigrated to America and he made his living as a chemist. He improved methods for developing photographic films and also developed superior emulsions for film. In 1909, he invented Bakelite. It was the first synthetic resin, and bakelite compounds were used to make electrical insulating materials, radio cabinets, and pipe stems.

Leo and Ce'line raised two children, George and Nina. Every family seems to have at least one adventurous soul, and George carried that title appropriately. While on a 1919 summer recess from Cornell University, he came up to the Adirondacks with a friend, Bradley Middlebrook, to canoe the upper reaches of the Hudson River. Their travels eventually led them to Blue Mountain Lake, where they made the acquaintance of Ernie Blanchard. The boys canoed the waters of the Eckford Chain and Raquette Lake, fishing and camping in various places.

Freeland Jones, a caretaker for Tioga Point on Raquette Lake, would occasionally give the boys a tow with his motorized boat, "The Go'er." They also enjoyed a friendship, and it was Freeland who told the boys of a small leanto-like cabin that might be for sale, "cheap!" The cabin was about three quarters of a mile in and along Bear Brook from Utowanna Lake. The cabin belonged to Ernie Blanchard (not his Bear Pond cabin), and at this time, it was one of his illegal cabins on State land. The boys checked it out with Ernie and then bought it for $25. It wasn't much of a cabin, but it would do for George's summertime visits to the area. George was never really happy with it, though. He always felt a little too closed in by all the surrounding woods.

A few years later, he noticed that Daley's Utowanna Hotel was up for sale due to delinquent taxes. The hotel and 40 acres of land were very close to the western end of Utowanna Lake. The buildings and most the acreage lay on the north shore.

John J. Daley used to own and run "The Hemlocks" on Long Point, Raquette Lake. It was destroyed by fire just before the turn of the century. He sold the property to Collis P. Huntington for $12,000. In 1903, he bought the property on Utowanna Lake and built Utowanna Lodge. It was right on the steamboat line and when the lodge was open, you could buy a ticket in Grand Central Station that would deliver you right to its front dock. Daley's was well run, comfortable, and set a good table, but it couldn't attract enough business to make a good living. Eventually, it went the way of the tax sale.

George was young and didn't have much money, but his mother, Mrs. Leo H. Baekeland (Ce'line), did; so he told her of the property sale. Ce'line came up in her high button shoes and formal attire of the day to look over the property. She bought it that year (1923) for $4,000 in back taxes.

There was no workable plumbing at the time she bought the property, so for baths and a first class meal, she would go to Antlers or North Point on Raquette Lake. There were only three buildings on the property: the main building or lodge, a leanto down by the lake, and another building up behind the lodge that was used as a workshop.

Ce'line decided what had to be done to make it into a comfortable, functional summer home. A caretaker was needed to make the necessary repairs and improvements. George's acquaintance with Freeland Jones secured the position of Baekeland's first caretaker for him.

Nina Baekeland married George Roll, and they had four children, Ce'line, Baeke, Ninette, and Peter. George and Cornielia Baekeland had a son, Brooks. All of the Baekeland and Roll children were up to camp at an early age, and most can remember Freeland Jones. Ce'line roll, now Ce'line Karraker, has these childhood memories of Freeland Jones and early years at the Baekeland camp.

FREELAND JONES

Freeland always seemed to be a little overweight, and he constantly reeked with the odor of the Wornaki Brown tobacco that he regularly smoked. He wasn't the cleanest person in the world because he never seemed to change his clothes, and always had the same stinky long underwear on. He used to upset Grandma Baekeland regularly by forgetting to button his fly after a trip to the outhouse. He was real good with us children though, and would always give us some attention.

Free would sometimes take us for short hikes into the woods and teach us woodcraft. He would show us how to build a leanto shelter and how to build a comfortable bed from spruce and balsam boughs. First, you put the spruce boughs down for spring, and then you put on the balsam boughs for softness. He would also teach them how to build a fire and, of course, there was always food to toast up. While toasting and eating their food, Free would always entertain them further with a story or two. The Baekeland children just loved this, and they all had warm memories of old Free. Unfortunately for Free, Grandma Baekeland didn't share those same warm feelings. It seemed to her that Free was drinking more and more, and it was seriously affecting his duties at the camp. When she fired him, the kids all cried their eyes out, but that was the end of Freeland at the Baekelands.

HIENEY GUTLIF

Mrs. Baekeland hired Hieney Gutlif to replace Freeland. Hieney was also a drinker, but he was a very hard worker and liked by all. Hieney was always cheerful and seemed impervious to the cold. Ce'line remembers spending a winter week in camp when the temperature fell to 40 below zero. Hieney would come walking into the lodge, with only a shirt on for a jacket, smiling and asking how everyone was on this fine winter day.

Hieney was also a good mandolin player. There were gatherings down by the leanto on summer evenings by a cozy bonfire. Hieney would play his mandolin and everyone would be singing. Later on, when the fire burned low, ghost stories would be told! Hieney worked at the Baekeland camp for a good many years.

The Baekelands hired many local people over the years to make improvements and build additional camps for their growing family. John Blanchard and Orrin Lanphear did most of the construction and all the Lanphear boys, Edgar, Stanley, Jerry, and Frank worked there at one time or another. When Ce'line was a teenager, she remembers looking out one of the camp windows and saw the Lanphear boys walk by. Her first thought was, "Wow, where did all those good looking guys come from?!"

Grandma Baekeland loved her camp on Utowanna Lake. It was her custom to take a swim in the lake every day she was in camp. She did this right up into her old age, and it didn't matter what the weather was, she took her daily dip. Leo Baekeland was another story altogether. He was only up to camp for one weekend. He called the place a firetrap and couldn't wait to get back home.

The camps are maintained in a very rustic style on the exterior, and they are well set up and comfortable on the inside. Ce'line remembers riding the Marion River Railroad and taking ferries up the Eckford Chain and also across Raquette Lake. She likes Utowanna Lake much better today, though, because it's less busy and much more peaceful. Her early years at Baekelands gave her a great love for the wilderness, and she feels very much at peace while at camp. While I was standing on the Baekeland dock, it was very easy for me to imagine the Oneonta going by with a load of passengers and heading up the Eckford Chain.

A HUNT TO REMEMBER

When George Baekeland was still a young man, he used to enjoy hanging out with Ernie Blanchard. Ernie would take him trapping, and he also hunted with him occasionally. In time, George became a good woodsman. One fall during the late '20s, the woods between the Marion River Carry and Sargent Ponds were recovering from a recent forest fire. The partridges that year were quite plentiful, and with the brush burned out, they provided some real easy shooting. Ernie and George decided to take advantage of the situation, so they grabbed their shotguns, and began hunting in towards Sargent Ponds. They started dropping birds right from the start. They hunted all the way in to the area of the ponds and had bagged a good number of birds, but it was now getting late in the day. The shooting was excellent and they both hated to quit, so they hunted a little more.

They were on the hillside just east of the big pond when darkness began to settle in. They had no flashlights, so George asked, "Well, what do we do now?" They happened to be near a huge old tree that had fallen down and was scorched by the fire. The stump was still upright and slightly hollowed, but full of dry wood slivers. Ernie said, "We've got lots of birds to eat!" Then he walked over to the big old stump and set it on fire. The stump burned all night long, and the two men roasted birds while Ernie told George many of his adventures while he was hunting, trapping, fishing, and guiding. They visited until dawn and then hiked back to camp.

Years later, George spotted Ernest working along Route 28. He pulled his car off the road and the two men began to visit. George reminisced about good times spent with Ernest's father, and mentioned the Sargent Ponds bird hunt. George said, "You know, that was one of the best times I ever had in my life — the time your dad and I hunted till dark, and then spent the whole night out roasting birds and visiting until dawn!"

EDGAR'S BLUE RIDGE HUNT

Edgar Lanphear was caretaker at Baekelands for a few years during the 40's. He used to hunt the nearby woods regularly in the fall and enjoyed some pretty good success. Edgar always had a curiosity to see what the top of Blue Ridge looked like, so one November day, he grabbed his deer rifle and headed out cross country for the ridge. There was close to a foot of snow on the ground, and the base of the ridge was a good two miles in. He crossed very few deer tracks on his journey in, and when he began climbing the steep slope of the ridge, he didn't see any. However, once he got up on top of the ridge, he ran into a lot of tracks. This was before the big 1950 windfall and the ridge top was fairly open at this time. He began hunting in a westerly direction and hadn't gone far when he jumped out four or five deer. One of them was a buck, but the shot would have been too difficult to try, so he passed it up.

Instead of trailing the spooked deer, he turned around and began hunting east. He hadn't gone far again when he spotted a big buck that was bedded down the slope. "God, I must have hunted right past him!" he thought. As he brought his rifle up for the shot, he noticed that his peep sight was full of snow. The big buck wasn't very far off, and he noticed that the heavy beams on the basket-type rack almost touched where they met by the ends. He blew softly on the peep sight to remove the snow and got most of it out, but not all of it. He could see the buck through it, so he squeezed off a shot. He missed him clean and the buck quickly disappeared in the surrounding cover.

Ed walked down to check for blood or cut hair that might indicate a hit. When he saw the size of the deer's bed and the huge tracks he was leaving, he then realized just how big the deer actually was. He got real let down and discouraged, so he just started heading for home with no further thought of hunting. There was a big storm front moving in, and there were fresh deer tracks everywhere on the way out, but all Edgar could think about was that damn big buck that he'd just missed up on top of Blue Ridge!

THE BIG DRIVE

Peter Roll was in the habit of coming up to Baekelands every fall to do some hunting with his guests. Their success varied with the seasons, but they did hang up some nice deer. It was during the 50's that the state decided to open up the last day of some seasons for a deer of either sex day. Pete decided to hold a big drive on one of these days, and they would hang up a lot of venison. There was Jerry, Edgar, and Frank Lanphear, Bill Eganhoffer, Harry Waldron, Peter Roll, and a number of his guests. They had nine people out on the watch line. The drive was started in the afternoon and it wasn't long until shots were fired, then more, and more. The shooting continued off and on throughout the drive. When the drive was over and everyone came in, it was learned that almost everyone had gotten some shooting in, but not a single deer was taken! Everyone laughed for years afterwards about this drive, but that's just how it goes sometimes!

Harry Waldron was the caretaker for Baekelands from 1951 until the late 1980s. George McCane took over after that and, at this writing, is the current caretaker. Property taxes for camp owners in the Adirondacks have skyrocketed in the last 15 years. So also has the cost of materials and labor for general maintenance. In an effort to hang onto the family properties at Baekelands, the buildings are now rented to the general public for periods of time each year.

THE LANPHEARS OF RAQUETTE LAKE

Anyone who has ever spent any time in the area of Raquette Lake has certainly heard of the Lanphear family. Orrin Lanphear (Ott), was born in Lake George, New York in 1889, but moved into the Central Adirondacks shortly afterwards. At the age of 12, he took a job as chore boy at his uncle's logging camp on Blue Ridge. His uncle was Stillman Lanphear and his camp was located on the north side of the ridge, high up on the east side of what we call the Big Notch. Ott remembers hiking down to Potter Pond on Sunday afternoons to do some ice fishing and shoot his rifle. Potter Pond isn't very big or deep, and Ott used to cut his fishing hole right over the deepest part of it. He used to make some nice catches of trout, and when light conditions were right, he could see the trout swimming around under the ice!

In 1911, Ott married Hazel E. McCane, who was from the Cedar River area. They settled at Raquette Lake, first at Pug Bay, and a little later at Poplar Point. The couple had seven children: Edna, Edgar, Stanley, Gerry, Frank, Jean, and Shirley. Ott worked at just about everything: caretaker, carpenter, guide, trapper, and he also rented cabins. Ott was a very capable man and he passed this knowledge on to his sons. Ott was also an excellent woodsman and a crack shot with a rifle.

THE BARNYARD DRIVE

The boys can remember one fall weekend of the hunting season in 1925, when they were very young. Their father and two other guides, George Newton and Bart Connley, were guiding a party of five clients. On the first day out, they got a nice eight-point buck. The next morning they intended to hunt a section of land over on the north shore of the lake. On the way over in the boat, they decided to put on a short drive behind North Point that was between Bradreth Brook and North Point. It was only a 10- or 15-minute drive, but it would sometimes produce a buck. The watch line was put out and the drive began shortly afterwards. What happened next was hard for even the guides to believe. Several deer were started by the drivers, and they included four nice bucks. Three of them were dropped by the clients, and a nice 10-pointer tried to slip back past Ott, but didn't make it. They had four bucks on the ground in less than 10 minutes, which filled all their clients' tags in a little over a day! Everyone was in a good mood, and they returned to camp with a boatload of bucks. The little drive near Bradreth Brook was always referred to as "The Barnyard Drive" after that.

Ott's sons learned woodsmanship from him at an early age. They learned the country around the lake in all directions, where a cabin could be found if needed, and how to make do if one couldn't be found. Edgar remembers scouting for beaver sign on snowshoes one winter with Ott. They left their home on Poplar Point in the morning and spent the first night in one of Mossy Maxim's line cabins (Pine Stump). The next day, they shoed up through the Wakley Mountain-Blue Ridge Valley. They found Ernie Blanchard's Aluminum Pond cabin, and at that time it was in pretty good shape. Once the boys were competent in the big woods, they were off on their own, hunting, fishing, and running their own traplines.

When Gerry was 16, he used to run a trapline from Camp Kill Kare, up along the foot of Wakley Mountain, over to Aluminum Pond, then on to Falls Brook, and come out of the woods by Marion River. If he didn't find a lot of activity in his traps, he would be out to Marion River by noon! That's covering an awful lot of country in a short while!

When the boys were attending school at Raquette Lake during deer season, they would often talk their teacher into excusing them for a day or an afternoon of deer hunting, if conditions were good. They would hunt the country between Raquette and Sagamore Lakes, and in those days it was nothing to see 20 to 25 deer in a day.

DR. LEWIS

Back in the late 1930s, there was a certain Dr. Lewis that used to come up from down state every fall to hunt in the Raquette Lake area. His favorite hunting region was on the west side of the Sagamore Lodge Road, which runs pretty much north and south. On a routine day's hunt, he would hunt westerly off towards Rock Pond, and when he was ready to return, he would simply use his compass and head east. This always brought him back out to the Sagamore Road and he never had a problem.

One Tuesday, he decided to try a different area, so he drove up Route 28 to a point just past the Marion River Cabins, and parked his car on the south side of the road. He planned on hunting the area around Bear Brook Swamp for the day so he headed south into the woods, just after full light. His wanderings brought him up along the east side of the swamp and he was in by the big Alder bed when he decided to head back out to the road. He had been so used to just heading east to get back out to the road that it never occurred to him that heading east in this locality was wrong. The route he was taking would lead him into the swamps and hills that lay along the foot of Blue Ridge.

Dr. Lewis was 72 years old, and it was cold out with a good foot of snow on the ground. When he didn't return to his lodgings that evening, people began to worry. Wednesday morning they sent someone out to look for him. They found his car, but it had been snowing during the night and they had trouble following his tracks. A larger search party was formed and Thursday morning they went in after him. Gerry and his brother, Stanley, were asked to join in the search, but they were guiding a party of hunters at the Baekeland Camp and couldn't get away. Gerry told the ranger that if they could find the guy's tracks, they would go in after dark and try to bring him out if the search party wasn't successful. Meanwhile, the temperatures stayed bitter cold and there was light snow in the air both day and night.

Dr. Lewis seemed to be traveling in small circles, crossing and re-crossing his tracks, and sometimes crawling through the snow on his hands and knees. All this meandering, plus fresh snow falling steadily, was making progress on tracking the man very slow. Despite all his wandering, he still was moving in an easterly direction. On Friday evening, the ranger looked up Gerry and Stanley. They had trailed Dr. Lewis to a point that was half-way down the length of Blue Ridge and near the head of Loon Brook, along the foot of the ridge. They had marked the tracks where they had left them and he asked the boys if they would go in that night and try to get him. The ranger didn't think the man could last another night.

Gerry made a few phone calls for some more help, then they got together some flashlights, lanterns, sandwiches, and thermoses of hot soup and some whiskey for the trip in. They entered to woods at Loon Brook and took the upper trail to the falls. Then they followed the ranger's tracks south almost to the foot of the ridge. They found the flagging the ranger had left by the doctor's tracks and began to follow. When they got to Loon Brook along the foot of the ridge, they could see where the doctor had crawled on his hands and knees across the brook. Once across the brook, he entered an old logging camp clearing and began rooting around in some old bottles and tin cans he had crawled through in the snow.

Five men were tracking him now, Gerry and his two brothers, Stanley and Frank, and Art Baker and his son, Art. When Dr. Lewis left the logging camp clearing, his track freshened up quite a bit. He began to head off towards the northeast away from the foot of the ridge. The tracks led them over to the hill that is just above Wilson Pond. He got into some fairly steep going and grabbed a seven-foot spruce tree to hold onto. The doctor fell backwards, snapping the young spruce tree off. They found him there lying in the deep snow, with the spruce tree right on top of him. They took the tree off him and he was wringing wet with sweat. Gerry shook him and said, "Are you all right, Doc?" Doc answered back, "Oh yes, I guess so!"

They swung him around so that his feet were downhill, and when they tried to pull him up into a sitting position, he stood straight up. His pants were frozen rock hard so that he couldn't bend his legs. They built a huge fire so that everyone could get warmed up and thawed out. They also got some hot soup into the doctor and a cup full of booze. The country between Wilson Pond and the road wasn't very easy walking, especially after dark with a man who could just barely walk! Gerry wasn't sure if it was because of the rigors of the last three days, or the cup of booze!

They started off towards the road, and had only traveled a short distance when Gerry spotted a light glowing in the woods down the hill. Gerry and Stanley went down to investigate and found a couple of hunters in an illegal cabin. Gerry explained to them what was going on and all he wanted to know was if their tracks led out to the road. They said, "Yes, but it's still a three-and-one-half-mile walk." A long walk for an exhausted 72-year-old man. It was a judgment call on Gerry's part, so he decided to try the walk out. He told the fellas not to worry, he wouldn't turn the cabin location in to the ranger.

They returned to the group and after a brief pow-wow, two of the men headed out cross country for the cars. They would meet them at the Wilson Pond trail head when they got out. They finally got the doc over to the trail, but he was traveling so slow that Gerry was beginning to get darn good and cold. Gerry asked the doctor, "Would you mind if I carried you?" "You can't carry me, I'm too damn heavy!" "Well, we can try. I've carried out buck just as big as you!" The doc weighed 210 pounds so they got him up on a log and he climbed on piggyback style. Gerry carried him all the way out and didn't recall stopping for a break!

When they got out to the cars and back to Raquette Lake, Dr. Lewis said that he wasn't really lost, he was heading east! Gerry replied, "You were heading right for the Indian Lake cemetery, and you were only 25 percent of the way there!" The doctor pulled out his money belt, which was loaded, and he gave each one of the men $20, which was a damn good tip in the late 30's. The doctor never returned to hunt at Raquette Lake again.

Frank had killed a very large six-point buck with huge antlers and massive bases the day before. When he joined the search, he wasn't able to go back in after it until Sunday. When he finally did go back in to get it, he couldn't find the buck. The fresh snowfalls and wind had changed everything. He followed fisher and fox tracks in that area all winter, hoping they would lead him to the carcass, but he never did find his lost buck.

THE WAR YEARS

In 1940, Stanley Lanphear went to enlist in the U.S. Army. He failed the physical examination when they discovered that he had "Bright's Disease." This is a disease of the kidneys, and in young men at that time, it was often a terminal illness. Unfortunately, Stanley died from it later that same year.

Edgar, Gerry, and Frank all served honorably in World War II, and thankfully all returned to their home at Raquette Lake. Edgar was severely wounded by shrapnel, and received the "Purple Heart" in recognition of his bravery. The 1940s also saw the boys marry and settle down in the area. Gerry married Mary Bird in 1940, Edgar married Anne Gibbs in 1946, and Frank married Doris Murray in 1949.

Gerry spent his life managing and caretaking various properties and also guided hunting and fishing parties. He was a very popular fishing guide on Raquette Lake. One season, he kept track of his catches during May and June. He tallied 400 lake trout caught during the 60-day period. That was with a three-fish-per man limit, and sometimes one party in the morning and another in the afternoon.

A NEW GAME WARDEN

In October of 1950, Frank Lanphear was appointed area Game Protector, a position he held for the next 32 years. Franks' territory ran from Inlet to Blue Mountain Lake and from West Canada Lake to the north end of Brandreth Park. Frank had replaced Ray Bourke who had vacated the position in 1945. Leo Minne was the Old Forge warden who helped in covering the area from 1945 until Frank was assigned the district.

Ray Bourke had pinched Frank years earlier for his only game law violation. It was in 1940, and at that time, the license year started on the first day of January. Frank was out hunting rabbits with his brother-in-law just outside the village on January 1. Frank had just shot a rabbit and Ray had heard the shot. When he came over to investigate, he found Frank with the rabbit and no license, a simple enough oversight on Frank's part. Ray didn't see it that way though. He wrote Frank up and it cost him a $10 fine.

Frank made a damn good game warden! He knew and understood the woods, and being a Marine, he could be tough when he had to be. He was also fair and understanding when it came to enforcing the law. He was a well-respected warden. The most common violations he found were untagged deer and loaded guns in a motor vehicle. Selling deer was another frequent violation during the '30s, '40s, and '50s. It was real tough to get a conviction on that type of violation though. The law enforcement community knew it was going on, but deer populations were very high in that period, and they didn't think it was hurting the herd any. They didn't approve of it by any means, and they enforced the law whenever they could.

Frank was also expected to work with other officers, in their districts, one area at a time. Long Lake one weekend, and Indian Lake the next, etc. Sometimes in checking remote areas and trails, there would be three officers together. It was a large area, and at that time there were a lot of hunters. Many a night they would be out until two or three in the morning looking for poachers, and then out all the next day patrolling. The officers weren't paid for this extra time, but they would get it back during the slow months of winter. Road hunters were always a big problem. Sometimes they would shoot a doe, for no apparent reason, and just leave it!

Frank was working with Jack and Jim Hall over in the Cedar River Country one fall. They were checking out a tent camp registered by a group from Ticonderoga. It was located some distance beyond the end of the Cedar River Flow. The officers had come up the length of the flow with a boat, and then hiked in to where the tent was. There was no one at the campsite when they arrived, and the first thing they noticed was deer hair on the tent floor. Frank said, "Sure looks like they got something!" They searched the grounds and found a can that had been sunk into the ground, and then covered with leaves and ferns. It contained a large quantity of fresh venison. The men then went down by the river to eat their lunches and await the return of the hunters.

While Frank sat eating his lunch, he noticed two logs that were laying parallel to one another, and they had the top of a spruce tree forced down in-between them. He couldn't help but think, "Now how in the hell did that spruce top get down between those logs?" After he finished his lunch, he went over and pulled out the spruce top. Under the top was the hide and head of a small doe. They ticketed the hunters when they returned, and put the evidence in one of their pack baskets for the trip out.

On the trail near the end of the flow was a leanto occupied by several hunters from the New York City area. They came up to the leanto from behind and then set down the pack basket. Then they walked around to the front and introduced themselves. Jack asked them how the hunting was, and they responded, "Not so good, we haven't seen any deer yet." Jack then grabbed the pack basket from behind the leanto and pulled out a doe hide and head stating, "Then who does this belong to?" The men stared at the evidence in astonishment. Then they all began talking and arguing at once. "Where in hell did that come from? It's not ours. We didn't kill the deer!" Things were in a real panic for a few minutes, and when it finally calmed down, the officers explained, apologized, and left. Darkness had settled in by that time and it was one of those inky black nights. The trip back down the flow was long and miserable, and they kept hitting stumps or running aground. However, the thought of those guys panicking over those doe remains kept the men laughing off and on all the way back to their cars!

THE SEARCH FOR EDWIN CRUMBLEY

It was August 10, 1951, and Edwin Crumbley was camping at the Golden Beach campsite on Raquette Lake. Ed was a 69-year-old druggist from Fort Ann, New York. He enjoyed his hunting, fishing, and camping trips in the Adirondacks and had been coming to the Raquette Lake area for the past 15 years. Steven, his nine-year old grandson, was with him on this trip, and occasionally they would fish some of the local streams for trout. They each carried a .32 caliber cartridge casing with them. If they wandered apart or wanted to go home, they would blow across the open end of the casing, which would produce a shrill whistle. Ed was hard of hearing, but this was one noise that he could hear quite well.

It was Friday morning and Ed asked Steven if he would like to spend the morning fishing for a trout up along Bear Brook. Bear Brook flows under Route 28 just east of the Marion River Cabins. Steven had made several friends at the campsite, so he decided to stay with one of their families. Ed put his trout fishing gear in the car and told his grandson that he would be back around lunch time, if he didn't get eaten by a bear. Lunch time came and went, and Ed still hadn't returned from fishing. His grandson was getting worried, so he went to the park ranger and told him his story. They waited a while longer, and when it was getting late in the day, the ranger called Frank Lanphear.

The ranger explained the situation to Frank, and Frank got in touch with his brother, Gerry. They grabbed some hand lights and a rifle and drove up to Bear Brook, where they found Edwin's car. They hiked upstream along Bear Brook and by then it was dark. When they got up as far as the first big beaver meadow, they fired off some shots and hollered quite a bit, hoping for an answer, but there wasn't any.

The next morning, a major search was organized, a search that would last for many days. One of the first clues that the search party discovered was that of a fresh spruce bough bed in the area of the first big beaver meadow. It might have been used by him on the first night out. If that were the case, why weren't their shouts and signal shots answered? They reasoned, due to the stress of his situation, he might not be thinking right, and even hiding from the searchers.

As the search progressed, there were as many as 200 people in the woods looking for Ed. People came from all over to help look or support the search party in one way or another. Many people were from the Fort Ann area and a good number were local people. Art Gates and his son, Bob, were there. Bob told me that it was the first year after the big wind storm of November 1950, and there were rafts of spruce trees down everywhere. They had the younger men get up on the trunks of these windfalls and walk along looking down into them. They also checked the deeper areas of the stream and made an effort to drain the beaver ponds to see if he hadn't drowned. A few days into the search, they found his fish pole and reel beside the remains of a fire he had built. A State Trooper came in with a pair of bloodhounds, and they appear to follow a trail up through the middle of the swamp through the biggest alder bed, which was just east of Bear Pond. The upper end of it was flooded pretty good with active beaver meadows, and the dogs were having a lot of trouble in finding enough scent to trail. It was a difficult area to cross, so the trooper pulled off the dogs and brought them back out. Gerry thought the trooper made a mistake by not bringing the dogs over to the hardwoods, on the west side of the beaver meadows.

Ray Colligan and Gerry owned a piper cub airplane. The few signs left by Cromley indicated that he was still able to build a fire. The two men planned to fly slowly, just above the tree tops after dark in hopes of spotting a fire, even with the heavy summer foliage on the trees. The afternoon before the flight, they flew around the entire search area, throwing out thousands of books of matches all over the area so he was sure to find some of them.

That evening, as planned, Ray and Gerry were out flying over the tree tops looking for any flicker of light from the woods just below. They had systematically covered the east side of the swamp and then Bear Brook Swamp itself, and were now beginning to hit the west side. They were flying over the outlet of Slim Pond and heading towards the swamp, when the cabin of the plane suddenly filled with the scent of an evergreen fire. The fold out window had been open during their search, so they both got a good whiff of smoke. Ray was doing the flying and his first instinct was that he might have a motor problem, then he realized what it was. He hollered to Gerry, "Do you smell that?" "Yes, it smells like a spruce fire!" They circled around several times, but couldn't detect its source. The next day, searchers looked through the area, but couldn't come up with anything. After this effort, hope began fading, and the number of searchers dwindled rapidly. It was extremely sad to give up the search for Edwin, but after two weeks, there was little hope of finding him alive.

CLOSURE

Seven years later, a hunter staying at the house of Orrin Lanphear, Fred House of Cicero, New York, found something he thought might be a clue to Cromley's disappearance. He had been hunting the upper reaches of Death Brook, which is just north of Slim Pond. He stopped to take a rest against a large tree, and while looking around, he noticed something shiny on the ground. He bent down and picked it up and he discovered it was part of a canvas fishing vest. It had sinkers and leaders in it, but this area was far removed from areas a fisherman might travel through. He remembered the big search for Cromley, and thought he may have stumbled onto something. It was Sunday afternoon and Fred had to be back in work tomorrow morning. He marked the tree well and then went back to Raquette Lake and told Ott what he had found.

Ott called Gerry, and the next day they hiked up into the area. Fred had accurately described the place where the tree was located, and Ott and Gerry knew that country well, so they located the tree with no problems. The men brought a rake in with them, so they carefully began to remove seven years of accumulated leaves and forest duff. It wasn't long before they found a gray sweater, laid out on the ground with all the buttons in place. It was similar in style to what the older game wardens used to wear. They found a tie clip, some sinkers, and a .32 caliber empty shell. They also found what later proved to be two finger bones, a rib bone, and a wrist bone.

The next day, they returned with the State Police, and a group of volunteers from the Cortland State Teacher's College. They all had rakes or potato hooks and they looked all over the place but couldn't find anything else. They shipped the bones off to the B.C.I. Unit at Albany, New York, and they confirmed that they were human bones from a male, about 70 years old, around five-feet seven-inches in height, and so much weight. Cromley's son, Paul, said, "It described his father perfectly." Paul hiked back into the woods at a later date and erected an iron cross on the spot where they found his father.

THE MARION RIVER CARRY

The Marion River Carry is a well-established portage between the waters of the Eckford Chain and those of Raquette Lake. Originally, it was known as Basset's Carry. Fred Basset put up a small building there and hauled freight over the carry for travelers. He also offered meals and some modest accommodations. In 1890, W.W. Durant had taken over the carry and provided a small hotel there as well. He built a dam across the upper end of the Marion River in order to raise the water level of the Eckford Chain. In 1892, he put up a sawmill at the carry in order to provide lumber for both water systems. Much of the lumber produced was used for the building of Eagle's Nest Country Club, Sagamore Lodge, and Camp Uncas.

By 1900, Durant had built the Marion River Railroad, which consisted of 1,300 yards of track, a small locomotive, and about three small rail cars in tow. When steamboats were the main haulers of passengers and freight on these waters (until 1929), the Marion River Carry was a very busy place. In the early 1930s, when the carry had been all but abandoned, Glade Keith wandered into the remains of the old sawmill. He said, "There was quite an abundance of tools, saw blades, and various parts, just laying around for the weather to claim. Some seemed to be in pretty good shape at that time!"

THE MARION RIVER CABINS

In 1946, Herbert Birrell bought 700 acres of land at the carry, and the following year, built a restaurant and some rental cabins along Route 28. During most of the '50s and into the early 60's, Gerry Lanphear and his wife, Mary, ran the Marion River Cabins and Restaurant.

It was their policy to feed the local deer population during January, February, and March every winter, just to help them through the tough part of the winter. It was also nice just to have them around and enjoy the natural beauty of the wild animals. There were 12 to 15 animals that always came around at that time, and there would usually be an antlered buck or two in the group until they lost their antlers.

One January, there were four antlered bucks that showed up, including one big 10-pointer. The deer seemed to know just who they could trust, and who they couldn't. If anyone other than the family drove into the yard, the whole group would be up and into the swamp in no time. They wouldn't take any chances with newcomers! The big 10-pointer was in the habit of bedding up, almost under their back porch. Their daughter, Marcia, could walk out onto the porch, with the big buck bedded only ten feet away, and she would talk to him. The big buck would lay there listening to her and move his ears, just like he was understanding most of what she had to say.

THE DELUXE BUFFET!

One year, they swapped some Christmas trees for some fine second and third cutting alfalfa hay. They started feeding 12 to 15 deer in January. The deer really liked that hay, and a week later, they had close to 20 deer feeding there. A few days later, 25 deer were showing up, and more came after that. They peaked at 72 deer and had to order more alfalfa to get the deer past the dangerous part of the winter.

One day, the caretaker from the Eagle's Nest stopped by for a visit. When he pulled into the yard, all the deer took off for the swamp, except for seven. When he got out of the car, he recognized them as deer he had been feeding up at Eagle's Nest. He told Gerry, "You've got some of the deer we've been feeding up at the Eagle's Nest!" That was the only winter they offered to feed alfalfa hay.

THE ROAD HUNTERS

One November evening at the Marion River Cabins, Gerry and his wife heard a shot ring out from down the road. It was well after dark, so Gerry went outside to investigate. At first, he didn't hear or see anything unusual, but after a few minutes, he saw a car come up the highway and stop. A fella ran out of the woods and jumped into the car, then it sped off towards Blue Mountain Lake.

This was private land, and legally posted, so Gerry went down to where the fella had come running out of the woods. As soon as he got close, he could smell the fresh kill and offal pile, so he didn't have any trouble in locating the deer. It was a doe, and doe season didn't open until the next day. He had also killed the deer on posted land and after legal hunting hours.

Gerry called up his brother, Frank, who was the district game warden. Frank looked things over and listened to what had happened. He said, "They'll be back Sunday night to pick up the deer, and I'm going to be waiting for them!" Frank took the doe back to Raquette Lake, and hung it up, then he returned with it late Sunday afternoon and put it back where the poacher's had left it. Frank and Gerry then backed the patrol car just out of sight off the road and sat there listening and waiting. "If they show up, I run down first, and then you drive up behind their car with all your lights on."

Along about 8 o'clock, a car came down the road at a good rate of speed and then braked hard when the driver recognized the spot he was at. Frank got out of the car and ran down after them in the dark, with his flashlight out. Meanwhile, the men had located the deer and were pulling it up towards the car. Frank turned on his light and said, "I'll take that deer fellas!" They both dropped the deer and one ran up to the car while the other ran off into the woods. Gerry had quietly pulled up behind the car, and now he switched his lights on. The guy in the car sped off, so Gerry stayed with the deer while Frank went after the car with his siren wailing and red lights flashing. He brought him back shortly, but the fella in the woods was still missing. Frank told the guy, "If you want your buddy to spend the night in the woods, it's up to you, but you and I are going to see the judge in Indian Lake." While they were talking, Gerry saw the other fella cross the road up by the cabins. They all walked up that way, and the guy came over and gave himself up. The judge took the deer away from them and fined them $100 each.

HERB BIRRELL

Gerry worked for Herbert A. Birrell for many years. Birrell was a prominent New York City lawyer, with much of his money invested locally in real estate. Their relationship was much more than employee-employer, though. They were also extremely good friends, and Gerry was his personal guide whenever it came to local fishing and hunting. Additionally, Gerry hunted with Herb in Africa, the western United States, and in Canada.

A FIFTEEN-POINT BUCK

It was during the '50s, that Gerry took one of his biggest whitetails. It was starting the second week of November, and the woods were unusually dry and noisy, making hunting conditions poor. Gerry hunted south of the Marion River Cabins that day, staying in the area of Bear Brook. He had observed some good signs, but saw very few deer. As the day wore on, he slowly began working his way back out towards the road, hunting his way along. It was very late in the day, and he was only a few hundred yards away from the road when he could hear a deer coming. It wasn't very far off, but the sun had already set and the shooting light was almost gone. When the deer finally came into sight, he could see right off that it was a good-sized buck. He had some trouble seeing the front bead on his .35 Remington in the weak light, but when he was sure he was on, he fired.

He could hear the big deer bounding off through dry ground clutter. His hooves were making a hollow rhythmic sound on the dry ground and fading as he went. Then he heard a rattle, rattle, rattle, and a mighty crash, and he knew the buck went down. When he found the buck in the last light of the day, he saw a beautiful 15-point buck. It was a classic even 12-point with three smaller legal points on a big heavy rack. It was only a short pull to the road, and a little while later it was hanging beside Herb Birrell's 12-pointer. He had taken his buck only two days earlier in a different locality.

THE BEAR BROOK CAMP

In 1953, Frank helped Gerry haul in some camping gear to set up a camp along the foot of Blue Ridge. It would be near the headwaters of Bear Brook. The camp was owned by Herb Birrell, and Gerry would guide Herb and his friends out of it during the next two years. They took five bucks out of the area while using the tent, two along the foot of the ridge, and three between the tent and the road. Gerry always enjoyed hunting in there, but he hated to kill anything because it was always such a damn miserable project to get a deer out. He thought the hunting was just as good out near the road, from what he could see.

LATE DAY CONFUSION

The second year the tent was set up, Gerry was in there with three other fellows. He spent one day high on the ridge with Herb and one guest, but by late afternoon they hadn't had any shooting. Gerry said he was going to go straight down to the tent, but Herb and his guest decided to head in an easterly direction and then stay above Bear Brook on their way back. Gerry got back to the tent and met up with the other hunter, then the two men coffled down and visited until dark. Herb and his guest didn't show up.

A while after full dark, Gerry went out and fired off a signal shot. The answer came from way off to the east near Loon Brook. Boy, Gerry sure wasn't looking forward to going after them because his fanny was dragging from going up and down the ridge all day. He told the other fella at the tent to fire a round off every 15 minutes so that Herb would return fire and guide Gerry over to him. He left the tent as fast as he could go, and it took him over 45 minutes to get over to where they were. Gerry asked him, "What in the hell are you doing way over here?" They replied, "We are on the tent brook!" Well, Gerry told them that they weren't, and they started to argue about it. Gerry returned with, "Well, I've got two flashlights on me now that I didn't have on me during the day, now where do you suppose I got them?" It took them well over an hour to hike back to the tent, and only then did they believe him.

PROPERTY DISPUTE

Bears were a constant problem at that campsite. It was almost like the bears considered it their own personal property. They tore the tent up good several times. Gerry put their canned goods in the deepest part of the brook in order to hide them from the bears. When they got heavy rain, which was often, they would have to retrieve all the cans that were washed downstream. They called this their 50-yard refrigerator! By the end of the second season, the bears had trashed the tent to the point where it wasn't worth fixing. They left it where it was, thoroughly disgusted!

BLACK BEARS ARE TOUGH

Gerry's brother-in-law, Ray Colligan, hunted with him sometimes. One day, Ray got himself a buck and after dressing it off, hung it above the ground to cool. He came in the following day to drag it out and discovered that a bear had taken the buck down and had eaten quite a bit of it. Ray had never killed a bear, but this one seemed like a good one to start with. He hiked back out to his camp and left word with his hunting partners that if he was late in getting back to camp that night, not to worry. He would wait as long as it took to get this bear.

He returned to the kill site later in the afternoon with his rifle and a good flashlight. There was a big old tree not too far from the carcass that had a broad limb coming out from it about ten feet above the ground. Ray climbed up onto this and began the long wait for the bear. The air was a little frosty, but he was a good warm-blooded fella that could withstand a little cold, so it wasn't so bad. About 9 o'clock that night, the bear made his appearance, but not on the remains that Ray was watching. If he'd only checked out the area a little better, he would have found a good-sized piece of deer cached just down the hill from the piece he was watching. He could hear the bear coming and then stop and start eating down the hill, and out of range. He could hear the bones popping and cracking for a long, long time. Finally, the bear stopped and came up the hill towards Ray. He could hear the bear getting closer and closer until he was standing right under the tree Ray was in. He switched on his light and shot the bear right down through the back. The bear took off running and bleeding real bad. Ray followed him a short distance, but then decided to come back in the morning with help.

He returned at first light with his brother, Steve, and they resumed tracking. The bear had run perhaps a half mile when he rolled and rolled around in about a 12 foot circle, leaving an awful lot of blood on the leaves. There was a dusting of snow on the ground so it helped them in tracking.

When the bear left the rolled-on area, he headed in the direction of Lost Brook Swamp. There was a big pine log that lay across the brook at the far end of the swamp, and every bear in the region seemed to want to cross that log. Ray told his brother to circle around and watch that log in case he jumped the bear out again between here and the swamp. It took his brother longer than he thought to get the log in sight, and just before he got to it, he could hear the bear going through.

They tracked the bear all day, and every so often he would make one of those big roll areas. They left the track at dark on the side of Squirrel Top Mountain, and weather conditions that night eliminated all signs of the bear. He never did get a bear in all his years of hunting afterwards, but hanging onto a tree, a light, and a rifle while trying to see your sights on a dark night makes for a tough shot!

BEAVER TRAPPING

Back when beaver trapping was profitable, Gerry used to spend a considerable amount of time trapping them. Most of his trapping was done in the Whitney Park area, north and west of Long Lake. Over the years, Gerry figured he's taken over 1,500 beavers and a lot of otter. Herb Birrell used to keep him company on some of these ventures. Herb would stay for a week or two, and sometimes up to a month. He would do the cooking while there and bring in lots of books to help pass some of the time. They had a perfect setup for what they were doing. They used Whitney's big camp on Little Salmon Lake. Gerry would clean skin all his beaver, but no matter how good a job he did, there was always a little flesh and fat left on the hide. The attic in the camp was a huge, open wooden floor, and Gerry used to stretch and tack down the hides, flesh side up, to this floor. Every night when the lights went out, the resident mouse population would come out and eat off the remaining flesh and fat from these hides. Gerry said, "They made a faint little noise, like fit, fit, fit, fit, fit, as they ate, and you could hear them any time you might wake up during the night. By the time the hides had dried, the flesh side would be as smooth as silk. The mice never damaged the fur or bit into the hides so the pelts were all in top condition. I might add that the mice were also in top condition by the time the trapping season ended!

LANPHEAR COUNTRY

The years pass by quickly with many changes in the order of life. The Lanphears made their appearance at Raquette Lake very early in the 20th Century. In 1997, only two of the Lanphear boys are living. They are still active and capable men. Frank still takes his share of the lake trout from the waters of Raquette Lake; and Edgar, well into his 80's, still gets an occasional buck from the nearby woods. The next time you drive by the lake or take a tour on the W.W. Durant, look around you, you're in Lanphear Country!

*Ce'line Kurraker at
her Baekeland camp.
Photo by Bob Elinskas.*

*The Baekeland camps blend in well with their natural surroundings.
Photo by Bob Elinskas.*

The Lanphear boys grew up in an age where guiding was big business. L to R Frank, Stanley, and Gerry Lanphear. Lanphear family photo.

Results from the "barnyard drive" plus one from the day before.

The Raquette Lake guides L to R Ott Lanphear, George Newtown, and Bart Conley. Lanphear family photo.

District game warden in 1974 – Frank Lanphear. Lanphear family photo.

Gerry Lanphear (left) and Herb Birrell with two fine Adirondack bucks. Lanphear family photo.

Ernie Blanchard was real close with his brother-in-law, Art Gates. The two men had spent many a day in the woods together deer hunting, guiding, trapping, and working on line camps. Art was born in an Adirondack logging camp just before the turn of the century. His father was a logger and his mother was a logging camp cook. When Art became old enough, he began working in the woods as a logger as well. He left the lumber camps at the age of 26 when he married his sweetheart, Hazel. Art worked at a variety of jobs which included carpentry, caretaking, guiding, trapping, and ice cutting. Art and Hazel raised four children and gave all of them a college education.

SUBSISTANCE HUNTING

Like most of the residents of that time, Art hunted through necessity, not sport. Blue Mountain Lake was a small community of year-round residents and these people used to look after one another, especially when money was scarce. Ernie and Art used to provide venison to needy families whenever the need arose. Art used to keep a pair of dogs at his home just for this reason. They were used to start and run deer. They were a small, short-legged, mixed-breed of dogs, and to look at them, one would never even consider them to be deer hounds. Their job was to find deer and then slowly trail them, while the hunters would be watching the best escape trails in the area. One of Art's most dependable spots for producing deer was in the channel between Blue Mountain Lake and Eagle Lake. He would turn the dogs loose in one particular area and then move up into the channel to watch. More often than not, he would have a deer in 10 to 15 minutes.

FIRST HUNT FOR BOB GATES

When Art's son, Bob, was only 13 years old, he was regularly bugging his father and Ernie to take him out deer hunting. After the legal season had closed and things in general had quieted down, they took him out. The hunt was in the area of Mud Pond, between Blue Mountain and Long Lake. The locals called that area the hay marsh, because of all the open beaver meadows. Young Bob couldn't have been guided by two more capable hunters in all the Adirondacks.

When they arrived at the marsh, Art stayed out by the car with his two small deer hounds leashed. Ernie and Bob hiked down through the beaver meadows to a run that Ernie knew would be good. When they reached the run, Ernie explained where the deer would come from and told him not to shoot until the deer get real close. He also emphasized to concentrate on only one deer at a time. Bob was using a 32-20 pump rifle that held 12 shots, and Ernie told him to hunker down behind a big sod clump to await the deer.

When Art felt sure the men were in position, he turned the dogs loose. Once the dogs started barking, it didn't seem very long at all until Bob could hear some deer coming. When he peered up over his sod clump he could see a whole herd of deer heading his way. When they were almost on the other side of his cover, he started shooting. He dropped one, then another, and managed to wound two more before they got out of sight. When he checked his rifle, he found that he had fired all 12 shots! Art and Ernie tracked the two wounded deer down and finished them off. It was quite an exciting hunt for a 13-year-old, and one that Bob would never forget.

FREELAND JONES' HARD TIMES

Freeland lived in a small house on the Durant Road. In Free's later years, he fell on hard times. There used to be a long bench in front of Fuller's garage and during the warm days of summer, the old timers used to gather there to visit while smoking a pipe of tobacco. Old Free used to meet there regularly and load up his modest-sized pipe. When his pipe smoked out, he would knock the ashes from it and put it into his pocket. Almost always one of the group would ask him if he wanted a refill of tobacco from their pouch. Free would agree and then take a much larger pipe from his pocket and pack it full. He would then return it to his pocket. The donor would ask if he was going to smoke it and Free's reply was always, "Oh sure, but later, not just now!"

A REAL BAD DAY ON BLUE MOUNTAIN

One day, Freeland approached Ernie and said, "I've got to have some meat! I'm out of money and down to just vegetables, and there's no strength in them!" Ernie said he'd pick him up in the morning and they would do the drive on what they called "sunset." The drive involved the rock ledges that are quite visible from the village and just above the businesses of Potter's and Steamboat Landing. The area just above those ledges is a popular bedding area for some of the local deer population. The plan was to drop Free off where the Maple Lodge Road comes out to Route 30. Free would then wait for 45 minutes while Ernie, Ernest, and Art drove over to the far side of the ledges and hiked up the slope to position themselves along three good runs that left the bedding area. Free would then walk through the bedding area towards the watchers, striking trees with a stick as he traveled. It was a quick and easy drive and had dependably produced deer many times in the past.

They left Free with Art's car to wait out the 45 minutes in, and Ernie drove his car around to the trail head where his group hiked up the slope and got themselves into position. Once Free started moving, it usually wasn't long before a deer would come along one of the runs they were watching. The men waited in place for quite a long while and no deer showed.

They were beginning to worry about Freeland's welfare so Ernie came down the slope to talk things over with Art. As Ernie drew near, Art said, "Do you smell anything?" "Yeah, it smells like shit to me!" "Well, that's what I thought!" Ernest was coming up the hill to join the two men and overheard the conversation and he could smell it too. Shortly afterwards, they could hear the sound of a stick hitting a tree and then the portly form of Freeland Jones appeared. When he walked up to them, he stunk like hell and was covered with shit from his neck down. Ernie said, "Free, where in hell have you been?" He then explained that when he crossed Route 30 to start the push, he walked across Mrs. Morrison's backyard, and the ground over her septic tank caved in. Free went right up to his neck and it took him a good half hour just to get out of it. Art, Ernie, and Ernest all started laughing, which didn't make Free feel any better for his ordeal. What really hurt him was that Ernie wouldn't let him in his car, so he had to walk all the way home, and there wouldn't be any meat for the pot when he got there!

THE GUIDE'S SEASON

When the woods were full of down-state hunters, some of the local people were a little nervous about going into the woods to do their hunting. In addition, the people that guided, housed, fed, and otherwise catered to them, were too busy during the regular season to go out and get their own deer. They needed those last few dollars to help get through a long winter when money is scarce. It was this need that brought about the "Guide's Season." There was nothing official about it, and it was all done very much on the Q.T. The week after the regular season closed became the guide's season for those people who couldn't get out during the regular season. Some of the game wardens knew what was going on, but unless someone brought their deer out to flaunt before the public, they didn't want to know anything. The winter economy was tough enough on the locals.

Bob Gates used to guide for Ernie, and he did this right up until the time Ernie couldn't guide any more. Bob said Ernie always prided himself on his ability to remember the woods. He would sometimes say that you could show him any tree, no matter where or how far back in it might be, and a month or so later he would take you back in and show you the same tree. He was never challenged because they knew he could do it!

WHERE'S MY BEER!?

There was one time, though, that Ernie wasn't so sharp. It was common knowledge that Ernie loved his home brew. Whenever he planned on hunting a certain area regularly during the coming season, he would sometimes cache a number of bottles of the brew back in the woods where he could later slack his thirst.

One fall he packed in two burlap bags that were partially filled with bottles of brew. He carefully buried them and then mentally marked the spot so he would find it during the upcoming deer season. A few weeks later when he returned for a cold bottle, try as he would, he couldn't find the cache! Every time he came through that area, he would look for his cache and it bothered him something awful that he couldn't find it. The home brew is still in there, somewhere.

ERNIE'S LAST YEARS

When Ernie started to noticeably slow down, some of his friends would kid him about it good-naturedly. One of the stories they used to tease him with went like this: After last fall's deer season, Ernie was found to be crying at a local bar. When the bartender noticed, he came right over and asked him what the problem was. Ernie sobbed, "I'm getting to be an old man!" "Why Ernie, what makes you say that?" "Well, I only got 16 buck this fall." "Ernie, that's a good number of deer. What's so bad about that?" "I saw 17!"

By the 1950s, Ernie was entering the twilight of his years. His guiding and trapping activities had all but come to an end. Now he was afflicted with prostate cancer, and for some reason, surgery was not one of his options. He would have to live with it as best he could. He had plenty of family living in the area should he need help, so that was a comfort to him.

THE LAST DEER HUNT

Ernie's last deer hunt occurred in the fall of 1959. His health wasn't very good so he relied on his sons, Ernest and Albert, to provide him with some fresh venison every fall. The two men had been working pretty steady right through November, and the few times that they had hunted, didn't produce anything. Now the end of the season was rapidly approaching and Ernie, who had his heart set on eating some fresh venison, was getting visibly agitated. Just before the season ended, Ernie said to the two of them, "Well, I guess I'm not going to get any venison unless the old man goes and gets it himself!"

In the morning, he grabbed an old octagon-barreled 30-30 rifle, some shells and a lunch, and had Albert drop him off at one of his old haunts. Ernie told him, "Now by jeez, you pick me up just at dark. I don't want to be out here after dark!" Albert returned for him just after dark, and old Ernie climbed in. "Well, did you get anything?" The old man replied with a smirk, "Well certainly I did! I got what I came for!" Ernest came back later with a light, backtracked him to the deer, and brought it out.

Ernie died on October 12, 1961, at the age of 84, and was laid to rest in Indian Lake Cemetery. He was born in the age of the guide boat and while most of the Adirondacks were still covered with virgin forest.

He saw the old forest and the early loggers, and the formation of the Adirondack Park. He also saw the building of some of the grand hotels and Durant's "Great Camps." He saw the implementing of new game regulations and the whole area opened up by new highways, outboard motors, and airplanes. Ernie was well read and could talk intelligently on almost any subject. His incredible knowledge of woodcraft and animals, gained from living off the nearby woods and waters, had served him well. Except for two seasons of manning the fire tower on Blue Mountain, Ernie had never worked for a paycheck. He was a remarkable man, and truly one of the last great guides of the Adirondack Park.

In 1990, one of Ernie's old clients stopped in for a visit with Ernest during the hunting season. The man was well up into his 70's, but still in pretty good shape. He hiked back into the site that he and Ernie used to hunt out of. The remains of the old stove they used were still there. He got a stick and stirred around in the leaves, uncovering some pots and dishes they had once used. Old memories began to come to mind. He had some great memories of that camp and Ernie from a time that has passed from us all.

Art Gates in doorway and Ernie Blanchard at the Aluminum Pond cabin.
Art Gates family photo.

Cascade Pond with Blue Ridge in the distance.
Photo by Bob Elinskas.

Ernie Blanchard in the late '50s. Blanchard family photo.

Ernest and Carrol Blanchard, Photo by Bob Elinskas.

THE BROWN FARM

The Brown Farm is steeped in a rich tradition of logging, hunting, and fishing. The Browns, who currently own and live on the farm, are direct descendents of J. Prentiss and Louisa Brown, the first family to settle in the Cedar River Valley.

J.P. Brown was born on March 2, 1827, at North River. He was a professional logger. In 1847, he married Louisa Sarah Bennett, and in the late 1850s they moved into the Cedar River country. At that time, there was no village at Indian Lake, and he used his oxen to help clear a road into the Cedar River Valley. He put up a small building of logs and then brought his family in from North River. About three years after he moved his family into the area, another logger by the name of Sprague extended J.P.'s road a little further up the valley and set up a logging operation. The men lumbered together and opened up 50 acres of meadowland that they sowed to oats. They also put up a barn to house their horses. The barn and property eventually became the property of Harry McCane.

In 1866, Prentiss and Louisa moved their family farther up the Cedar River Valley. This time, he helped to survey a square mile of land consisting of lots 74, 75, 95, and 96. Prentiss made a contract with Orson Richards, who represented the lumber company that owned the property. The deal was to clear that section of marketable trees, in exchange for the title on the square mile of property to be cleared. He did this, and it became the site of his permanent home, The Brown Farm.

J.P. and Louisa had 11 children, five boys and six girls: Henry, Leonard, William, Fred, Josiah, Sarah, Sophia, Harriet, Jennie, Henriette, and Edwinna. It was during this era that Ned Buntline was living at Eagle Nest on Eagle Lake. Ned had built the fictional character of "Buffalo Bill" after a buffalo hunter named Bill Cody. Ned's fictional books became very popular and much sought after. Prentiss Brown used to take Ned's current installment of "Buffalo Bill" from Eagle Nest to North River to put it into the mail and pick up his incoming mail. It was a two-day trip, one to North River and back, and one cross-country to Eagle Nest and back. He held this job until Ned eventually left Eagle Nest.

Prentiss also helped to establish the Town of Indian Lake and attended the first town meeting. He was elected Justice of the Peace and held that position for many years. He was a staunch Republican and never missed voting or a town meeting from the first town meeting until the time he died. He was also a devoted Christian and a member of the Methodist Church. He had a big hand in building the first church in Indian Lake and in organizing the first Sunday schools.

It was recorded in Stoddard's Guidebook to the Adirondacks in 1883, that Prentiss Brown was a proprietor of a lodge known as "Sportsman's Home." The rates were $6.00 per week, and special arrangements had to be made for transportation from town out to the lodge. The lodge attracted the hunting and fishing public as well as loggers who might be working in the nearby woods, or in times of river drives.

J.P.'s five sons all became well-known and highly skilled guides. There were a great many entertaining stories brought home by this guiding family in the late 1800s and early 1900s. This was before the age of radio in that district and their guests were always entertained with a never-ending supply of incredible wilderness adventures. William Brown's daughter, Gertrude M. Brown, used to delight in listening to all the stories that her father, uncles, and Grandfather Prentiss would entertain their guests with. She wrote many of them down, and later published a small book of them, including some of her own poetry, entitled, *The Browns*. She also published some of them in, "High Spots," a quarterly publication of the Adirondack Mountain Club. Most of these were printed during the 1930s. The following selection is taken from her book, *The Browns*, to give you a feel for the early North Woods tales.

> One day I took my gun and went a-hunting. I tramped all day through the woods and never saw a thing. Towards night I came out on the shore of Stephan's Pond, and was about to start for home when I saw a big buck. I raised my gun to shoot him when, just beyond I saw a big black bear. I wanted both but could not decide which to shoot. On looking again, I could see that the buck's neck was in line with the bear's heart. I took careful aim with the big bored Winchester rifle and fired. I killed them both. The bullet cut the jugular vein on the big buck and passed through to hit the bear right in the heart. At the same time, the ramrod flew backwards out of the rifle and split the limb on which six ducks were sitting. The limb closed on their toes, holding them fast. The recoil of the gun sent me backwards into the water. When I climbed back out of the water, my pack basket was full of trout.

Gertrude writes, "That was one of many stories told by my father, uncles, and grandfather during those early days of guiding."

Josiah Brown was one of the better storytellers in the family and was once voted "the biggest liar in Hamilton County" by one of the local civic organizations. Josiah married Bertha Shaw and they remained on the farm after the other children had moved off. They worked the farm and helped J.P. and Louisa through their old age. Josiah and Bertha had five children, Fanny, Myron, Ernest, Dora, and Earl. Ernest married Elizabeth Ovitt, and they remained on the farm helping Josiah and Bertha. Elva, the daughter of Ernest and Elizabeth, now owns and runs the farm. Elva married Arthur W. Brown of Port Leyden (not related), on June 27, 1956, and they had four children, Marie Elizabeth, Edgar Arthur, Irene Lois, and George Herbert. These children were also raised in the traditional "Brown Farm" environment.

The farm has three rental cabins that are usually full during the hunting season. In earlier years, the house also would be full with boarding hunters. The cabins are quite rustic, but their regulars come back year after year! In a pinch, the farm has accommodated up to 33 people, but that was packing it in pretty tight. At one time, they used to board river drivers. Elva said you can still find a few of the floorboards that were marked by their caulked boots. Stock on the farm includes dairy cows, work horses, pigs, chickens, and goats.

Ernest used a team and wagon to bring hunters out into the woods before dawn. The wagon had brackets that would hold lanterns to light up the roadway. The light wasn't for the benefit of the horses as they could see quite well without the light, but the driver and passengers had to see limbs that might be hanging into the roadway or a possible windfall across the road.

"THE COSSAYUNA GANG"

One group of regulars, "The Cossayuna gang," has hunted the farm since 1952. It all began with a "chance" meeting with Ernest Brown. Bill Morrison of East Greenwich, New York and a life member of the group gave me this account. In the region of East Greenwich, Argyle, and Cossayuna Lake, New York, a certain group of mostly dairy farmers and friends used to gather each fall to hunt the local deer population. One year, member Alf Thygeson dropped a big 10-point buck and the group formed a club shortly afterward calling itself, "The 10-Point Fish and Game Club of Cossayuna." The club enjoyed hunting the local hills, but they often talked amongst themselves about getting a lot up in the Adirondacks and building a small cabin to hunt out of.

The talk became serious enough so that one summer, four of the members took a ride up into the mountains to see if they could find a lot to buy and build on. Towards the end of the day, they found themselves riding down the Cedar River Road. Eventually, they came in sight of a house with an older man standing on the porch. The men stopped to visit for a while and learned that they were talking to Ernest Brown. He was using a pair of crutches to get around because of an injury he received during World War II. They told Ernest of their desire to buy a lot to build a hunting cabin on. Ernest told the men that they would be foolish to spend lots of time and money on a lot and cabin. He explained that he took in boarders and also had three cabins that are rented out during the hunting season. "When you come up, it'll only cost you $5 a piece per day for room and board, and you'll have this property to hunt on, plus the forest preserve. Why would anyone want to monkey around with a camp?" Well, it sounded like a real good idea, so they kept in touch with Ernest and made arrangements to come for the first three days of the 1952 deer season.

That first year, 13 members of the club came up and they all had a really great time. They brought back three whitetail bucks for their effort. It became an annual event for the club, with as many as 19 members coming up at one time. They always reserved for the first three days of the deer season. Since most of the men were dairy farmers, it was hard for them to get away from the farm for much longer. Breakfast would always be served up at the house, well before dawn, and each man would have a nice bagged lunch made up for him, which included a big fresh apple grown on the farm. Edgar Brown remembers the group as all being hard hunters, hunting from first light until last. Elva's mother, Elizabeth, was a very good cook, and always had a delicious meal ready for the men when they returned.

SECOND CHANCE BUCK

Porter Burgess was the oldest member of the group and a real sharp hunter. Bill Morrison was never far away from him on the hunts, and he can remember Porter dropping at least seven bucks over the years. Porter carried a Model 8 Remington auto in .35 caliber. Whenever he got in any shooting at a buck, it was usually two quick shots and both bullets would always be right in the heart or very close to it.

One time they were hunting off to the west of the farm, up on Round Top Mountain. They had a line of watchers spread out and when the drive was under way, three doe and a beautiful buck came walking by Lynn Huggins. Lynn shot at and missed the buck, which was an easy shot. Lynn had made a rush trip up to Brown's the night before and had forgotten his rifle. Not wanting to go all the way back for it, he bought a new 30-30 in Indian Lake the night before, but didn't have time to sight it in, and it cost him a real nice buck!

They put on two more drives in different areas, but with no success. Later in the day when they started to hunt back towards the farm, Bill Morrison suggested that they drive Round Top again on the way back, and they all agreed. Shortly after the drive got under way, Bill heard two quick shots and thought, "Port's got a deer." He did, and it was the same buck that was missed earlier by Lynn. The beautiful eight-pointer tried sneaking back past Porter, and this time, he didn't make it. It was the biggest buck the boys had ever taken out of Brown's.

It was a long, and sometimes steep, pull back down to the Cedar River Road. They used a rifle sling to pull the buck with and twice when the buck came up against a log, it broke, sending both pullers headlong off down the hill and giving the onlookers a big belly laugh. When they finally got to the road with the buck, they were about two miles down the road from the farm.

It was getting close to supper time, and they hated to be late for supper! Bill said, "Now what are we going to do? It's a long way back to the farm!" The dead buck lay in the knee-high grass, just off the edge of the road. Port said, "Nothin' to it, let me handle this." Porter was always a real comic and a lot of fun to be with. He could hear a car coming up the road and heading in the direction of Brown's. As soon as the car came up the road and into view, Port held up the deer's head so the rack was plainly visible above the grass. When the occupants of the oncoming car saw the rack, they brought the car to a stop to have a real good look. The driver got out of the car to see the whole deer, and Porter covered the antlers with his jacket. The driver said, "What's the matter?" Porter said, "There's only one way you're going to get a good look at this buck, and that's to give one of us a ride up to the Browns to get our car so we can take him home!" Everyone had a good laugh, and they got their ride to Brown's.

Bill Morrison thought of the Brown Farm as being just like home. He knew the country well on both sides of the river. He also knew everyone and watched the Brown children grow up. Edgar and George were both excellent shots and good hunters. He can still see George as a genuine daredevil, racing around on a three-wheel ATV, and once in a great while, taking one hell of a spill. He also thought Edgar was a damn good welder. The last year that the original group went up to hunt was in 1990, and there was only Bill Morrison and Leon and Arnold Abrahamson. The "Cossayuna gang" always counted their stays at the Brown Farm as time well spent!

BROWN FARM MEMORIES

Elva remembers her father telling of early times on the farm. Once, there were as many as four of the old-style crank telephones in the house. One line ran through the Wakley Mountain, Blue Ridge Valley, to Camp Kill-Kare, and another ran around the east end of Blue Ridge and then cross country to Eagle Nest, on Eagle Lake. When the lines were in operation, it wasn't unusual to get a call from Kill-Kare with a request to ring Eagle Nest on the other line in hopes of finding a certain party. If that person was located, then the speakers and receiver would be reversed and held together while the parties conversed.

A good foot trail ran the length of the line that went to Camp Kill-Kare. Ernest Brown and Harry McCane used to hire out for an occasional job at the camp, and they would use this foot trail to commute — a distance of nine miles.

Ernest Brown died in November of 1969, and his wife, Elizabeth, died in 1974. Eleven years later, Arthur, Elva's husband, died of respiratory complications in 1985.

The Brown Farm is uniquely different in that it is surrounded by miles and miles of wilderness, both public and private. Over the years, they have had a wide variety of bear experiences. Edgar has come home to find one standing on the front porch, and it isn't uncommon to sight one crossing the back pasture while looking out one of their windows.

THE NEIGHBORHOOD WATCH

A number of years ago, the people along the Cedar River Road were suffering from a rash of burglaries. A neighborhood watch program was set up, and Elva and her kids did their part by keeping watchful and also inspecting some of the nearby camps that were just out of sight of the road.

One afternoon, Elva and Edgar went out to inspect some of these camps to see if they had been tampered with. Edgar was only 13 years old at the time. Elva would check out the front and one side of each camp, and Edgar would check out one side and rear of the camp, looking for signs of a forced entry. On one of these inspections, Edgar ran around to the rear of the camp and came face to face with a very large black bear. They both stood looking at one another for maybe 30 to 45 seconds, and then the bear slowly turned and walked off into the woods. When Edgar ran back out to the front of the building, Elva took one look at him and knew something had happened. She said, "When I looked at him, it appeared that every hair on his head was standing straight up!" Then he told her of his "close encounter" with the bear.

THE BURGLAR

The Browns had a small collie dog named Cassie. Cassie had the run of the house during the day when people were up and around. However, at night they were trying to break her of lying on the furniture, so she was tethered near the rear door by her mat with water and food bowls nearby. One night in early summer, they were all awakened by a tremendous crash and then the hysterical yipping of Cassie! They all rushed downstairs and headed for the back door. The back door had been open slightly, but now it was wide open! They turned on the backyard floodlights and went out onto the back porch. Both of the large flower boxes had been knocked over, and when they looked out on the rear lawn they saw a large black bear. He was busy eating all the scraps from the garbage can, which had been inside their back door only minutes earlier. He looked up briefly and gave them all a look that seemed to say, "What's all the fuss about?" Edgar went back in for a rifle and scared him away with a couple of shots. They didn't want to encourage this bear to come back, especially since he was bold enough to go in through the back door for the garbage can.

NO SLEEP DUE TO BEETS

Edgar works in North Creek at the Garnet Mine. One of the fellas that works with him grows a big garden every summer. One day, he approached Ed and asked him if he wanted any beet greens. Edgar said, "Beet greens, what do I want beet greens for?" The fella told him that horses love them and he knew that Edgar kept a team on the farm. Ed thought he would give them a try, so after work, he headed over to the guy's house and had about eight bushels of beets dumped into the back of his pickup truck. When he got home it was getting late, but he drove out into the pasture and kicked off a good pile of beets, but not all of them.

He headed for bed around 10:30, and it was one of those warm summer evenings when you go to sleep with all the windows wide open. Around 1:00 a.m. he was awakened by the damnedest noise. It sounded like someone was dragging their fingernails across a chalkboard! He lay in bed trying to figure out what it could possibly be, when suddenly he realized it was coming from where he had parked his pickup truck! "Oh no, I'll bet it's a damn bear!" he thought.

It was his brand-new pickup, and only a few months old. He grabbed his shotgun and a few slugs, a flashlight, and was out the door. He shone the light all around, but no bear could be seen. He walked over to his pickup truck and what a hell of a mess it was! There were muddy bear tracks and scratch marks all over it! That bear must have been in and out of that truck 20 times or more. Edgar swung the light around one more time, and then back by the house where he had just come from appeared two glowing eyes on a coal black form! God, those eyes looked two feet apart! He thought, "I don't think I have enough gun!" The bear moved slowly to his left and away from the house, giving him a safe shooting lane. He really didn't want to shoot the bear, but he didn't want him coming back and doing more damage than he already had. When the shooting was over, the giant bear turned into one that wouldn't weight 300 pounds!

INVISIBLE INK

One fall, on a damp and rainy day, one of their hunting guests killed a large black bear. Because of the rain, the hunter elected not to fill in his harvest ticket for the bear until after he got it back into camp and hung up. When the bear was hung, he immediately went into the house and began filling out his tag. Elva personally watched him fill it out and then go over and attach it to the bear's head. A few hours later, the game warden stopped by and spotted the bear hanging over by the cabin. He asked Elva who got it and if it was properly tagged. Elva told him who and said that it was then the warden went over to examine the bear. Meanwhile, the hunter that had taken the bear was sitting on the front porch of the cabin, contentedly smoking a pipe and taking all this in. The warden looked over the bear and then looked at the tag. He hollered over to Elva if she was sure he had filled out the tag. She replied, "I stood right here by the kitchen table and watched him fill it out, and it was done proper!" The warden hollered back, "Well, there's nothing written on this tag!" The pipe-smoking hunter who had bagged the bear held the pipe in his mouth so that it stuck straight out from his face. Edgar said, "When the warden said there was nothing written on the tag, the end of his pipe immediately fell about two or three inches!" The mystery was solved when it was discovered that the hunter had used a felt-tipped pen to fill out a damp tag. After the bear was tagged, the additional rainfall quickly washed off the markings on the tag. The warden let him off but warned him never to use a felt tip on a tag again.

THE TRACKING BEAR

George was hunting the Panther Mountain area one time on eight inches of snow. It had rained the day before and then froze hard forming a very noisy crust. It was a lousy hunting condition, but it was either hunt with it or stay home. He was hunting high on a hardwood ridge and was moving across its slope when he stopped to sit on a log and look over the terrain. As soon as he sat down, he could hear the sound of crunching footsteps slowly heading his way. He thought it must be another hunter. Who, besides me, would be crazy enough to hunt way back in here on a day like today? Shortly afterwards, he made out the form of an approaching black bear.

The bear was walking parallel to George's tracks and just down the hill from them. Then he hooked up the hill and came onto George's fresh tracks. His head jerked up as he caught the scent stream, and he started looking nervously all around. Then when he was satisfied that there was no danger, he seemed to calm down, and stuck his nose deep into one of the tracks. He began following George's tracks in this manner, sniffing one track after another. George wasn't interested in shooting the bear, but he had to smile at the bear's preoccupation with his tracks. When the bear got to within 30 feet of him, George suddenly stood up and shouted as loud as he could, "Get the hell out of here!" The bear swapped ends immediately with snow, ice, sticks, and leaves flying all over the place, as the bear tore a path off through the hardwoods. He even bent over a decent sized beech sapling in his haste to get out of there. George chuckled off and on the rest of the day every time he thought of the sight of that bear swapping ends and cutting a new trail off through the hardwoods.

Elva is no stranger to a rifle and has been shooting since she was eight years old. She also enjoys a little deer hunting and has taken several bucks herself. The biggest buck she has taken should have been a nice eight-pointer, but one side of its rack was deformed and only carried a spike. Whenever she gets one, she'll dress it out and then have the boys drag it out for her. If the boys are real handy, she'll have them dress it out too! In the fall of 1997, Edgar and George had little time for hunting due to various reasons so they didn't get any deer. Elva, however, went out and bagged herself an eight-point buck!

ELVA'S DEER

Elva is very protective of the deer around the farm. The first time I met Elva, it was in the fall. As we talked by the front door, there were three doe and a six-point buck feeding under her apple tree in the front yard and only a few feet from the road. She excused herself and the next thing I knew, she was roaring after them on a four-wheel drive ATV like she was driving cattle. Up the bank and down through the pines they all went in high gear! She came back as quickly as she left, saying, "If those God darned road hunters see that buck, they'll be around all the time trying to get him!" She had just finished saying that, when the same four deer came back and resumed feeding under the apple tree again!

The Browns feed deer every winter. They have fed as many as 77 deer at one time. They very seldom see any real big bucks at the feeder, though. Elva enjoys feeding the deer and knows every one of them. The deer also know and trust her. When she puts out the daily ration of cracked corn for them, she calls and talks to them. They come streaming out of the woods and gather around her. If anyone else puts out the food, they are very hesitant to come out.

The Brown Farm is located near the S.E. end of Blue Ridge. Photo by Edgar Brown..

One of 3 rental cabins on the Brown Farm. Brown family photo.

"The Cossayuna Gang"
Standing L to R Al Durkee, unknown, Dick Hall, Bruce McMorris, Bill Wood,
Stanley Waite, Charles Bailey, Alf Thygesen, Don Bain. Sitting L to R Willard Reed,
Jim McNeil, Bill Morrison, Jim Phalen, Phil Waite, Arnold Abrahamson, George Reid.
Porter Burgess. Laying L to R Larue McClay, Ed McMorris. Bill Morrison photo.

Elva feeds her deer. When she calls, they come running!, Photo by Bob Elinskas.

HEADQUARTERS CAMP

Bill Wakley was the original builder of "Headquarters." In the 1870s, he extended the Cedar River Road six miles past the Brown Farm, to what was then called the Cedar River Falls. There he built a dam, put up a saw mill, and built a large hotel named Cedar Falls Hotel. The hotel was locally referred to as "Headquarters," and as time went on, that's the name that stuck.

The buildings on the property have suffered from a large number of fires down through the years. The property has also been leased by a variety of proprietors. The original dam at Headquarters was rebuilt in 1902, so that a large volume of logs could be sent down the Cedar River and eventually to Glens Falls on the spring run off. The dam was rebuilt again in 1919. This time, they used a stone-filled, log-cribbed structure. The dam and flow were used to drive logs to market at Glens Falls through 1948. After that, they were brought out by truck.

By 1953, the dam was in very poor condition and not holding back very much water. The buildings were not being maintained and were also deteriorating.. Finch & Pruyn and International Paper Company had jointly owned the Flow and Dam site since 1889. In 1964, it was sold to the state. The dam was rebuilt in 1970 and a public campground now occupies the site.

Frank Pelon ran Headquarter's Camp during the first part of the 20th century. He also tended the dam and catered to the various logging firms that were operating in the area. Wildlife was plentiful, and Frank did an excellent business every fall with the hunters.

THE MITCHELS OF INDIAN LAKE

In the 1920s, John Mitchel leased the property from Finch & Pruyn and International Paper. He ran it seasonally as a hunting and fishing lodge. John was well liked, and he also did an excellent business. During those years, Headquarters consisted of three cabins and a main lodge. It would accommodate up to 37 people.

Ed Mitchel, John's nephew, lived in Indian Lake and was a great, great grandson of Sabael Benedict. Benedict was an Abenaki Indian, originally from Maine. He is considered the first permanent settler of the Indian Lake area. Ed began guiding out of Headquarters Camp in 1934 at the age of 19.

Like many young men in the North Country at that time, he adjusted his age to "21" in order to procure the needed "Guides License." The going rate for guides at that time was $7 a day, but Ed had to give Headquarters $5 a day for room and board. Two dollars was what he got to keep.

GAINING EXPERIENCE

The biggest buck he can ever remember was one that his father killed, up in the Cedar River Country, near Buell Brook. It was late in the season and Ed and his father, Ed Sr., were out looking for some venison of their own. The two of them had guided clients all season, and this was the first chance they had to get out for themselves. They had split up and went their separate ways early in the morning, when Ed Jr. cut a huge track, right at the start. He started tracking the deer and it wasn't long before he jumped it out of its bed. It was a big buck and Ed got off three or four shots at it as it ran off, but didn't hit it. He tracked the buck all morning and into the middle of the afternoon, jumping it several more times. Each time the deer was jumped, Ed would get off two or three shots at it, but he couldn't manage to hit it. By the middle of the afternoon, he was getting low on ammo and enthusiasm for the chase! The buck was heading for the top of steep hardwood knoll along Buell Brook when he left the track and headed for the trail out, and that's when he ran into his father.

He told his father of his adventures with the buck. Ed admitted he was young and really didn't know a lot about deer hunting yet, but he knew he'd had enough of this buck. Ed Sr. said, "I'll go and get him." Ed Jr. replied, "Go to it." Old Ed picked up the track and when he knew the buck was heading for the top, he left the track and made a big circle around to the far side of the knoll, then he quietly and slowly stalked up to the top. After some earnest looking, he spotted the buck bedded and looking down his back trail. One bullet from his 44-40 anchored the big buck in his bed. Old Ed knew the game well, and was an excellent rifle shot. Very few deer ever got away from him, once within range. He hollered down to his son, who came up the hill following the big buck's tracks right into his bed. They tried to move the buck to a more open area for dressing him out, but they had a real tough time in moving him anywhere. He had a large heavy beamed rack that only carried seven points.

Ed's Uncle John had a horse that he kept at Headquarters, just for bringing deer out of the woods, and that horse was darn good at it. The horse would go just about anywhere in the woods and his uncle had a packing harness made up for it that would carry two deer at a time out, if need be. The horse never had driving lines on it, because it would follow you wherever you went in the woods. They brought the big buck out of the woods the next day. After it had hung for 10 days, they decided to weight it before they butchered it up. It went 265 pounds!

THE NIGHT SHIFT

Ed remembers a Dr. Rose from New York City getting lost one fall. He had been lost for two and a half days, way back in the Buell Brook region. Ed and his uncle John were out looking for him and were in about three and a half miles. It was 11 o'clock at night. They had fired some signal shots and had heard the fellow holler back at them. However, when they tried to close the distance and go to him, he would be back in the area they had left or off in another direction. Still, the fellow would holler after every shot. Ed and John finally guessed that the guy must be deliberately trying to stay away from them.

Uncle John said, "We'll get this guy!" They came down off the mountain a short way to where a trail ran off at an angle towards, but below where they had last heard him. John told Ed to go down the trail a distance and then cut in and listen for him when I shoot. The woods were reasonably dry and you could hear things pretty good in places. Ed did as he was told and when John shot, he heard the guy holler and then start to run. He was quite a distance off, but moving towards the trail that Ed was near. Ed got back on the trail and then tried to close the distance without the aid of his flashlight. Ed remembered it as tough going, and he got slapped pretty hard in the face several times while running down the trail. When he figured he was pretty close, he switched on his light and ran up to the guy.

The doctor didn't try to run away but started babbling crazy things and acted mad and belligerent about being found. When Uncle John showed up, the doctor started going crazy and acting wild. Uncle John grabbed him by the collar and slapped him real hard across the face three or four times. Ed was wondering whether or not it was the right thing to do, but it calmed him right down.

They gave him some hot coffee from a thermos and a bagged lunch. He ate it all down and wanted more, but they told him he'd have to walk for his next meal. It was about midnight when they started the walk to the lodge. The doctor was about 60 years old and very weak from his ordeal so it took them all night to get back. Breakfast was being served when they walked in, so they all sat down and had breakfast. Doctor Rose had come up with three other doctors and after he ate, one of them gave him a shot to help him relax and sleep. Ed saw him a day later and he seemed his old self again. While he was lost, he left a beautiful bolt-actioned 30-06 back in the woods somewhere. It had an expensive scope and a real fancy stock on it. They looked for it every time they hunted that area, and never did find it.

THE LAST BUCK

At the very end of one deer season, Ed, his father, and Uncle John were trying to close up Headquarters for the winter. There was one hunter left, and he had been in almost every weekend of the season. He had his "chances" at filling his tag, but one thing or another had gone wrong all season. Now, with the season about to close, he was turning into a real pain rather than a sport. While the sport was outside, Uncle John said to Ed and his dad, "Listen. Why don't you take him to the big swamp and maybe between the three of you, fill his tag."

Ed Sr. led the way and placed first the sport, and then his son on watch. He told Ed that he would circle the big swamp and then hunt down through the alders until he was across from him, and then whistle so they could meet up.

Ed Jr. waited there for about an hour and then he heard a shot go off in the alders only two or three hundred yards away. A minute later, he heard his father call. He went over and saw him standing over a small six-pointer. He gave his dad a compliment for getting the buck and then began to dress him out. After a few minutes, his father said, "There were two bucks. The other one was a damn nice 10-pointer, but I took the youngster. It's good enough for this guy!"

GOOD OLD UNCLE JOHN

Ed told me he never did carry a compass. The only directional device he had with him was right in his head. He did get turned around once in a while, but nothing he couldn't figure out after a time. He never spent a night out lost in the woods, but one time, he got quite a distance from Headquarters and spent more time back in there than he should have. While on the way out, it got dark on him while he still had a long way to go. He had no light with him so he tried to feel his way along the old tote road in the dark. The night was inky black, and he wound up taking one hell of a spill. He decided it wasn't worth getting himself hurt, so he groped around in the dark until he found enough wood to start a fire. Once the fire got going, he gathered in more wood by its light. Conditions were dry so spending the night shouldn't be too bad. Along about 9 o'clock he spotted a light coming up the old road. It was his Uncle John with a gas lantern. Ed wasn't worried about spending the night out in the woods, but he was mighty happy to see his uncle coming in for him with the light!

THE HALL BROTHERS

There was some real fine deer hunting in the Headquarters area during the '30s and '40s. Ed used to enjoy hunting the terraced slopes of Metcalf Mountain. His clients took many a buck off from its terraced inclines, and Ed took a couple of real big ones himself. He shot a dabbled gray buck there one time on a drive with Hattie and Albert Hall. The Hall brothers were part of a well-known Indian Lake guiding family. Their grandfather, George Hall, came over from England in the late 1800s bringing with him a large number of huge work horses. He got a large track of land to log off near Headquarters, and between logging and horse-trading, he made himself a pile of money.

There were four boys in the Hall family, Toddy, Albert, Tony, and Hattie (Harrison), and every one of them guided. They operated out of their home in Indian Lake village. Their parents were Theodore and Olive Hall. Hattie and Ed Mitchel were real good friends and often hunted, trapped, and fished together. Hattie told me that when Ed was just a three-year-old, his grandfather, Frank Mitchel, would put Ed into his pack basket and then take him for a ride on his back into the woods, showing him whatever he could. Hattie moved to Utica in 1949, and took a permanent job with Chicago Pneumatic. He married Josephine Zegarelli in 1952 and settled permanently in Utica. He retired after 25 years with Chicago Pneumatic in 1974. I asked him if he ever missed his days of guiding and trapping in the Adirondacks. He replied, "I'd just love to do it all over again!" Hattie died February 11, 1994.

Ed's Uncle John ran Headquarters from the late 20's until his death in 1945. After that Claude Savarie ran the lodge for a few years.

Ed married Geneva Beech in 1933, and their marriage produced eight children: Robert, Rita, Venetta, Janette, John, Peter, LouAnne, and Bruce. Over the course of the years, he held down a variety of jobs, which includes garage mechanic, caretaker for Governor Dewey's estate, working for the Sheriff Department, and 14 years for the Conservation Department as gate keeper at Headquarters. He also guided deer hunters for 46 seasons, from when he turned 19 until he reached 65 years of age. Most of his guiding was done out of Headquarters, Cedar River House, and McCane's.

THE GHOST BUCK

The biggest antlered buck that Ed ever killed was taken in the 1970s. At the time, he was guiding a hunter out of the Cedar River House. Ed didn't particularly enjoy taking a single hunter because there is a lot more work involved. He would have to take him out and place him, then circle and work the cover around him, and then go back to get him and place him again. It's much easier with three or four men.

He took the hunter up the Cedar River and on to Hudson's Mountain where he placed him on a watch that he knew would be good for seeing deer. Ed then left him and began making a big loop in the cover above him in an effort to get some deer moving towards his client. While making the loop, he jumped out three or four deer. They headed down the slope in the direction of his hunter, and Ed could see that the last one was a buck.

When the deer came down out of the thick spruce trees, they headed past Ed's client. They were moving slow, and the hunter had a good shot at the buck, but when the hammer fell on his lever action rifle, the firing pin struck an empty cartridge chamber. The guy had failed to load one into the chamber! Then he short-stroked the shell while loading one and wound up with a badly jammed shell sticking out of the action. The buck looked over to see what was going on and then followed the does down the slope and out of sight.

Meanwhile, Ed began working his way down the slope towards his client. He stopped to have a smoke and relax a few minutes and was looking around when he spotted what looked like a large rack of deer antlers, setting in a thick growth of spruce trees. The dense spruce thicket was just over a short rock ledge and up the slope and a good distance off. Ed wasn't really sure what they were, but they certainly looked like deer antlers. He watched them while he enjoyed his cigarette and would look away and then look back. There was no movement from the "rack" and now the thing was beginning to get Ed's curiosity cranked up. He snuffed out what was left of his smoke and thought to himself, "Well, there is one sure way to find out!" He was standing beside a hemlock tree, so using that for a rest, he brought his sights to align just under those big horn bases, if that was in fact what they were. When his 280 Remington went off, the horns disappeared. Ed thought, "By God, I shot a ghost buck!"

Instead of going up the hill to investigate, he went down the hill to get his hunter. His client told him how he had botched his chance for a buck and showed him his jammed rifle. Ed cleared the shell from the action and the guy asked him if he had shot a short while ago. Ed told him he had shot a set of horns, so they headed up the slope to investigate. It was almost lunch time so they would look and then have lunch. They returned to the spruce patch that had held the mysterious set of horns and searched it thoroughly from stem to stern, but no deer. Ed decided to give it up when he found a big rock to build a lunch fire against. He hollered down to his hunter to come up and have lunch by the rock. When he started up towards Ed, he almost stepped on the buck, which was stone dead. He shouted up, "Here's your rack!"

What a rack it was! It was a classic, rustic, heavy-beamed rack with 14 perfectly matched long points. It was the biggest and most handsome rack he had ever taken. Ed said that if he was going to mount any of the heads he had ever taken, that one head would have been the one. However, he was guiding this hunter at the time, and by law, it was his to claim. It took them all afternoon to snake the deer down to the Cedar River and then pull him across. The water was knee deep and ice cold, but they made the road by dark. He caught a ride up to his car and they finally got the deer back to the lodge.

The hunter was from New York City and when he realized that Ed was giving him the buck, he told Ed that he would take the buck home to show all his family and friends and then have it mounted. When it was completed, he would have it shipped back up to Ed for him to keep. In addition, he also paid him for three days of guiding. The following year he got a notice from a taxidermist that the head was completed and was being shipped, but Ed never got it or heard any more about it.

Ed always had a fascination with wildlife of all sizes. During his many years in the Adirondack environment, he has had many close encounters with the resident animal population. Some of these encounters he tried to develop further, by bringing the animal home in hopes it might become a family pet. The following episodes illustrate that wild animals are better off left in their own environment.

YOUNG REYNARD

Ed has driven the length of the Cedar River Road many times while guiding clients and commuting as gate keeper for the Conservation Department. Early one fall while driving home from his shift as gate keeper, he spotted a young red fox trotting up the road ahead of him. The fox had heard Ed's car coming, so he stopped and turned to watch. To Ed, it appeared that the young fox was going to wait and watch him pass by. Instead of passing the fox, Ed pulled up along side of him and stopped. Then he said, with his dry sense of humor, "I'm going as far as Indian Lake if you want to ride." Then he opened his door to make the offer "in jest" complete. To his utter amazement, the young fox came right in under his legs and jumped up on the seat! "My God," Ed thought, "he took me at my word and came right in." He had Ed kind of scared because he didn't know if he could be rabid, and he really hadn't expected this kind of a response. Nevertheless, he put the car in gear and headed down the road with his new passenger.

Ed didn't quite know what to make of it yet, and he was entertaining thoughts of taking the fox home, when about two miles down the road, the fox started to cough or gag on something. A while more and the fox started to cough and gag so bad that he thought it was going to heave up on the floor. Ed thought, "The heck with this!" He brought the car to a stop, then got out and opened the passenger door. He pushed young Reynard out and down on the road edge. Another man had driven up behind Ed's car when he pushed the young fox out of the car, and it ran up on the bank. The man asked, "Where'd you get him?" Ed told him about picking up the fox a few miles back and then putting him out just now. The guy shook his head, "If I hadn't seen you put the fox out of your car, I would have had a lot of trouble believing that one!"

BORN WILD

On a trip down the Cedar River Road, Ed noticed a sow bear with two tiny cubs crossing the road ahead of him. There was a steep cut bank on the far side, and mother bear jumped up on top and walked off into the woods. The first tiny cub scrambled up to the top and just made the top without sliding back down. Ed stopped his car by the last cub as it made its attempt at climbing the steep cut bank. It got almost to the top and then started to slide back down. The mother was off into the woods out of sight, so Ed thought it might be a good time to get a real close look at a black bear cub. He jumped out of the car and ran around to where the cub was making its second attempt at the bank. It was just a small cub, so Ed picked it up by grabbing it right behind the shoulders. Ed said, "It was like picking up an armful of mad wild cats!" The cub was bawling, clawing, scratching, and trying to bite him, all at once. Above all this commotion, he could hear mamma bear coming back at a high rate of speed, and it was obvious she was in a very bad mood! Ed dropped the cub and very quickly got back into the car, leaving mamma and her family in a cloud of dust.

"PETE"

Ed used to keep a boat over on Wakley Pond to use for some occasional trout fishing. One Saturday, Ed and his son, Robert, were trolling for trout along the lengths of its shoreline. Down at one end of the pond was a small bay, and while trolling towards it, Ed noticed what appeared to be a couple of chips of wood floating on the surface. However, when the boat would pass close by, there was nothing to be seen on the surface. This bothered Ed, since he was sure it wasn't his imagination. He was sure he'd seen something! On the next pass around the pond, he again spotted what appeared to be wood chips floating on the surface. He told Robert that on his next pass by the small bay, to cut into it a little to have a better look at what he was seeing.

Bob cut into the bay at his father's instructions, and they slowly passed by the spot where the two wood chips were last seen floating. As Ed peered into the clear waters of Wakley Pond, he suddenly made out the forms of two tiny baby beaver making a slow descent to the bottom of the pond. He grabbed the landing net and going down as deep as he could, he managed to net one of the tiny beavers. Ed picked him out of the net and guessed he wouldn't weigh more than half a pound. The baby was friendly and cuddly, and would curl up right inside Ed's woolen shirt. Ed made a nest for him inside his lunch pail and brought him home that way.

They named the beaver "Pete," and for a while they kept him in a cardboard box in their living room. They nursed him with a baby bottle and when someone was home, he had the run of the house. Beavers only defecate in water, so twice a day he was put into a wash tub of water they kept on the back porch just for that purpose. It didn't take long for him to learn how to nibble on the tender birch and popple twigs the kids began bringing him. Each twig would be five or six inches long and Pete would turn it over and around several times before working on it. When he finally started eating, he would start it into one side of his mouth, spinning it slowly and chewing on it as it went in. When it came out the other side, it was all stripped of bark.

The kids loved playing with the beaver and Pete loved the attention. While it was still nursing, the kids would paint his claws with nail polish, put a ribbon and a bonnet on him, and take him uptown for rides in their doll carriage, complete with blanket and bottle of milk! With all this food and attention, Pete was growing real fast. Later in early summer, he was moved out into a cardboard box on the back porch, where he could come and go as he pleased. Pete would disappear into the tall grass and slashings that bordered their backyard, and forage along a shallow stream and a couple of ponds that weren't far away.

Along about mid-summer, game protector, Jack Carol, paid Ed an official visit. "Ed, I understand that you've got a wild beaver staying at your house." "Yes, that's right

Jack." "Well, have you got a permit to keep one?" "Don't need one." "Well, what makes you so different from anyone else? You've got to have a permit to keep a wild animal!" "Well, I agree with you Jack, but I'm not keeping it!" "Can I see the beaver?" "Sure." They walked around to the back of the house. "Where does he stay?" "In that cardboard box on the back porch. There is no door on the porch and no fence. He comes and goes as he pleases." "Where is he now?" "Probably down along the creek looking for lunch." "When will he be back?" "I'll call him for you." "Pete! Here Pete!" A few minutes later, Pete, sleek and healthy, came walking out of the tall grass and up to the men. Jack looked at the porch with no door, the cardboard box with a hole in it, the unfenced yard, and a healthy, well-mannered beaver. A sheepish grin spread over his face and he stated, "Well Ed, I can't see any problem here. See you around!"

All went well for the balance of the summer, with Pete growing rapidly in length and weight. He would occasionally spend a night inside the Mitchel house, and Ed said he would mind you just like a well-trained dog would. When the deer season finally rolled around in the early fall, Ed would get up around 4:00 a.m. and put some coffee on so he could fill his thermos and enjoy a cup before leaving for one of the lodges along the Cedar River.

On one of these mornings, Ed was enjoying his coffee when he felt something loose on the floor under the kitchen table. He moved the table cloth aside to see what it was, and there on the floor was an accumulation of oak chips, with 1/2 of the oak table leg chewed through by good old Pete! Another leg on the other side had already been started also! Suddenly, spending the winter with a full grown beaver didn't seem like a good idea. Reality was setting in and he could foresee many problems.

Instead of going guiding, Ed put Pete into the pickup and headed for Wakley Pond. He slipped his boat into the pond with Pete in it and headed for the far end where he had picked up Pete originally. Once there, he slid Pete into the water. He was hoping Pete would get busy exploring or looking for food so he could make a bee-line back to his truck, but every time he tried, Pete would be swimming right alongside the boat. It was beginning to look hopeless when the mother beaver surfaced about 100 feet away, and Pete eventually saw her. Pete swam out towards her and the mother swam around Pete two or three times before moving in close to say hello. Finally, they both submerged and Ed headed for the truck in high gear!

THE LONG DISTANCE RUNNER

Late one fall, while keeping the gate at Headquarters, a marathon runner stopped in for the night. The fellow was attempting to run the Northville-Lake Placid trail, a distance of 133 miles, in two days. Everyone said that it couldn't be done, but this guy said it could and he was out to prove it. His only night on the trail was to be spent at Headquarters Camp, and he came running up the road into camp at about 6:00 p.m. There was a doctor and two nurses there to check him out when he came in. Ed thought the runner was in better condition when he came in than the doctor and two nurses were when they met him. After spending the night, he was off and running again by 6:00 a.m. and he made it all the way into Lake Placid that day.

NO LINE BUCKING

One year when the State was holding a special antlerless deer season in the Moose River Plains area, Ed had to go into town the night before to pick up the special permits so they could be sold at the gate the next morning. Ed stayed the night in town, and early the next morning he headed back down to Headquarters. When he came in sight of the gate, he could see that a good-sized line of cars and trucks had already formed. He went to pull around the end vehicle when he was stopped by three or four angry hunters. "No line bucking around here buddy, wait your God damn turn like everybody else!" He rolled down the window and started to explain, but he was cut off by several remarks that were just as unfriendly. "Alright," Ed thought, "I'll just have to wait." He backed behind the rear car and after a while, several more cars pulled in behind him. With the line at a stand still, many of the hunters got out of their vehicles and were walking around. A couple of the hunters walking by recognized Ed, "Say, aren't you the gate keeper?" Ed said, "Yes, but they won't let me pass, told me to stay in line!" The hunters ran down the line moving people and cars. Five minutes later, the gate opened!

Paddy Pelon on Cedar River Flow. Early 20th century photograph.
Photo compliments of Bill Zullo.

Headquarters camp guides.
L to R Crum Fish, Tom
Davison, and Ed Mitchel, Sr.
Photo compliments
of Bill Zullo.

Headquarters Camp as it appeared in the 1930s. Photo compliments of Bill Zullo.

*Cedar River Flow Campground now occupies the site of the
old Headquarters Camp. Photo by Bob Elinskas.*

Cedar River country near Headquarters Camp. Photo by Bob Elinskas.

Ed Mitchel, Jr. at his Indian Lake home. Photo by Bob Elinskas.

MC CANE'S LODGE

In 1909, George and Meta McCane moved into the Cedar River Valley. George was a logging contractor and he worked for Finch & Pruyn. They bought the former Potter farm, a 320 acre parcel of land and paid for it by filling logging contracts. Their land was about five miles down the road from Route 30, and it included the 50 acres of land originally cleared by Sprague and J.P. Brown, plus the stock barn. In 1917, George put up two new buildings and opened up "McCane's" as a sporting lodge. Two years later, he built a bigger building that would be used as the main lodge. The couple did a good business with the lodge in season and George continued to log in the off-season.

George died in 1941, and it was then that Harry, his son, and Amy, his daughter-in-law took over. Harry ran the lodge in the same manner that his father did, and he logged in the off-season. Harry and Amy raised five children: Ester, Julia, Frances, Harriet, and George. Eventually, they sold the lodge to their daughter and son-in-law, Royce and Frances Wells in 1970.

Royce and Frances didn't move in until 1974, and before they made the move, they almost lost the whole lodge! In 1973, a rare Adirondack tornado touched down on the property and headed straight for the buildings. The twister destroyed one of the original buildings and severely damaged the roof on another. It twisted the top off from a huge maple tree that was growing close to one of the buildings and stripped the flag off the flagpole. A man fishing in the nearby Cedar River witnessed the whole event. He said, "You could see the twister sucking huge amounts of debris way up into the air and then floating it off two miles or more away." The lodge itself sustained heavy damage, but if the tornado had struck on only a slightly different line, everything would have been gone.

Frances and Royce were married in 1950, so Royce had been around for quite a while before taking over the lodge. He still remembers his very first hunt out of McCane's. Just as soon as he entered the woods, he jumped out six deer. He thought to himself, "Boy, this is the place to hunt!"

Hunters staying at McCane's could hunt the farm and the Forest Preserve, but they had to buy a guest button from Finch & Pruyn for $10 to hunt their lands for one week. Hunting was almost always good and a normal take for a day's hunt would be two or three bucks. Royce remembers one day when they brought in six bucks. They hunted both sides of the Cedar River. A cable car system was used to get the hunters back and forth across the river. It consisted of a bucket big enough to hold two hunters. Once the hunters were loaded, they would then pull themselves across by a separate rope. It wasn't always a simple matter to cross. Sometimes the hunters would be overweight and out of shape, then they really had to sweat to get themselves across.

Most of the deer were brought out by horse. George and Harry always kept a couple of horses on hand for just this purpose. The heaviest buck to ever come out of McCane's scaled in at 248 pounds.

Royce used to love to sit and listen to Ralph, Harry, and John McCane talk of their past deer hunting experiences. They were all good deer hunters that could hit what they shot at. Some of the guides who used to work out of McCane's were Bill Cross, Bert Randuesin, Larry Wardell, Royce Wells, and Ralph, John, and George McCane.

Ralph McCane was probably the best guide in the house. His biggest problem was that he liked to drink and smoke too much. Many a time he would hunt hard all day, and then stay up late visiting and drinking until two or three in the morning. Then he'd get up early and do it all over again. He was very tough on himself physically. Ralph was heading into the woods one morning with a bunch of guys that were going to do some driving for a watch line. He had been out drinking almost all night in town and now he was hurting. Every little stream they would come to, Ralph would stop and get himself a drink. Finally, one of the drivers asked him, "Ralph, why do you need so much water?" He replied, "I'm trying to work up some steam!"

THE G.E. ENGINEERS

Harry told of one drive they put on over near Stephens Pond. He put out the watch line and the last watcher was right down close to the shoreline. Harry was about 100 yards above the watcher. As the drive progressed, Harry could see a deer coming in the distance. It was a buck, and it should pass close enough to the shoreline watcher so he would have a shot at it. The watcher never saw the buck, though. When the buck passed by and into a safe shooting lane, Harry shot it. The deer was hit hard, but it ran down to the pond and out onto the thin ice, crashing through as it went. It got about 50 feet out from shore and died there, just barely floating in a hole in the ice. The dead buck was in water too deep to wade in and surrounded by ice that was too thin to walk on.

They were guiding a group of G.E. engineers out of Schenectady at the time, and nobody wanted to go into the icy water on a cold day after the buck. The problem was solved when they engineered the "Stephens Pond buck retrieval stick." The stick was made from two long hardwood poles that were tied end-to-end securely and had a rope loop fastened at one end. The end with the loop was then slid out over the thin ice to the buck's head. Then the stick was rolled until the loop caught on the buck's antler, and once secure he was then slowly hauled in.

BEARS AND BEARS AND BEARS

One of McCane's hunters was still hunting across the top of Blue Ridge on a November afternoon. Suddenly, he spotted a black bear only a short distance ahead of him. He dropped the bear with one shot and all at once there were bears running all around him, and real closc! The hunter got real scared and every bad thing he'd ever heard about bears started flashing into his mind. He started shooting, and when it was over, there were four dead bears laying around him. When the other hunters in his party came up to investigate, they found him shaking uncontrollably. He left McCane's the next morning and never came back.

LOST ON BLUE RIDGE

Another hunter was hunting up near the top of Blue Ridge on its east end. He took a shot at a big buck and wounded it. He began trailing the buck and that's when it started to snow. He pressed the buck hard, following it up over the top and into unfamiliar country. The snow was coming down hard and steady when he finally gave up the chase, only now he wasn't sure which way to head for home. Snow was hanging heavy on all the trees. He was in a big wilderness area and short on daylight with no idea of where to go. He spent the next two days wandering around the slopes of Blue Ridge, tired, hungry, and bewildered. He had fired off all his ammo and threw his rifle away. Early on the third morning of his ordeal, he came across the fresh tracks of a huge black bear. The tracks scared him and sobered him up enough so that he could travel in a straight line. He came out of the woods at Camp Kill-Kare, off the southwest corner of Blue Ridge. A major search was going on for him on the east end of the ridge.

CLASSIC BUCK ESCAPES

Royce enjoys hunting with his brother-in-law, George McCane. George is an excellent hunter, and the two men have tagged many a buck together. Both men enjoy hunting the higher elevations of Blue Ridge, and they both believe that's where the largest bucks in the area hang out. George has nailed some real nice ones up near the top, but he has come to believe that many of them are leading some kind of a charmed life when it comes to escaping his meat pole. He began learning this at a very early age while hunting with Royce.

Young George was hunting high on the ridge one day, looking for any signs of movement on the slopes above him. It was pouring down rain, dark and gloomy, and the only thing that wasn't wet and cold was his enthusiasm for the hunt. Suddenly, he spotted a big deer heading down the ridge in his direction. He wasn't sure yet if it was a buck or a doe when he lost track of it in some spruce trees. When it reappeared, it was only a short distance off, and the two spotted each other at the same time.

It was one of the most beautiful bucks he had ever seen, but he hadn't brought his rifle up and the buck was watching him on full alert. He slowly brought his rifle up, but the buck wasn't about to wait. He bolted out of there, and George got off a quick shot. The bullet grazed the buck's back, and all George got was a hand full of hair. Missing a buck like that really hurt George, but that's part of the game. A couple of days later, a west wind was blowing down from the ridge and Royce told George, "I heard a deer snickering up on the ridge today," he was saying, "Is George coming up to hunt today?"

Another close encounter on Blue Ridge happened while George was hunting up near the top on a real steep slope. The slope had several rock ledges on it and was covered with a fairly thick growth of young evergreens. He had been hunting along very quietly, when he came up to a spruce windfall that blocked his line of travel. He ducked under the fallen spruce tree, and when he began to straighten up, a buck jumped right over the top of him from the ledge above. He landed only 10 feet away and let out a deafening snort before bolting out of sight. George was caught so off guard that he didn't even get off a shot. It was a sight that he will never forget, and to this day, he can clearly envision the buck, crowned with a beautiful rack, bolting off into the spruces. There were several more classic buck escapes over the years, and we tend to remember the escapes better than an actual kill. I'd guess that's what keeps us going back in for another season.

To this day, the top of Blue Ridge is extremely thick, and there's a lot of country up there. They have tried driving sections of it from time to time, but the area is so big, you really have to be quite lucky to see whatever you might be moving. On one of their luckier drives back in the 60's, they moved three bucks past three different watchers. One fella killed a beautiful 10-pointer, another fella missed one that he thought was much bigger than the 10-point they got. The third fella was an older gent, and a big eight-point came by him. He thought about it before shooting, and he decided that he didn't want the trouble that a buck would give him in getting it back out to the road. He didn't shoot. George agrees that if you shoot a big buck way back in and want him out whole, you're in for an awful lot of real hard work.

Royce remembers the '50s as being a real good decade for hunting. There were lots of deer around and it wasn't uncommon to find areas where the bucks got into some bloody, knock down, drag out fights. There would be hair, blood, and skirmish tracks all over the place. Also, areas loaded with hooking and scrapes were common, but not any more.

In the old days, hunters used to hike into some pretty remote areas in pursuit of their deer. Nowadays, they hunt pretty close to the road. Not too long ago, George and Royce guided a party of seven young hunters. They tried to take them up towards the top of the ridge where they had seen some pretty good buck sign. The boys got half way up and they started complaining, "What are we way up here for? Isn't there anything down lower and closer?"

Finch & Pruyn ended commercial hunting on their properties in 1960. You must be a member of Cedar Valley Club in order to hunt the land now. The Northville-Lake Placid trail runs through the McCane property. The wooded property northeast of the buildings where the trail runs is McCane's. Then it's Finch & Pruyn property for another half mile to the State lands. The "hiking only" public may use the trail at their convenience. There is no hunting, fishing, or trapping allowed on any of the private lands, and they will not let hunters access the State lands by way of the trail or any way across their property. Royce and Frances have both recently retired so McCane's Lodge is no longer open.

McCane's Lodge, early '30s. Photo compliments of Ted Comstock.

McCane's immediately after 1973 tornado. McCane Lodge photo.

This cable car was used by McCane patrons to cross the Cedar River.
McCane Lodge photo.

Putting out the watch line. Ralph McCane is center person, McCane Lodge photo.

Bring out a buck with horse power. McCane Lodge photo.

Stephens Pond
The buck died in water too deep to wade and around ice to thin to walk on!
McCane Lodge photo.

George McCane and a 10 pt. Blue Ridge buck. McCane Lodge photo.

Frances and Royce Wells at McCanes. Photo by Bob Elinskas.

THE CEDAR RIVER HOUSE

The Cedar River House was located near the southeast corner of Route 30 and the Cedar River Road. It was built in the early 1870s by Richard Jackson, and he called it his "Arctic Hotel." It was a popular stagecoach stop and well known for good food, lodgings, and sports afield. The property changed hands several times in the following years, and it was renamed Cedar River House.

In 1920, William Goulet was working in Rochester, New York as a street car conductor. While working there, he made the acquaintance of a co-worker named Arther Blanchard. Bill was suffering from asthma, and Art was quick to recommend that he move to the Adirondacks. The air was pure and clean and would surely be beneficial to his health. Art's father, Charles, lived in Blue Mountain Lake and there was more family there that might help him get a start in the area. Bill thought about this, and in 1921, he came up to look things over. He stayed with Charles Blanchard and worked for Art's brother, Ernie, at Maple Lodge.

In the spring of 1922, he bought the Cedar River House from Frank Wood for about $13,000. As soon as the deal was closed, he sent for his wife, Rose, and their four children, Rose, Florence, Edward, and Bill. The property consisted of 320 acres of land, the lodge, a large barn for livestock, and several out buildings. It was, in reality, a lodge and small farm. They raised cattle, sheep, turkeys, and chickens for meat, eggs, and wool. They also kept a team of horses to help with the farm chores. With the lodge and a farm to run, the Goulet family were very busy people.

Mrs. Goulet was an excellent cook and a former baker. The meals she provided were first class. They advertised their services in the Albany, Troy, and Schenectady newspapers and early rates for room and board were $18 per week, two to a room; $21 single; and $10 for children under 12 years old. Their first summer in business was almost a disaster. They had invested all the money they had in buying and setting up the business. In early summer, there was a murder-suicide at the lodge, and only a short while later, there was a suicide in the nearby cemetery. They received some bad publicity in the newspapers and their business fell off sharply. They were near the point of bankruptcy when the hunters saved the day. They enjoyed one of the busiest hunting seasons the lodge had ever seen. From then on, there were no further financial hardships.

In 1927, Rose gave birth to their last child, a son, George. Bill and Rose managed the Cedar River House for 25 years. In 1947, Rose died and Bill sold the business to Dewey Brown shortly after. Bill survived his wife by ten years and died in 1957.

At this late date in the century, Edward Goulet is the only surviving member of his immediate family. He fondly remembers his years at the Cedar River House, as his boyhood home of many great adventures. Life at the lodge was never dull. People were always stopping in to share the news of the day. Hunting, fishing, and trapping season were the most interesting to Ed though. He remembers one fall when some dogs chased a buck across their pasture and the buck got his antlers tangled in the barbed wire. One of their hunting guests went out and dispatched the buck with his rifle, and then later stood proudly by the buck for a picture. It was a mighty short hunt!

L to R, Charlie Jakevick, Ernie Brown, Frank Wood (former owner of Cedar River House), Jim Hennisey, and hotel guest that shot the buck caught in fence.
Goulet family photo.

BEAR PROBLEMS

The flock of sheep that Bill pastured on the farm was always subject to predation by black bears. Bill had a permit to either trap or shoot the bears if they were bothering his flock. Jack Farrel was the local game warden and also their next-door neighbor. He was also an excellent trapper. He volunteered his services one time when a bear started regularly raiding the flock. Ed followed his father and Jack out to the area that the bear had been active in. He watched Jack set a large bear trap between two rock ledges. First he dug a shallow hole and put some sheep meat into it. Then he placed the set trap over the meat and covered the trap with wool. He chained the trap to a six-foot hemlock log that had all the branches trimmed, so they stuck out from the log about eight inches.

The next morning when they checked the trap, it was gone. The spiny hemlock log made an easy trail to follow, and it eventually led to a large muddy area, that had a small balsam tree growing in the middle of it. It was only slightly bigger than a Christmas tree, but the bear appeared to have gotten himself and the trap good and muddy. Then he wrapped the drag chain around the tree, stripping most of the branches off in the process, and then pulled on the trap until he slipped free. A pretty slick getaway!

Things remained peaceful around the sheep pasture for a good six weeks. Then one day, a stranger stopped into the barroom and asked Bill if he was the owner of the flock of sheep pastured a short distance down the Cedar River Road. Bill nodded, "Yes," and the stranger told him that a large dog was chasing them all over the place and he ought to go down there and do something about it! Bill grabbed his rifle and some shells and didn't waste any time in getting over there. As soon as he stopped the car, the sheep began running for the road in high gear with a large black bear on their heels! Bill shot and killed the bear before he got to the sheep. The "dog" pulled the scales down to 380 pounds. This was a different bear than the one that had escaped the trap, since all four feet were in perfect condition.

A RIVER FULL OF LOGS

The Cedar River flowed right behind their lodge and down through the middle of their cow pasture. The spring log drive was always a fascinating event to witness. Loggers would be busy all winter in the woods near the Cedar River flow, and the cut logs would be hauled out on or right near the ice on the flow. When the ice melted off and waters were at their highest, the logs would then be sent downstream on a freshet of water from the impoundment. The logs would eventually wind up in the Hudson River and Glens Falls for processing. For a few days, the Cedar River would be full of logs as they floated their way to market. At first, there were only the saw logs of about 14 feet in length, but in later years, they floated 4 foot bolts of wood for pulp.

DEER SEASON

A busy deer season was important to an Adirondack lodge in those days because it helped carry it through those lean winter months. The lodge made sure there were enough well-marked trails for their hunters to use and an ample supply of capable guides also. Ed guided many parties out of the lodge. Every trip out was a new adventure and the luck you had on any hunt was never guaranteed.

One of the regular drives they put on was the "Mill Mountain drive." It was started right across the road from the Cedar River House. On one occasion, Ed's father had taken eight men out with him to put out a watch line. Ed sat on the front porch with four other hunters, and in about 30 more minutes they would begin to drive deer to the watchers. Ed noticed a man from the lodge go across the road and start for the woods they intended to drive. He said to the other drivers, "The watch line isn't even out yet, he's going to spoil our drive!" One of the drivers jumped up and ran after the fella. He told him that the woods he was heading for had been pushed pretty hard the last few days. The woods behind the lodge along the river might be a better bet. A nice eight-pointer had been spotted in the swale grass along the river only a day or two ago. The hunter thanked him and then headed for the woods behind the lodge. The big drive went on as planned but didn't produce anything. When they got back to the lodge, they found the hunter they had turned around, happy, soaking wet, and looking for some help. He had hunted along the river only a short distance when he got a shot at a big buck. He hit it hard, but not before the buck crossed the river and died on the far side. He waded the cold, waist-deep water to look at and dress out his dandy nine-point buck!

Ed did a lot of guiding in the Panther Mountain, Bear Trap Brook, and Unknown Pond areas. Toddy Hall and Ed were guiding a party of hunters in the Unknown Pond area. One of the drivers came upon a dead buck that had only recently died. It had a beautiful eight-point rack on it and he hated to see it go to waste. He cut it off at the neck and carried it through the drive. When he got out to the watch line, the story was told that he had shot the head right off the deer as it ran through the woods. Shot it with a high power military rifle! Word of this got out all around and it was the talk of the town, since quite a few people actually believed it. Later on, it was learned that Bill Brown had wounded a nice buck in the same area of the drive a few days earlier.

Fred Bullard, Ed, and his father were guiding hunters in the Ledge Mountain area. A large buck came through the watch line and was killed. The deer was very old and heavy. The antlers were only two and a half inches long and just as thick. It was an illegal buck since antlers have to be at least three inches long. Antlers such as these on an old buck are what they call a "Molly Buck." The meat didn't go to waste!

Hunting was generally pretty darn good in the '30s and '40s. Sometimes a single drive would produce two or three bucks. The biggest buck Ed ever guided a client to was Len Wooster's, when he took a wide, heavy-beamed 21-point buck.

TRAP LINE OBSERVATIONS

Ed did extensive beaver trapping in the '40s and '50s when fur prices were high. Most of his trapping operations were in the Rock Lake, Rock River, and the Dunn Brook areas. Running a line of beaver traps requires a lot of hard work. Even a skilled and very successful beaver trapper earns every dime he picks up at a fur sale. It's not just the fur check you pick up at the end of a season that makes it all worthwhile. A large part of it is all the time you get to spend out in the field. Spending time in the environment you love gives you more time to observe nature, and that's worth quite a bit in itself.

Ed was snowshoeing up an old tote road near Dunn Brook one spring when he noticed a lot of blood on the snow just ahead of him. When he walked up to investigate, he found that a large fisher had killed and eaten a porcupine there. Fisher love porcupines, and they're about the only animal that can kill one without paying a heavy price in quills. The fisher had eaten the entire carcass, leaving only the hide with quills attached.

He was snowshoeing across the ice on Rock Lake one day when he observed another bloody spot on the snow. Walking up, he could see the heads of three very large bullheads. They had all been eaten right up to their dorsal fins. There was a hole in the ice under the snow and fresh otter tracks that told the tale. The otter must have just left, since all three heads were still trying to breathe!

Another experience with otter happened on the late season ice of Cranberry Pond. Ed noticed that the ice over the spring holes were all honey-combed and showing signs of melting out. He was about 50 feet from one of these when he heard a faint sound coming from under the ice. Suddenly, some shell ice exploded in the honey-combed area, and an otter came up on the ice with a seven-inch bullhead in its mouth. The otter raised his head up high and began chewing and swallowing the bullhead. It looked like the fish was disappearing into the mouth of a meat grinder! These were much smaller bullheads than the ones on rock Lake, and the otter ate the entire fish. The otter went into the lake twice more and returned with a bullhead of the same size each time. He swallowed these also, tail first, in his meat grinder style.

Ed was walking along the Rock River one spring when the ice was breaking up and floating down the river in large chunks. On one of these icebergs that was on the far side of the river, was a very large and dead buck deer. It sported a huge rack of antlers, and even from where Ed was, he could count at least 12 points. He wanted to get to it so he could save the rack, but there was no way to safely cross that swollen river.

On another March day of a different year, Ed discovered a large buck along the Rock River. This buck had earlier shed his antlers, and was now so weakened by the winter that it could hardly move. Ed was moved with compassion for it, so he cut a large armful of fresh cedar boughs and left the deer feeding on them. When he came through the next day, the deer was gone. He hoped his act of kindness may have saved that buck's life.

MEMORIES OF ERNIE BLANCHARD

When it came to trapping skill, nobody could beat Ernie Blanchard. Ed used to pal around with his son, Ernest, when they were kids, and sometimes he would spend the night at the Blanchard house. He can still picture Ernie coming home from the woods after dark. He would often sit down to a big plate of beans and he'd always have a large glass of his own home brew.

Ernie knew the woods for miles around like nobody else. He had a lot of different trapping partners over the years, and they all spoke well of him. In later years, Ed's brother, Bill, went trapping with old Ernie in the Rock River country. They stayed in Dick Farrell's cabin on Cranberry Pond. The trapping venture had just nicely started, when along came a warm and extended spring thaw. Water levels rose so high that any kind of travel, especially on the ice, became too dangerous. They finally gave it up. This was the first time of any length that Bill had spent with Ernie, and he was greatly impressed with his incredible knowledge of animals and trapping.

One year, there was a demand and a high price being offered for live fishers. Ernie and Dick Farrell were running a line of fisher traps together and wanted to cash in on some of those high prices. One of the first fisher cats to be caught was held by a small trap, and the fisher appeared to be in very good condition. The fisher had backed itself into a hollow log that was part of the cubby hole set. Ernie and Dick knelt down by the opening, and Ernie reached in to pull out the live cat. As soon as he reached his gloved hand in, the fisher bit into it and wouldn't let go. Ernie pulled the fisher out and got a hold on it with the other hand, and still, the fisher wouldn't let go.

Ernie didn't realize it at the time, but Dick was getting all nervous and excited about dealing with that live fisher. The men had a small single bitted ax with them, so Ernie told Dick to tap the fisher on the nose so it would give up its hold. Well, Dick struck the fisher with the sharp side of the ax, and struck it with such force that it killed the fisher an put a deep cut into Ernie's hand! At that time, Ernie wasn't very happy about the dead fisher or his cut hand, but they laughed about it for years afterwards.

Ernie was having a few beers in a Raquette Lake bar one spring towards the end of beaver season. He was visiting with a good friend of his who was also a fellow trapper. His friend was telling him about a big beaver that he just couldn't fool with a trap. This guy was a good trapper and had tried every trick in his book, and still the beaver had eluded him. Ernie told him to sit still a minute while he went out to his car. When he returned, he put a small bottle of lure into his friend's hand. He told him to pull all the traps he had around in the pond, and then make up one simple shoreline drowning set. "Put a little of this lure on a stick, just beyond the trap," Ernie said. "The next time you go in to check the trap, you'll have that beaver, and what's more, he'll have a big grin on his face when you find him!"

The trapper went and did just what Ernie told him to. The next morning when he hiked into the pond to check that trap, he could see right away that it was gone. When he peered into the murky waters of the beaver pond, the first thing he spotted was the toothy grin of a large dead beaver. "Damn," he thought, "that guy is good!"

Ernie used to trap the marshy areas of Flow 34 before it became Lake Durant. In the early 1850s, Otis Stephens built a dam there for some Glens Falls lumbermen. When lumbering operations were over with, the gate was left open so there wasn't any volume of water being held back. The marshy area was a magnet for fur bearers, and Ernie was quick to capitalize on it. One spring, he took over 500 muskrats out of the marsh. In later years, the Civilian Conservation Corps rebuilt the old dam at the outlet. It was a much larger dam and it created a large and permanent body of water. It was officially christened Lake Durant in August of 1936.

Ernie would never trap an area dry, and he was one trapper that was capable of doing it. He would always leave enough animals to re-populate, and then not trap that region for at least a couple of years. He was an excellent martin and fisher trapper. The Blue Ridge area was his favorite for trapping these furbearers. During the war years of the 40's, Ed Goulet drove the Blue Mountain school bus. He couldn't serve in the military because he had asthma, so he replaced Norris LaPrarie. On one of his runs, he had to pick up Hieney Gutliff's son at Baekeland camp five miles south of the village on Route 28. Many times during this period, Ernie Blanchard would ride the school bus down part way to Baekeland's, and then strike off into the woods checking his traps.

After one long day on his trap line, Ernie was hiking his way back out to Route 28. He still had a good mile to go, when he started feeling dizzy and his vision blurred. Ernie knew right off that something was wrong, but he kept his cool. He found a nearby tree that he could sit down by and rest his back against. Then he drew his knees up to his chin and pulled his parka over his head. He rested there for quite a long time and eventually fell asleep. When he awoke, it was dark in the woods, but the stars were out. He felt better and slowly made his way out of the woods. He rested for a few days, but the experience had scared him. After that, he was reluctant to go very far into the woods alone, as he used to. Ernie trapped right up into his 70's. He would often ride his horse, "Kit," to run the much shorter lines of his older years.

A LOST CHILD
AT LAKE DURANT

During the early 1950s, Ed became a New York State Forest Ranger. One evening in early summer, he got a call for volunteers to participate in a search for a missing child at the Lake Durant campground. A family from Rochester, New York, was camping there and between four and five o'clock, they discovered that their five-year old boy was missing. They had searched the campground but couldn't find him anywhere, so they notified the authorities. A small search party was assembled immediately and sent out into the nearby woods, but with no result.

A call went out to assemble a huge search party at first light, and Ed would be part of that search. The assembled group was made up of state troopers, game wardens, forest rangers, and a large number of concerned local people. One of the state troopers took charge. He formed a search line and had the group go in a big semicircle into the woods, first north and then south. Ed went along with this plan for a while, but he felt in his heart that it just wasn't getting much accomplished. Ed was very familiar with the area, so he dropped out of the search line and sat down on a log to think about the whole situation. While thinking about where the little boy may have wandered, he remembered a small brook that wasn't far from their campsite. He had this strong premonition that the boy may have followed that brook.

He hiked over to the brook and began to follow it into the woods, while looking for any signs of the boy's passing. Ed had a small knapsack with him with sandwiches, cookies, and a thermos of hot tea. He followed the stream for three quarters of a mile, diligently looking for any clue from the boy, especially in the mud and sand along the stream bed. He saw beaver and deer tracks, old and new, but no sign of the boy. His hunch was still strong, so he continued on. When he rounded the next bend in the stream, he spotted a little blue sneaker sitting on some mud. It was fairly new, and now he felt sure he was on the right track. Ed followed the stream carefully for a few hundred yards more to an old beaver meadow that was growing thick with waist high, blue joint grass. Ed was walking through this tall grass, when up ahead he saw the grass move. It was the boy!

He had been laying in the grass when he heard Ed coming. He jumped up, thinking Ed might be a deer. When their eyes first met, he thought the boy might start running, but he didn't. A few moments later, they were friends. The boy was starved, but Ed told him he could only eat a little at a time. The boy had lost both of his sneakers, and his feet had been cut and bruised so bad that he had to be carried. His face had been all bitten by black flies and mosquitoes also, but underneath it all, he was still a strong healthy little boy! Ed began to carry him out, and when they were close enough to the campground for signal shots, Ed fired off three shots. He gave the boy more to eat and drink and a short while later, LeRoy Springs showed up to help. LeRoy carried the boy to others, and they got him back to the campground and his family. Ed just wanted to go home, so he went right to his car and left quietly.

The next day, the parents drove over to Indian Lake and looked up Ed. They were so grateful! When the little boy saw Ed again, he ran right over and jumped into his arms. It was all very humbling to Ed, and he was very pleased and grateful that the search had ended as quickly as it did. Ed knew all too well that the great forest can be extremely unforgiving! For the next few years, the family would stop by briefly to say hello whenever they were in the mountains on vacation. He often thinks back on how lucky he was to find him. It was one of the greatest experiences in his life.

THE CEDAR RIVER GOLF COURSE

The idea and inspiration for a golf course at Indian Lake came from the town's first permanent dentist, Dr. Russell Beekman. Dr. Beekman and his wife, Gertrude, moved to Indian Lake around 1929, from the New York City area. His practice was first located in Farrell's Hotel, and then later in a building across from Bill Zullo's 1870 Bed and Breakfast on Route 30. Dr. Beekman and Gertrude were avid golfers, and now they would have to travel a considerable distance in order to play a round of golf.

The Beekman's circle of friends included Dr. Hubert Carroll, the town physician, John Farrell, owner of Farrell's Hotel, and Buster Lewis, a summer resident who was co-owner of the Nassau Inn at Princeton University. Buster was the only other known golfer in town, and both he and Beekman had vocally wished that there was a golf course near-by. It wasn't long before the open farm pastures of the Cedar River House caught Dr. Beekman's eye, and he fielded the idea of a golf course there with his friends.

They all thought a golf course in Indian Lake would be beneficial for the whole town. They approached William Goulet and offered to help put up money and help with the planning. Bill was receptive, since he was quite willing to develop his property. The Town of Indian Lake was willing to help because it would increase tourism. They would provide water, free of charge, for watering the fairways and greens. Dr. Beekman, Buster Lewis, and William Goulet, worked out the plans for laying out a nine-hole golf course.

Work on the course began in 1930, and a great deal of the labor done was a community effort. John Rust, a neighbor and good friend of the Goulet's, helped with labor, materials, and machinery in building the suspension bridge between #5 tee and #5 green. Rust was the contractor that built the state road between Raquette Lake and Blue Mountain. He also made major improvements to Route 30 between Indian Lake and Blue Mountain in 1925. A lot of local people would walk the course just to cross his suspension bridge. Some of Dr. Carroll's contributions were from people who owed him money for his services.

When the work was originally started, most of it was done with horse power. They had a team drawing a crude scraper to smooth out the fairways and prepare areas for greens and tees. They also hauled dirt for the greens using a "False Bottom" wagon. The bottom of this wagon was lined with 2-by-4s that could be removed one at a time. In this manner, the load of dirt could be unloaded without shoveling it off. It saved them quite a bit of extra work in building the tees and greens.

Later in the project, Bill bought an Iron Mule from John Rust. The Iron Mule was a special built Fordson tractor with a huge dump box on it. They used this in place of the wagons. The Goulet family worked very hard in putting one green at a time in. The eighth green was built in the shape of a heart, and they got a lot of nice compliments on it after completion. The Iron Mule was used to mow the fairways at first, but then they traded it for a newer standard Fordson tractor. In time, this also was traded for a new Farmall tractor. Ed's main job was to mow the fairways and the roughs, while his dad and brother, Bill, did the greens. They would all get up early every morning and whip the dew off the greens with long bamboo fish poles.

In the first two years the course was open for play, it was quite a challenge for any golfer to come in with a respectable score. Bill Goulet was more of a farmer at heart than a greens keeper, so he would let the roughs get high enough so he could cut them for hay! This made all the poor golfers quite mad. A good golf ball in those days cost 25 cents, and greens fees for 9 holes was one dollar.

When James Beha was teaching at Indian Lake School, he would release some of the students from gym or study hall if they would go over to the course and pull wire brush from the fairways and roughs. Wire brush is a tall, fast-growing weed very common in open areas of the Adirondacks.

When the course opened up, quite a few area people began playing golf, including the Goulets. Beekman was a good golfer, but he had a bad temper. One day while playing a round with his wife and some friends, he hit two bad shots in a row. He was so frustrated he threw his wife's clubs in the Cedar River. Everyone laughed but Gertrude, since he hadn't thrown his own clubs in.

Ed's brother, Bill, developed into a great golfer, and he gave lessons for a while. He later built his own golf course in Rochester, New York. His youngest son and daughter, and their mother, still run that course.

Dewey Brown ran the Cedar River House from 1947 until his death in 1973. His son then took over the business and ran it for only two seasons. He sold it to Mr. and Mrs. Robert Below, and Mrs. Below's son, Richard Clark. On April 21, 1976, the entire contents of the Cedar River House and related items were put on auction. Hundreds of people from all over the east showed up for the sale. A few days later, the historic old stage coach stop was torn down. It had been a beautiful landmark and a reminder of ages past. Many people, both local and from afar, were bitter about the decision to remove it.

The current owner is Dr. Peter J. Goldblatt of Toledo, Ohio. Ed believes that the course is now in the best condition that it has ever been in. He wishes that his mother and father were here to see what they started so long ago.

Ed Goulet married Edna Brown in 1939. Edna's father was Howard Brown who was the forest ranger at Lewey Lake for 40 years. Her great grandfather was Prentiss Brown, of the Brown Farm. Ed and Edna raised six children, Keith, Karen, Linda, Kathryn, Elaine, and Edward (Beaver). The couple ran "Goulet Wood Products" in Indian Lake for 18 years. Ed also worked as a contractor, cabinet maker, guide, forest ranger, and managed the Indian Lake water and sewer system for a while. They moved to Florida in 1967 to be near a daughter that was suffering from asthma. In 1976, they moved to North Carolina where they ran a campground for a number of years. They are both retired now and enjoy the warmer climate of the southern states, which is good for both of them. Their thoughts still drift back to the friendly people and the rugged mountains of the Adirondacks, where they made their home for so many years.

The Cedar River House in 1925. Goulet family photo.

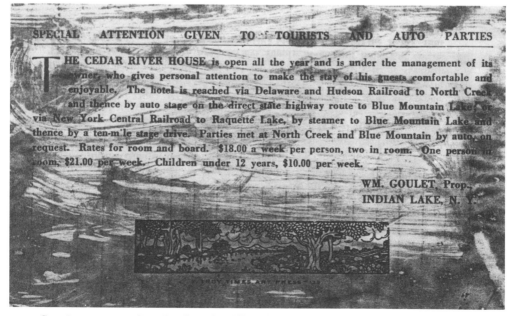

SPECIAL ATTENTION GIVEN TO TOURISTS AND AUTO PARTIES

THE CEDAR RIVER HOUSE is open all the year and is under the management of its owner, who gives personal attention to make the stay of his guests comfortable and enjoyable. The hotel is reached via Delaware and Hudson Railroad to North Creek and thence by auto stage on the direct state highway route to Blue Mountain Lake, or via New York Central Railroad to Raquette Lake, by steamer to Blue Mountain Lake and thence by a ten-mile stage drive. Parties met at North Creek and Blue Mountain by auto on request. Rates for room and board. $18.00 a week per person, two in room. One person in room, $21.00 per week. Children under 12 years, $10.00 per week.

WM. GOULET, Prop.,
INDIAN LAKE, N. Y.

*Services were advertised in the Albany area and also sporting magazines such as **Field & Stream**.*

William Goulet and the 380 lb. bear that was chasing his sheep. Goulet family photo.

Late '20s hunting party at Cedar River house. Goulet family photo.

Cedar River golf club house, motel and 9th green. Photo by Bob Elinskas.

Ed and Edna Goulet. Goulet family photo.

WAKLEY LODGE

Wakley Lodge and golf course is found two and one half miles down the Cedar River Road from Route 30. It was originally opened by Cora and William (Coop) Wakley in 1918 as a sportsman's lodge. Coop is the son of William S. Wakley, who originally built the Cedar Falls Hotel, or "Headquarters." Coop ran the lodge and also a small farm on the premises. In later years, when William Goulet took over the Cedar River House, the two men would often help each other with the summer farm chores. Bill always considered Coop a good neighbor.

Coop was also a good stone mason, and over the years, figured he had built over 100 area fireplaces and chimneys. He would also deliver fireplace wood to many area accounts. The hunting season was big business at Wakley's. The Cedar River area was well known to sportsmen, so little, if any, advertisement was done. There were five main hunting lodges in the Cedar River area, Cedar River House, Wakley's, McCane's, The Brown Farm, and Headquarters. During the season, they were all full. In those days, the sawmills and logging operations would shut down for the hunting season so everyone could take advantage of the extra money that the hunters brought in.

All the lodges hunted their own self-assigned areas, and they never hunted in another lodge's district. It was an honor system which worked because it was never broken. Coop was a small man in stature, but it took a good man to keep up with him in the woods. Many a big client would look skeptically at Coop's small frame, only later to find himself struggling to keep up. Coop killed a huge buck back in the 1930s that field dressed 315 pounds. He was also an excellent fisherman and one of the few that could consistently take trout from the Cedar River.

Coop once sold the lodge and property (about 300 acres) for $12,000. However, the person couldn't make the payments, so he took his property back. In his later years, he was hospitalized down in Albany for a while. Many of his former clients stopped into the hospital to visit with him. There were a number of prominent people among his visitors, including the mayor of Albany. It was very heartening for old "Coop" to see so many familiar faces in an unfamiliar city. Coop passed away in August of 1957.

A NEW CABIN
ON CEDAR RIVER

Coop helped a lot of distant sportsmen to get started with a seasonal camp. Cliff Anderson came up to hunt as a guest of the Cedar River Club with some friends. While there, an argument broke out among them, dividing the group. Cliff's half of the group decided to leave, but not before approaching Coop Wakley and asking him if he wouldn't sell them some land to build a seasonal camp on. Cliff and four other hunters bought a three acre parcel down by the river. The following year, with Coop's help, a new log cabin, complete with fireplace and large upstairs sleeping loft, was built. The group enjoyed many a fine deer season after that with no further arguments.

Cliff was from the Hornel area and a mechanical engineer by profession. He married his wife, Marjorie, in 1921, and they raised three children, Thomas, Suzanne, and Prudence. As the hunting group at the cabin grew older, and either died or lost their desire to hunt, Cliff would buy out their share of the property. By the time he and Marjorie were ready to retire, he owned the whole piece. They built a retirement home a short distance from the cabin, and it has a spectacular view of the river.

Marjorie would often accompany Cliff on many of his hunting trips and keep the home fires burning at the cabin while he was out hunting. On the way up, they would normally pass through Geneva, Utica, Old Forge, Blue Mountain and then Cedar River. On one trip up in the '40s, when they got to Utica, Marjorie suggested that they try the route up through Speculator and then Indian Lake. Cliff was game, so off they went, and when they got to Speculator, it was dark. They headed north on Route 30, and when they got out of town, the road they were on put her into a state of shock! The country had weathered several heavy cloudbursts from storms the day before, and the road looked like it was rarely, if ever, traveled. Big boulders stuck right up into the roadway in many places, and when they topped some of those hills, it appeared that their Buick was going almost straight down on the far side! It was an experience she would never forget.

Cliff loved his deer hunting and always preferred to hunt alone. One on one was his most enjoyable deer hunting adventure. He was a good deer hunter and always got his buck. There was one year in the early '50s when he almost didn't. The weather had been dry, so hunting conditions weren't the best. Few deer were spotted that week and none of them sported a rack. Now it was pack up time, and how he hated to leave without a deer to bring home. Marjorie was with him on this hunt, and she could plainly see his deep disappointment.

The road between Indian Lake and Speculator had recently been widened and paved so they decided to take that route out of the mountains. Cliff was heavy-hearted and quiet on the drive south, and conversation was minimal at best. It was the first time he wouldn't have a buck to show when he got home. They were on Route 8 heading south and in the area of Piseco Lake, when a car approaching from the other direction waved them down. There was a woman behind the wheel, and she just had to tell someone about the big buck she had just seen feeding along a logging road only a half mile back. She said, "He is huge, and you can see him right from the road!"

Cliff followed her instructions, and sure enough, he was there and only a short way off. He quietly got out of the car and slipped one shell into the chamber of his rifle. One shot later the big buck was down on the ground. The woman who flagged him down came back to see the buck, and even helped to load him on the car! Well, with a buck on the car, there was quite a change in the atmosphere in that car for the rest of the way home. Cliff was talking a mile a minute and just as happy as a clam. When he got home, he drove all over town, showing it off and telling how he got it.

BEAR FEVER

One season, Cliff got a bear. It was his first and only bear. When he first spotted it in the woods, it was slowly heading his way. He had a Winchester Model 71 lever-action in .348-caliber that he was always cool and deadly with, but a bear was something else. As the bear got closer, he would work the action to make sure he had a shell in the chamber, and each time he did this, it would eject the live round that had been in the chamber out on the ground. When he finally shot the bear, it was with his last cartridge, the rest were on the ground! He went for his hunting partner to help get the bear out to the road, and after they wrestled it onto the car, they made a quick trip into town for some groceries. At the checkout counter, the lady said, "You boys got a bear, didn't you?" "How did you know?" "Because they stink like hell, and I can smell it all over you two!"

Cliff Anderson died in 1967. After his death, Marjorie sold all their property in Hornel and moved to Cedar River permanently. When I talked to her in '94, she was 92 years old, happy, active, and content. I asked her if she had any regrets about moving up here permanently, and she replied, "Not a one!"

DICK & ETHEL FLETCHER

On December 10, 1955, Dick Fletcher married Coop's daughter, Ethel, and the two have run Wakley's for over 40 years now. In the 1950s, when they took over the business, hunting was still their biggest money season. Dick remembers when they used to guide up to 100 hunters out of Wakley's. They couldn't accommodate that many people at the lodge, so there were local motels and tourist homes that used to handle the overflow. Putting on large drives was a good way to hunt the area effectively. Dick said 40 hunters would go out with four guides in one direction and 40 hunters and four guides would leave in another. Then one of the groups would begin driving to the other. With a group that size, it wasn't unusual for six or seven bucks to be hanging in the barn by nightfall.

The lodges along the Cedar River Road hunted a lot of the leased property of the Finch & Pruyn Paper Company. This property continued to produce good hunting well beyond the "doe days" of the '50s, because they didn't allow the taking of doe deer from their lands. Dick was never a licensed guide himself, but he would show the lodge guests the trails to hunt from, and point out areas to work that had produced deer in the past. The worst part about running a hunting lodge was that all to often, at the end of a long day, a hunter or two would be missing. So what do you do? You grab some lights and a rifle, and go back out and shoot signal shots, and start looking for them. Those days got to be just too long!

Wakley Lodge has suffered from two devastating fires since its beginning, and Ethel clearly remembers both of them. The original lodge burned in 1932. It was rebuilt and remained until February 1958, when it was again destroyed by fire. Reconstruction began in June of that same year for the new and current lodge. Dick added a large pond off the northeast corner of the lodge in 1967 and stocked it with trout. He named it Fletcher Lake.

WAKLEY GOLF COURSE

Dick was a natural born workaholic and always on the go doing one thing or another. It was his nature and lifestyle. On one of his visits to Dr. Carroll, he was told to slow down his pace somewhat, and do something to relax. "Relax," Dick replied, "How can I relax?" Dr. Carroll replied, "Why don't you try playing some golf?" Dick laughed out loud at that, but he did think it over. A good friend of his, Howard Brown, was an avid golfer, so he got Howard to give him some lessons and they played a few rounds.

Dick loved it! He joined a golf league at the Cedar River House and played for three years. One day, at the end of his round, he thought, "Why not build my own course?" He had the land, the know-how, the ambition, and the desire, so why not? He talked it over with Ethel, then he and Howard began putting plans together and taping out tees, fairways, and greens. Then he rented a bulldozer and a log skidder, and he began working on his own nine-hole golf course. Needless to say, Dick didn't relax too much while construction was going on!

Dick put his heart and soul into the project, and it shows! In August of 1971, his par 34, nine-hole golf course opened to the public. It's a delightful course with challenging holes, beautiful scenery, and a chance to see wildlife that occasionally cross the fairways. The award-winning fourth hole is as challenging as it is beautiful and has appeared in a national golf magazine. It was a lot of hard work, but an excellent investment for the lodge, and one that they have never regretted.

Dick and Ethel still take on a few hunters every fall, but they aren't like the hunters they used to accommodate, up at 5:00 a.m., out at gray dawn, hunt all day, and back by dark. Today's hunters tend to sleep late and get back early, and if the weather's bad, not go out at all. Wakley's used to be open all year round, but now it's open from melt-off until December.

The original Wakley Lodge. Fletcher family photo.

Wakley's before the 1958 fire. Bunkhouses for hunters are left of main lodge.
Fletcher family photo.

Hunting party at Cliff Andersons. Cliff is standing in front of buck.
Coop Wakley is bottom row far right. Coop built the cabin and put in the fireplace.
Anderson family photo.

The Cedar River near Wakleys. Photo by Bob Elinskas.

The new Wakleys with 9th green in front and Fletcher Lake on right.
Photo by Bob Elinskas.

Dick and Ethel Fletcher. Photo by Bob Elinskas.

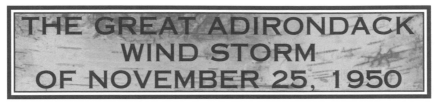

THE GREAT ADIRONDACK WIND STORM OF NOVEMBER 25, 1950

On November 22, 1950, a bitter cold arctic air mass began to move down through Canada towards the United States. The following day, it drifted into the central part of our country and began to move southeast. A low pressure system with very warm and moist air was centered over North Carolina and Virginia. By November 24, the two contrasting air masses had combined to form a powerful storm, which rapidly increased in size and strength. The normal drift of this storm should have taken it east-northeast, which would have put it out in the Atlantic for much of its duration. However, this path for the storm was blocked by a nearly stationary high pressure cell out in the Atlantic Ocean.

The monster storm proceeded northward up the Appalachian Mountains dumping huge amounts of snow on the west side of the mountains and heavy, flooding rains on the east side. The winds associated with this storm were unusually strong and entered New York on November 25, while gaining in intensity. Wind gusts of almost 100 miles per hour were commonplace throughout the state. Coastal gusts were recorded at 108 miles per hour! The Albany County Airport reported a sustained wind velocity of 66 m.p.h. for over five minutes. Many weather stations reported recording the highest wind velocity ever.

Over 20 inches of snow had fallen in western New York counties, and heavy rains fell from the Mohawk Valley south. The windfalls caused by the high winds in the Adirondacks were of staggering proportions, with many acres completely flattened. Electric and communication services statewide were severely interrupted. The mammoth storm affected 22 states and had accumulated property damage of over $500,000,000, which was an astronomical figure back in 1950! For the state of New York, it was the most damaging storm on record.

History recorded this storm as the Great Appalachian Storm of 1950, but for Adirondackers, it was the Great Wind Storm of 1950. The storm wasn't a hurricane as many people believed it to be, but was in fact a monster nor'easter. There was very little rain accompanied by the wind in the mountains, and no one storm has ever left such a profound effect on the mountains as this one did.

IN THE WOODS

Donald Keith and Warren Ramsdell were hunting at Loon Brook during the last week of the deer season. The weather had been moderately warm and rainy for so late in the season, and there was no snow cover on the ground. By November 24, Don had taken a four-point buck and had it hanging out behind the tent. The boy's had one day left to fill Warren's tag, so they planned on hunting all the last day, and then take the tent down on the following morning.

The morning of the 25th dawned cloudy and breezy with just a scattering of light rain. The boys headed for the low hills just north of the foot of Blue Ridge. The breeze soon turned into a strong wind which rapidly grew in strength all morning. Deer were difficult to see that day and the men blamed their luck on the strong wind raking the tree tops. By early afternoon, the wind gusts were becoming incredibly powerful, and trees and limbs were falling all around them with each consecutive blast. Both men were visibly nervous about the present condition, and by late afternoon, they were back at the tent. They couldn't pull in a radio signal from the tent at that time, so there was no way for them to check the forecast. They weren't looking forward to a night in the tent under these conditions, but they were hoping that the storm would move out of the area after dark.

Several trees had already come down in the vicinity of the tent, and before nightfall, the boys warily looked over the nearby trees, wondering if any of them might come crashing through the tent after dark. Both men were pretty scared and kept a watchful eye on the canvas walls of their tent each time a tremendous wind blast would buffet their area. They talked about going out to the road, but the way things were, they didn't know if they would be any better off. The sleeping area of the tent consisted of a couple of bales of straw that were spread and then covered with a canvas. The men lay in their blankets that night as the heaviest winds of the storm pounded the woodlands. They could hear trees falling to the ground near and far. Warren remembers several big ones coming down quite close to the tent, and when they hit the ground, he swore the vibration would lift them right off the straw!

In the morning, after a frightful, sleepless night, they found windfalls all around the tent. They considered themselves damn lucky for not getting hit with one! Warren told me 45 years after the storm that, "As long as I live, I'll never forget that damn windstorm of 1950!"

Edgar Lanphear was hunting in the neighborhood of Potter Pond with his brother-in-law, Dick Beckingham. He thought the deer were terrified of the big winds and were real spooky. In spite of conditions, Dick managed to wound a buck, but lost his trail when attempting to track it. Conditions were too dangerous to continue the hunt so they headed out. As the wind ripped through the treetops above them, the root structures they were walking on would rise and fall. Edgar saw the top of a huge tree snap off, and when it fell, bury its jagged end deep into the ground. Ed thought the hardwoods were spared a lot of damage because their leaves had already been shed. If the leaves were on, they would have been pushed a lot harder by the wind.

Ed Edwards and Jim Turner were hunting on the north side of Blue Ridge that day. Jim was watching a good run that ran from the bottom lands up into the heavy spruce cover on the higher elevations of Blue Ridge. Ed was hunting the cover below Jim, thinking that if he started something, it might head up past Jim. Jim remembers seeing a huge old owl that day. It came flying down out of the high country and through the hardwoods right past him, real close. Its size was very impressive to young Jim. Being on the lee side of the mountain, Jim didn't think the wind was all that bad, until they started out to the road from their tent. The wind was powerful out there, and with all the new windfalls, it was tough going all the way.

Verne Turner was hunting the Salmon River area, just north of Blue Mountain. Conditions weren't bad during the morning, but in the afternoon, the wind got downright violent. Trees were coming down all around him, and he was very lucky not to get hit, having had several close calls. Every time the wind would gust into his immediate area, he would hear timber crack, and then he would look around real quick! He had an awful time in just getting back out to the road through all the new windfalls.

Over in the Cedar River country, Harry McCane had a party out near Panther Mountain. In the afternoon, trees were coming down all around them, and they were very lucky no one got hurt. Royce Wells was hunting in a lowland swampy area. He remembers standing on some of the spruce root structures and being raised up two feet or more when a big blow would come.

Near headquarters, Ed Mitchel had a party of hunters out in the Buel Brook region. They were about two miles in, when the real heavy winds hit. "God," he said, "You really had to watch for falling trees, especially the spruce trees! That big spruce timber — boy that wind was really laying them down!"

We all headed down the trail for the road, but the trail was filling up fast with windfalls. We only had one ax with us, so we'd bust a hole through the branches with it, and keep on going. When we finally got to the road and headed for Indian Lake, we had to frequently stop and cut windfalls out of the road. Over by Brown's Farm, we met the highway department coming in. They had chain saws to cut out the windfalls with. It was after 8:30 by the time we got back to town.

Ed said, "The woods were never the same after that. He used to take parties in on Hudson's Mountain, and boy they used to get a lot of deer up there. It was nice open spruce timber. I think a guy, in places, could see a deer farther than he could shoot. Not after the windfall, though. First came the windfall, and then they lumbered it. It's thicker'n hell in there now!"

Ernest Blanchard remembers trying to go over some of the trails he and his father used for deer hunting. He said, "After the windfall, you couldn't even begin to use them. The whole country looked different!

The top of Blue Ridge would never be the same in our lifetime also. What was once mostly open spruce timber, was now a thick tangle of windfalls. Many of the spruce swamps were also laid flat, but within the last 10 years, the mid-'80s on, they have begun to open up. The top of the ridge has a much shorter growing season and a colder climate. Most of the ridge top remains incredibly thick and unhuntable to this day.

The following excerpts, were taken from "Operation Blowdown" and written by supervising forester, Charles F. Baar. The article appeared in the December-January issue of the New York State Conservationist magazine, 1956.

"DAMAGE AND RECOVERY"

The November 25th windstorm did more damage to the Adirondack region than anything else previously recorded in history. It was particularly damaging to the Park's softwoods (spruce, pine, balsam, and hemlock). Hardwoods suffered losses also, but not as much as the softwoods. The heaviest damage recorded was in Herkimer, Hamilton, Essex, Lewis, and St. Lawrence counties. Heavy damage was reported on state campgrounds, truck and foot trails, telephone lines, fire towers, and fire observer and ranger cabins.

A ground and air survey was immediately undertaken to assess damage to standing timber. The final figures indicated that over 400,000 acres had wind thrown timber down amounting to 25% or more of the trees on each acre. Some of those acres were completely flattened! Volume estimates indicated a wind throw of over a million cords of pulpwood, and about 40 million board feet of hardwood timber (some other estimates ran much higher).

Since much of the damage was done on forest preserve lands, which are protected by the state constitution to remain inviolate and forever wild, the Department of Conservation was helpless to act in this emergency. The Conservation Department and state foresters were extremely worried about the acute fire danger a windfall of this size would produce. They also would like to salvage as much of the natural resource as possible in reducing the fire hazard.

In December of 1950 the Hon. Perry B. Duryea wrote to the State Attorney General, the Hon. Nathaniel L. Golstein, for a legal interpretation of the law, to see if the windfalls could legally be removed to reduce the fire hazard and could the pulp and saw logs harvested be sold. The Attorney General ruled that only the dead trees could be removed, and that an absolute minimal of live trees, of no material degree, could be cut to facilitate the removal of the wind thrown fire hazard. As for the sale of the timber and pulpwood, the authority must come from the state legislature.

In January of 1951, the New York State legislature enacted a new law giving the Conservation Department the necessary authority to proceed with essential cleanup operations, and through an amendment to the finance law, set up a Forest Preserve Protection Fund, which in effect, was a revolving fund with a first instance appropriation of $200,000.00. All income derived from the salvage operation was paid into this fund, and all operating expenses required by the Department in carrying out the clean up and salvage operations were paid out of it.

This law remained in effect until June 30, 1955 and was subsequently extended until March 31, 1956.

Once the Department got the legal go ahead, the race was on to reduce the fire hazards in the most critical areas and get the timber to market before it deteriorated to the point where it was no longer marketable. Excellent progress was made in 1951 and 1952, but by late '52, blue stain and ambrosia beetles (wood borers) had rendered the hardwoods unsaleable. By 1954, most of the softwoods were being refused at the sawmills and pulp mills also.

When the program legally came to an end on March 31, 1956, 245,057 cords of pulpwood, and 40,147,830 board ft. of lumber had been removed. Gross receipts from these sales totaled more than 1.1 million dollars. Smaller local sales pushed this figure to $1,264,850.90. Most of this money was used to run the program and to restore and improve existing facilities within the Park. Some of it was used to purchase more Park land, both in the Adirondacks and in the Catskills.

THE FIRE BREAK TRAIL

It was in the late summer of 1951 that a forest fire broke out on the north side of Wakley Mountain. A crew of fire fighters was dispatched in an effort to extinguish the blaze. They went into the woods by the Brown Farm and then took a logging access road west to the area of Dish Rag Pond. From there, they attempted to go cross country to the fire. The windfalls in that district were so bad that they couldn't even begin to make any distance towards the fire. They gave up and came back out. The next day the fire was put out by several soaking thunder showers.

For many years, there had been a usable foot trail through the valley, leading from Brown's Farm to Camp Kill-Kare, some nine miles distant. The Great Windfall obliterated the trail, making any access to the valley almost impossible. After the forest fire incident on Wakley Mountain, the Conservation Department decided that the foot trail through the valley should be re-established, at least until the fire hazard from the windfalls was over.

Two trail construction crews were formed, one at Raquette Lake headed by Ranger Moses Leanard, and one at Indian Lake, headed by Ranger Ed Goulet. Leanard's crew consisted of Gordon Aldous and two other Raquette-lakers, and Ed's crew was Guy Aldous (Gorton's brother), George Osgood, and Cecil Blanchard. Their job was to clear out a well-marked, serviceable trail between Kill-Kare and Brown's Farm through the Wakley-Blue Ridge Valley. Moses would start at the Kill-Kare end, and Ed would start from the Brown Farm, joining the two trails wherever they met. All of the men were comfortable in the woods and looked forward to the project as an interesting change of pace.

On the Brown Farm end of the project, a serviceable logging road ran into the valley, a distance of four miles and ended near the outlet of Dish Rag Pond. In early 1951, a logging company was awarded a contract to remove all the saleable wood from the windfalls in the valley. However, the windfalls were so heavy and in such a tangle, that they were just too difficult to remove. After spending several weeks at it and losing money every week, they just gave it up.

When Ed and his crew came in to the end of the logging road, they found a quantity of lumber left by the logging crews. They built tent platforms and erected three tents by the outlet brook of Dish Rag Pond. They made some rough camp furniture and sunk two five-gallon lard tubs into a nearby spring hole for refrigeration. The large main tent had a sheet metal stove in it for cool weather and a kerosene stove for cooking.

The actual trail work began in May of 1952. They had a large Maul chain saw, and several axes and bucksaws, all furnished by the state. The men would work eight hours a day for a 40 hour week and be home weekends. Guy Aldous was the camp cook, so he would be excused one hour early to prepare the evening meals. He did all his cooking over an open fire, except when the weather didn't cooperate. Ed would go home on Wednesdays after work to file the payroll and be back in time for work Thursday morning.

The trail work progress varied considerably. In some places, the trees were bent over and across one another, creating one hell of a tangle. Some of these trees would measure more than three feet across. Also, it was very difficult to scout ahead for the best possible trail route. To Ed's knowledge, the area they were in had never been logged before. It would be hard to describe, attempting to cut a trail that would last, through entanglements such as these. Daily progress ranged from a few yards up to a few hundred yards.

They saw wildlife every day, mostly partridges and deer. A young fawn used to hang around their tent site, and it became quite tame after a while. At that time, there were still a few trout to be found in local streams, and they would often supplement their meals with fresh trout. It was while working on this trail that Ed heard his first pack of Adirondack coyotes. George Osgood had heard them earlier in other areas, so he knew just what they were. They could hear them at times both night and day. It reminded Ed of a wolf pack out hunting.

On July 21, the boys were all in camp relaxing after the day's activities. Suddenly, they became aware of a low, ominous roar. The sky turned black, as dark sinister clouds rolled in over their campsite, darkening the surrounding woods. The roar rapidly increased in volume, and it began to hail incredibly hard. The hail stones were about one inch in diameter but oval in shape. They came down with a deafening roar, stripping all the leaves off the hardwoods and plugging up the outlet brook with shredded leaves and ice. The men in the tents weren't sure the canvas roof could withstand the pounding, so they had chairs to put over their heads, just in case! When it was all over, a huge pond was formed right in front of the tents from the plugged outlet brook, and there was at least three inches of hailstones covering the ground. Ed went down to check on the jeep, and it was a real struggle to walk anywhere on all those hailstones. It was the worst storm he had ever experienced while in the woods. Four days later, hail stones could still be found in some of the shaded areas.

When the trail got over near Aluminum Pond, Ed and George Osgood decided to build a raft and fish the pond with it. The summer days are long, so one sunny day after work, they built a raft, and a few days later, they returned to fish. The men began working the pond with their lures but were only getting a few medium-sized trout for their effort. The highlight of the day was watching a huge eight-point buck, whose antlers were still in the velvet, walk into the pond and begin feeding on lily pad roots. It paid no attention at all to Ed and George. The buck would completely submerge his head, and then come up with a mouth full of lily pad roots. Ed thought only moose did this, but now he knows that deer do also. The deer, with his big velvety rack, made a beautiful sight while feeding in Aluminum Pond, one Ed never forgot!

The boys had also heard of Ernie Blanchard's Aluminum Pond cabin, and they were moved with curiosity to look for it. Neither man had ever laid eyes on it, and they wondered if it were even standing. They had found some of Ernie's old cubby-hole trap sites that he had built for fisher and martin, and now they started looking for his cabin. They knew it was away from the shore line and on the north side of the pond, so they started their search there. It wasn't long before they spotted an old spruce log that had been stripped of its bark, so they reasoned it wasn't very far off. A short while later they came upon the cabin. The 1950 windfall had dropped several trees near the cabin, and one of them had caved in the roof. The cabin, as they found it, was unusable. There were shelves, a bunk bed, some old canned goods, and aluminum pots and kettles that the porcupines had chewed on. There was also a large amount of traps and some were in their original boxes. (One of their acquaintances hiked in later and got all the traps.) They couldn't help but envision old Ernie in his younger days, coming into the cabin near dark, with a pack basket full of fur, and happy to have this cabin on his line so far back in and away from everything.

George and Ed got along great. George was a Gooley Club guide for 60 years. He was very knowledgeable in woodcraft, and he gathered ginseng from the forest and honey from wild hives. He took a buck and a bear at the age of 85. He died on October 13, 1991, at the age of 87.

IN RETROSPECT

After the big windfall, the cleanup effort enjoyed a great deal of cooperation from the highest political offices, right down to John Q. Public. The main worry of the state foresters at the time was of a huge existing fire threat caused by the windfall. I was just a 10-year-old boy when the storm struck, and at that time, I lived in Connecticut. By the time I was 15, I was a New York State resident, and I hiked through some of the areas that were cut out by the contractors. Those woodlands were still in one hell of a mess and made worse, I thought, by all the skid trails going every which way. The downed tree tops were merely pushed aside, and were still a fire hazard.

Since that time, I've spent many days in remote parts of the Adirondacks and witnessed, several times, the areas where severe down drafts have flattened a stretch of trees, leaving one hung upon another, and a mess you couldn't get through. It wouldn't take too many years where they would all break down, and you could once again hunt through there. In addition, the new growth and cover was beneficial for wildlife.

I don't have anything against loggers. I was a logger myself for a few years, but I hope we never again let commercial loggers onto Forest Preserve property, for any reason. The constitutional law states that, "They shall be forever kept as wild forest lands." Therefore, they are subject to the laws of nature! Let the trees rot down as they normally would, and if a fire occurs, then we'll have to deal with the fire. Many areas of the windfall were never cleaned up, yet I didn't recall hearing of any disastrous fire occurring in a windfall area. Even so, fires are very beneficial to wildlife. It's true that some animals are lost in the conflagration, but many more generations of wildlife benefit from the lush new growth.

In April of 1988, I hiked into the Wakley-Blue Ridge valley with my son Rick, Gerry Chesebro, George Gay, David Pavese and Don Adams. We camped an evening at Aluminum Pond and fished the pond and some area brooks, but caught no fish. We looked for Ernie's old cabin, but didn't find it, and we looked for traces of the old trail and didn't find any. The woods were real open in places, and there were several huge boulders that appeared to be sitting right on top of the ground. Ernie's old cabin and the windfalls and trails of old appeared to be long gone.

*After the great storm the woods were dramatically changed in many areas.
Bill Weedmark photo.*

You couldn't even begin to use the old trails! Bill Weedmark photo.

Once legal matters were cleared up, the race was on to salvage as much of the downed timber as possible. Bill Weedmark photo.

Salvaging pulpwood. Bill Weedmark photo.

Basecamp at Dishrag Pond. Goulet family photo.

Breakfast at Dishrag Pond. L to R George Osgood. Cecil Blanchard and Guy Aldous.
Goulet family photo.

*Ranger Ed Goulet talks to Wakley Mt. fire tower observer from Dishrag Pond.
Goulet family photo.*

*Looking East through the Wakley Mt, Blue Ridge Valley. Blue Ridge left, Aluminum
Pond left center, Lost Brook right center. Photo by Bob Elinskas.*

TONY DIPINO

Tony Dipino was born on St. Patty's Day, March 17, 1917. In 1933, he moved with his family to Syracuse, New York. He married Yolanda Fiorini in August of 1941, and their marriage produced five children, three sons and two daughters. Tony was a mechanic by trade, and he ran his own garage.

Tony began hunting at an early age and enjoyed a good share of rabbit and grouse hunting. Some of the first treks after big game brought him into the southern Adirondacks, near Woodgate. Tony and some of his friends would come up on Friday nights and camp near the end of the Bear Creek Road. They would pitch a tent and then cover the floor with about six inches of spruce boughs. Then two full-sized mattresses would be laid down on the boughs. There was no heat in the tent, and all the cooking was done outside on an open fire. The men used blankets to sleep in, but with no heat in the tent, Tony remembered some of those nights as being damn cold!

A REQUEST FOR HELP

During one hunt in 1939, Tony had taken a nice eight-point buck around noon, and they had the buck back into camp by late afternoon. After the evening meal, three or four men approached their campsite. One was a state trooper and another was a priest. The trooper addressed them stating, "Men, when you are camping in this area, you fall under our jurisdiction. If any of you get hurt or lost, we all have to help one another out." Then he went on to explain that earlier in the day a hunter had died of a heart attack, and the body was still quite a distance back in the woods. He said there was a fella staying in there with him, but help was needed in getting the body out. Tony asked where the body was, and the trooper replied, "Back in along trail number two." A man from one of the other tents shouted, "I know that trail so I'll lead them in!"

There were several other tents near Tony's, and the number of volunteers going in numbered fourteen. They all headed out at 5:00 p.m. with flashlights and lanterns, but somehow their guide got them off on the wrong trail, and they went a long way in before the mistake was realized. By the time they got things straightened out and found the man staying with the corpse, it was 2:00 a.m. They were at a place called Muskrat Pond, and the fella with the corpse had been trying to drag the body out and carry the rifles and all, too. The boys that had come in to relieve him didn't think he had been showing the corpse very much respect, and they were a little "put out" about it. However, they all teamed up to carry out the dead man, and once under way, they discovered that he was awkward and hard to handle. By the time the dead man was finally brought out to the road, he had lost a hell of a lot more respect from the 14 volunteers that had brought him out!

It was 5:30 a.m. when they got to the road, and the dead man's wife was among the people waiting for the body. She took the time to get everyone's name and address, and after the funeral a few days later, she invited everyone over to her home for brunch, and to thank them again.

A SOUTHERN TIER TRAGEDY

When the deer season opened in the southern tier of counties in 1940, Tony began hunting deer down south. In 1947, Tony witnessed a terrible accident. A father had shot and killed his son, mistaking him for a deer. Tony was only a short distance from the father when the fatal shot was fired. When Tony walked over and saw what had happened, and seeing the horrible pain and grief caused by a foolish lack of self control, it upset him tremendously.

Les York and Jay Conley were good friends of Tony. They were also in the garage business, and they used to meet regularly at a local tavern. When they saw how upset Tony was over the shooting accident, they invited him up north to hunt with them at Loon Brook for the coming weekend. Tony accepted the invitation, and he liked what he saw, both in camping and in the different hunting environment. It started an annual tradition for him that would last for the next 50 years.

THE DIPINO CAMP

Tony invested in his own 16' by 16' marine pyramid tent. He put in a big wood stove, a four-burner propane stove, table, chairs, and cabinets. Half of the tent floor was blanketed with a thick bedding of straw for sleeping on. It was quite a project to bring it all in before the season opened and set it up, and just as big a project to take it all down at the season's end, but it was very comfortable to hunt out of during the season. Some of Tony's regular hunting companions included his brother Frank, Les York, Jay Conley, Frank Saya, Ed Gratien, Dick Betis, Pat Grosso and Al Young. Peter Dipino, Tony's son, began coming up when he was 10 years old.

After hunting the area for 50 years, Tony has quite a collection of hunting stories. He and his group have taken a great many deer from the region under all types of weather conditions. Access into and out of camp can sometimes be very challenging. Heavy snowfalls have at times, made just getting their cars onto the highway again a major project. In bitter cold weather, they've had their share of jump starting cars and frozen gas lines also. In the big picture, it's a small price to pay for some quality Adirondack adventures.

In 1959, Tony bought the Freeland Jones house on the Durant Road in Blue Mountain Lake and put his tent into storage. They continued hunting the Loon Brook area even after moving into the village. On Father's Day, in June of 1985, the house burned to the ground, along with a great loss of personal property and most of the pictures he had collected of their hunts through the years. Late that summer, Tony, along with his sons and a lot of their hunting companions, built a new house on the same site. They started on the structure only four weekends before deer season opened. In four two-day weekends, they had it up and inhabitable by the time deer season opened. Evelyn Thompson, who lived next door, did the cooking for the crew.

In 1990, Tony sold the house to Ken and Bill Larkin and Tony's boys set up a new 16' by 32' army cook tent back at Loon Brook on their old tent site. Tony also hunted out of this tent, but it was a younger generation of hunters who ran the tent now. They called themselves the Smuck Hill Gang, which is a nearby area they liked to hunt regularly. The group includes Pete, Anthony, and Frank Dipino, Dick Walrath, Dave Foley, Russ Runkels, Scott Warry, Larry Barnes and Daryl Eaton. The big tent is heated by a dual 55-gallon drum stove, and is unquestionably the warmest tent in the Adirondacks, regardless of the weather conditions.

THE
GOLDEN HORSESHOE

In 1957, the boys had hunted hard all season, but for one reason or another, things just didn't seem to go right, so they had no deer to show for their efforts. Now they were down to the last weekend of the season, and the last day was to be a special day where you could legally take a deer of either sex. On the day before "doe day," Tony was hunting the section of Loon Brook between Potter Pond and the falls. He had hunted that section a few times earlier in the season but hadn't noticed enough sign to get excited about. Today, however, tracks seemed to be everywhere, lacing through the alders and bordering spruce trees. He had started deer several times during the day but hadn't seen them well enough for some possible shooting.

He got back to the tent just at full dark and told the boys what he had found. There was close to a foot of snow on the ground and there was a lot more in the forecast. Tony guessed that the deer were beginning to yard up, so he suggested that everyone go up there in the morning and work the alders.

Later in the evening, George and Parks Keith stopped in from the tent next door. George had hunted on the hardwood ridge above the alders that Tony was in that day. He said, "Every track I crossed seemed to be heading right down towards Loon Brook. Tony told them of their plans to hunt those alders on the last day and invited them to join in. They declined though; they had their minds made up to hunt off towards Bear Brook.

It snowed heavy that night with light, fluffy lake-effect snow, and by dawn, there was close to two feet of it on top of what they already had. At first light, Tony's crew was pushing through the snow and heading for the falls on the upper trail. The snow had stopped falling, but now a strong wind had come up and was blowing it all over the place. When they got to the alders, they spread out, and Tony took the south side, just up into the spruce trees. He had just started to hunt when he saw a buck out in front of him. He took a shot and the buck bolted out of sight. When he reached the tracks, he found a heavy blood trail, but it stopped bleeding real quick. He followed it only a short distance when he saw the buck standing in the alders below him. He dropped it in his tracks and went down to see his buck.

It was a nice nine-pointer and after he had looked it over real good, discovered that the buck had only been hit once. Well, this didn't add up, so Tony went back to where he originally started the track and found another blood trail going in a different direction. He only followed it a short distance, when he found a dead 11-point buck. Piecing the puzzle together went something like this. Tony shot the first time, hitting the deer through the lungs. The deer jumped over a nearby bedded buck, soaking him with his blood, and this was the deer Tony followed first. Tony had two nice bucks on the ground, and when he finally rounded all the guys up, they couldn't believe it. No one had heard any of the shots for all the wind and blowing snow.

They snaked both bucks over onto the trail near the falls, and while doing so, Tony spotted a good-sized lone track that appeared to be real fresh. He told Pat Grasso to flank the track, hoping he would get a shot at it, and Tony would stay on the track. After a while, he met up with Pat, and he told Tony that he'd seen the deer but couldn't tell if it was a buck or doe. Tony said, "This is doe day, you can shoot either one!" They went back to tracking the deer, and this time, Tony saw it and dropped it. It turned out to be another buck with big long spikes. They dressed it out and dragged it back to the tent. Now there were three bucks lying in front of the tent, and when the boys learned that Tony had also taken the third one, they began to tease him. "What the hell, Tony! Have you got a golden horseshoe strapped to your ass or what?!" Everyone was in a good mood; after a long, dry season, it was good to have some deer for the camp. They all had lunch and rested a while. Then, Tony suggested that they try hunting the alders below the falls.

They hiked in to the second crossing of Loon Brook on the lower trail. This time, Tony had the guys flank the alders watching some good runs, while he would hunt up through the thick alders. About a half an hour into the drive, Tony spotted an opening in the alders ahead. Through the blowing and swirling snow, he could make out the forms of two deer on the far side, and they were both bucks. Tony brought up his rifle thinking, "If I shoot the one on the far side and am lucky, then I might get a shot at the second buck also." Tony got both bucks with some quick shooting, and for the second time that day, he had two bucks down along Loon Brook. Again, no one had heard him shoot due to all the heavy wind, and again, they couldn't believe their eyes!

They had all five bucks back to camp by late afternoon, and everyone in the Dipino camp had his 1957 deer tag filled. Tony had taken an 11-point, nine-point, eight-point, six-point, and a spike horn, all on the last day of the season. When George and Parks came into camp a little later they exclaimed, "Oh my God, no wonder we didn't see any deer! They were all right here laying in front of Tony's tent!"

They took the tent down and got everything out to the road after full dark. The following day in Syracuse, they took all five bucks down to Frank Saya's Sporting Goods Store and hung them up in front of it. It made for quite a sight and ended the season on a happy note.

CAUGHT WITH THEIR PANTS DOWN!

It was late in the afternoon, one November, when Tony and Frank Dipino, Frank and Pete Saya, Ed Gratien and Art Bittle began a drive on the north slope of Smokey Roost Hill. It was the middle of the month with no snow on the ground and everything was frozen down hard. They were going to put on a silent push, with two men flanking the drive. Tony and Frank Saya were still walking in to their assigned places when several shots went off below them and off to the northwest. Shortly afterward, they could hear deer running their way, and then six doe went bounding by them, but no buck was spotted.

After the drive, they all regrouped above the falls, and Tony learned that his brother, Frank, had wounded a big buck at the beginning of the push. Frank and some of the others had tracked it down to Loon Brook, where they lost its trail. Tony listened to the whole story and then said, "Let's go down to where you lost the track and spread out on both sides of the brook and see if we can't locate him or some more sign. He can't be too far away!" It was getting pretty late in the day, and some of the guys didn't think there was enough time to look and still get back to camp before dark. Tony reassured them that he'd get them back even if it got dark.

They all went back to where the last sign was found, and then fanned out on either side of the brook. About 200 yards down stream, they found where the buck had fallen while crossing some frozen stillwater, and left a bloody smear across the ice. A short distance later, they saw the buck laying on the ground and apparently gasping his last breath. Tony hollered that they had found the buck, and a short while later, the group all stood before a big buck with its absolutely beautiful rack of antlers. After the boys had taken their first look at the buck, they could see that he still had a little life left in him, so Frank brought out his pistol to finish him off. When he started to take aim, Tony shouted, "Don't use that, you'll hit the rack!" Tony's loud voice must have brought the buck back to his senses, because he jumped to his feet and was off through the spruces with only a few, wild, Hail Mary shots thrown after him. They all returned in the morning and searched the entire area, but no further sign was ever found of that buck. Ed Gratien, who is a bit of an artist, symbolized the event with a sketch and a caption, "Boy, did he ever catch us with our pants down!"

Tony's sons have also had their share of adventures. Anthony, (Tone) wounded a big buck just west of their tent one fall. Pete and Tone took up the track and the buck led them on a grand tour off to the west. After a couple of hours of tracking, they spotted a different buck, so they dropped that one, dressed it and hung it up, and continued tracking. The buck took them through Bear Brook swamp, and then way off to the west. Late in the day, they jumped him out of some tall grass in a beaver meadow, and Tone put him down for keeps. The beaver meadow was less than a mile from the road! Afterwards, they retraced their route on a map and figured that they had tracked that buck a good seven miles. He was a big buck with 10 perfect points.

Frank Dipino became a big league pitcher and pitched for the Milwaukee Brewers, Houston Astros, Chicago Cubs and the St. Louis Cardinals. He made his home in Gilbert, Arizona, for many years, but always returned to the Loon Brook area every fall for some good old Adirondack deer hunting.

Frank was on watch one day during one of their silent drives. He was watching a pretty good run when, suddenly, he heard a commotion behind him. He turned around and saw four doe run out of some spruce trees and into the more open hardwoods. He heard more noise from the spruce trees and then saw a big 10-point buck come out and then walk up behind one of the does. The buck hit the doe in the ass with his antlers, so hard that it spun her around 180 degrees. The buck stood there eyeing the doe, but Frank had seen enough. He dropped the buck with a single shot and brought home a beautiful Adirondack trophy.

TRAGEDY AT LOON BROOK

On November 5th of 1978, Tony's group of hunters suffered a heart-breaking accident. They had all hunted hard that day, and the last drive they put on was up on Hodge's Rock Hill. It was a good two miles back out to the road, and everyone walked it out at their own comfortable pace.

Tony and his son, Frank, had left a little earlier in order to start preparing the evening meal. At this time, Tony was using the house he had bought on the Durant Road as his base camp. Bob and Ray Finney came out of the woods next, and they were driving up to the top of the hill to turn around, when Frank Saya and Anthony Dipino came out of the woods. Frank's hearing had deteriorated to the point where he had to wear his hearing aid all the time. This weekend, his hearing aid had plugged up, and he didn't have the tools with him to clean it out. For reasons we will never know, Frank walked right out across Route 28 and into the path of an oncoming car. He never looked up the road for traffic, and he couldn't hear the car coming because of his plugged hearing aid. At the last instant before being hit, he spotted the car, but it was too late! He jumped up slightly, and the impact rolled him across the hood where he smashed his head into the windshield, and was then thrown 40 to 50 feet from the vehicle.

Anthony had witnessed the whole incident and couldn't believe what had just occurred. It had all happened so fast, there was no way he could have prevented it. Peter Dipino, Scott Warry, Joe Grosso, and Dave Van Slyke came out to the road immediately after the accident. They gave whatever first aid they could, while others rushed into Blue Mountain to summon their ambulance and also to notify Tony and Frank. Everyone responded in record time.

Frank had suffered a major traumatic head injury, as well as a badly bruised body. He was rushed to Tupper Lake Medical Center, and Tony rode right beside him in the ambulance. Later, he was transferred to the Saranac Lake General Hospital, and then down to a Syracuse Veterans' Hospital. Eventually, he was taken to the James Square Health and Rehabilitation Center, where he remained until the time of his death. Frank went into a coma on the day of his injury and remained in it for over eighteen years, until death.

Before the accident, Frank Saya was a healthy productive worker, husband, and father of three children. He worked for General Electric in Syracuse, and also ran Saya's Sport Shop on Wolf Street where he sold and repaired all types of sporting equipment. He was loved and respected by all, and his accident deeply saddened everyone, especially the entire hunting group at Loon Brook.

Tony's Bear Creek campsite in 1939, just before going in after a dead hunter.
Dipino family photo.

Tony's original marine pyramid tent at Loon Brook. Dipino family photo.

Sketch by Ed Gratien.

Tony Dipino.
Dipino family photo.

A good weekend hunt. L to R Peter Dipino, Dick Walrath and Tone Dipino.
Dipino family photo.

The latest Dipino tent is a spacious 16' x 32' and is the warmest tent
in the Adirondacks! Photo by Bob Elinskas.

RALPH HOLDRIDGE

In the fall of 1947, the tall, lean frame of Ralph Holdridge entered the woods at Loon Brook for the first time. Glade and Ralph had been gun trading acquaintances as well as friends for many years prior. Both men shared a great wealth of knowledge in firearms, which included collecting, repair, and shooting skills. They also enjoyed the challenge, sport, and spirit of a good old Adirondack hunt. Glade and Ralph hunted together at Loon Brook for close to 40 years. In those years, they were the team that usually produced the bucks, even in the lean years!

Ralph is four years younger than Glade. He was born on April 27, 1908, and raised on the family farm in Columbus, New York. His father, Hiram Marlin Holdridge, was a farmer and logger. They lived close to the earth, and Hiram used to enjoy his deer hunting in the Big Moose area of the Adirondacks. When he was a boy, some of Ralph's favorite times were when friends would drop by to visit in their big kitchen. He enjoyed the stories told of hunting, fishing, gathering ginseng, and logging the best. Ralph would sit on the kitchen floor, near the warmth of the stove, with his back against the wall, and drink it all in.

He was always interested in firearms, and was raised in a home with a shooting range right outside the back door. His collecting and trading history is very similar to Glade's. Ralph worked for the State Conservation Department from 1930 to 1941. He left to start an independent trucking business, and worked at it until 1951. It was during his trucking years that he became very active as a gun trader. By 1951, he was making enough money at it to leave trucking and trade in guns full time. He would also contract log during the slow periods. This was his livelihood until a serious truck accident in 1986 ended his logging activities. In 1995, he didn't renew his federal firearms license, and called it quits on his gun trading career.

You can't help but like Ralph. He is always garbed in the casual attire of an outdoorsman, and topped with a weathered gimmie hat. A salt and pepper stubble of beard covers his square jaw and high cheek bones, and his sharp blue eyes can reflect the wisdom in his words or twinkle with his keen sense of humor. Ralph is a talented storyteller, but he won't stretch the truth for the sake of a good story. He has the ability to relate an event, and make you feel like you were right there beside him, watching the whole story unfold again. The man has taken over 60 bucks in his lifetime, and the greater share of them were the good, big bragging kind, from the deep Adirondacks.

Any visit with Ralph is always a treat. If you happened to be talking about guns, he may suddenly excuse himself and head for another part of his home, returning shortly with some related firearm. If you were talking about hunting, he may leave and return with two or three large sets of antlers, relating to the stories. Ralph was a seasoned woodsman and an excellent deer hunter before he began hunting with Glade at Loon Brook. His adventures before and during his years at Blue Ridge have kept us entertained at every storytelling. The following stories are among our favorites.

THE ONE-TOOTHED BUCK

Clieve Hodges, Glade, and Ralph were in at Loon Brook during the late '40s, putting in their week of deer hunting. There was snow on the ground, and Ralph had hiked in to the foot of Blue Ridge, and then began hunting up near Cascade Brook. It was one of the first times that he had hunted over into this area. One thing he noticed right away was that there seemed to be an abundance of big and wide-spaced deer tracks in the region — the kind of track where the hoof isn't picked too far off the ground between prints. The day was warming up and the four or five inches of snow on the ground was starting to settle. It was the kind of day where a man could cover the country pretty darn good and not get too tired doing it.

Along about the middle of the morning, Ralph struck a good big track that looked reasonably fresh. The track was just kind of wandering along, so he cut right in on it. By 'n' by, it led to a big old Maple stub that had a lot of those white Italian tree mushrooms growing on it. The deer had circled the tree about three times, eating whatever mushrooms he could reach. Ralph said to himself, "That's right old boy, you get your gut good and full, and you'll be laying down soon. Now, the only thing I've got to do is spot you before you spot me!" Ralph said, "Getting your eye on a bedded deer can be tough sometimes, because they don't always look like you think they might." He has killed five or six deer right in their beds, and when you're looking for a bedded deer, the tendency is to look right over them. This old buck didn't give him any problems though. He spotted him bedded up right out in the hardwoods behind a couple of flattened windfalls. His polished antlers were sticking right up in the air. Ralph pushed the safety off his Remington, and gave a whistle. The old buck lifted and turned his head, and as soon as he did, KA-BOOM, he died instantly from a broken neck.

Ralph walked over and took a good look at his trophy. The buck was pretty good size, 180 pounds or better, and had a reasonable amount of fat. The rack was a good respectable nine-point, but the right brow tine was partially broken, from fighting, no doubt. He had an old gray face on him, and when he looked in his mouth, all he could see was one front tooth. All of his back teeth were worn down below the gum line!

By the end of the week they had Ralph's buck, plus one more to pack for the ride home. On Route 12, south of Alder Creek, they had a game check station, so they pulled in and two young biologists came out to look over the deer. When they got to Ralph's, one of them very professionally opened the mouth and looked in, then offered it to the other biologist. He looked in, and then they both looked at each other, but didn't say anything. Ralph said, "Well, how old is he?" "We can't say for sure, we'll go get the boss." A much older biologist came out of the shack, and he took a good long look. He even stuck a mirror in there and squinted some more. Ralph again said, "Well, how old is he?" The chief biologist returned with, "I ain't going to tell you, because I don't know! I'll tell you one thing though, he'll never see 10-and-one-half again, and he could well be a couple of years older than that. It's a good thing you got him, though, because he would have had things pretty tough from this fall on."

Ralph used to love hunting those "high country" bucks on Blue Ridge. During most of his years at Loon Brook, that was where the greater share of his time was spent. We used to call the upper areas of Cascade Brook and the Big Notch, "Holdridge Country." He took some real nice bucks out of there over the years, but he didn't get all the bucks he came across. The following stories describe some of his high country adventures.

CAUGHT OFF GUARD

On one hunt in the late '50s, the weather had remained wet for most of the week. Nobody was having any luck seeing deer and time was running out. Towards the end of the week, the rain stopped, but the woods were still soaked, and a light mist hung in the air. Ralph had remembered seeing some good sign earlier in the Cascade Notch area, so he headed up into the high country above Cascade Brook. By mid-morning, he had wandered into an active bedding area, and put out at least 18 deer. One was a nice buck, but he didn't see it long enough to get a shot off. By noon, he had worked up a pretty good appetite, and started looking for a place that was dry enough to sit on. Finally, he spotted a sizable spruce windfall whose trunk had some bark rubbed off from it. It looked like it would make a fairly comfortable seat to rest on while chowing down.

Ralph laid his rifle across his legs and opened his lunch bag. He had an apple in one hand and a chunk of sharp cheese in the other, when he caught a movement only a short way down the hill. His eyes met those of a huge buck that was now staring right at Ralph. The buck's left foot was still off the ground, and the buck wasn't 50 feet away. Ralph counted 10 perfect points on one of the biggest racked bucks he had ever seen. Ralph thought, "Well, you sure caught me in one hell of a fix, with both hands full and my rifle pointed the wrong way, but if you blink just once, I'll get you!" The two stared at each other for close to a full minute, then the buck made his move, and Ralph made his. His rifle was up in record time, but that buck was gone! Later that day he met up with Jim Kling, and he told him where he had seen all the deer. That evening, he told Glade of his adventures also. The next day all three men hunted the same area, but came into it from different directions. By the end of the day, all three men had killed an eight-point buck, but nobody saw or took the monster 10-pointer.

THE CHRISTMAS TREE BUCK

Ralph was hunting high up in the spruce trees on Blue Ridge one November when he decided he'd had enough of them for one day, and slowly began his descent towards the hardwoods in the Big Notch. He was walking along one of those long horizontal ledges that are commonly found up on the steeper slopes, and looking for a safe way to get below it when he spotted a fracture in the wall just ahead. A slab of rock had been pushed out away from the base of the ledge a few feet. There was a nice bushy Christmas tree growing at its base, and the pitch of the slab wasn't too steep, so Ralph thought, "Heck, I'll just slide down the rock, and if I start going a little fast, I'll catch myself on that Christmas tree."

Ralph got up on the end of the slab, and sat down with his two feet flat on the rock. He then started a controlled slide to the tree. As soon as he reached the tree, he stood up and grabbed hold of the top to steady himself. When he did, an eight-point buck that had been bedded under its far side, jumped up and began to run up through the cut that the rock slab was laying on. The buck was really struggling to get up the cut, and Ralph, although surprised, thought, "Why heck, I can get this buck with one hand!" With the butt of his rifle against his shoulder, and his right hand guiding the rifle, Ralph let five shots go off at the not very distant buck! When the shooting was over, the buck was up through the cut and heading for the top of the ridge in high gear, no worse for wear! Ralph was left standing on the end of the rock slab, still hanging onto the Christmas tree. He was thinking, "We were both a little foolish. If I'd just stepped off the slab and used the rifle with both hands, I'd have plugged that buck, and if he'd just bounded down the hill, I would have been lucky to have even got a good look at him!

HOW DO YOU DO!

Ralph was hunting right on the very top of the back basin of the Big Notch. The south side of it is extremely thick with growth, but the very top has a thin mixture of stunted hardwoods, spruce trees, and a salting of small grassy meadows. Some of these meadows are lined with a bushy, stunted growth of black spruce trees. Ralph was slow poking through this when he came upon an awful lot of real fresh deer tracks. There was about four inches of snow on the ground, and as Ralph hunted and peeked, he could swear he was smelling these deer. "I could see all around, and it would seem so's a fella could get his eye on one," Ralph said. With things looking this promising, Ralph had his rifle in a high state of alert. He was just stepping around one of those dwarf bushy spruce trees, when he looked and spotted a nice buck coming around the other side of it. The buck wasn't six feet away! The buck never completed his first bound for safety. "The buck went WOOF, and I went KA-BOOM! We come darn near walkin' in to one another!"

The biggest bodied deer Ralph ever saw on the ridge was up above Cascade Brook. The first time he saw the buck, Ralph was trying to get through a windfall without breaking a leg. The deer went out just below him, and he saw him jump over some windfalls before disappearing. Ralph said, "He had a big pot belly on him, and his body reminded him of a 55-gallon drum running down the ridge!" Ralph was back up in that locale a couple of days later when he got the impression he was being looked upon, and the hairs on his head were trying to stand on end. He thought to himself, "There's a buck in here, and the sucker's lookin' right at me!" He turned around and began looking over the upper spruce cover, and he spotted him. "He had his lips curled back just like an old bull! I couldn't see all his rack, but I could see the main beams, where they swept up and away from his head. They looked about the size of baseball bat handles! Just as soon as I raised my rifle, that buck disappeared. I often thought of how much fun I would have had in getting that buck out of there!"

NORTH OR SOUTH?

Ralph was hunting up near the top of the ridge above Cascade Brook on one occasion, with a good cover of snow on the ground and a fair amount hanging on some of the spruce trees. The buck he was tracking didn't seem to be getting any closer, and to make matters worse, it was snowing again and coming down quite hard at times. Ralph thought it might be a good time to get the hell out of there. He left the track and began the slow process of going down through all the spruce thickets, windfalls and ledges. After what seemed like quite a while he broke out into the hardwoods, but something wasn't right. A break in the cloud cover enabled him to see a distant and unfamiliar skyline, and from what he could see of the valley floor, it appeared to be the Cedar River side of the ridge! He checked his compass again and north pointed right out across the Cedar River drainage. Now there are lots of examples in the books, on why you should always believe your compass, and earlier in the day, Ralph wouldn't have had a problem, but not now! He turned around and headed back up into the spruce trees that he'd just come down through. The second time, though, they seemed to be thicker'n nastier than ever. To make matters worse, going down the north side, his daylight was running out. It was close to 11 o'clock when he got back to the tent that night. Somewhere up on top of Blue Ridge that day, his compass had swapped ends, with north pointing south and south pointing north. He still has the compass, and north still points south!

Ralph carried his Model 8 Remington automatic for a good many of his hunting years. It has notches on one side of the stock for 17 bucks, and two on the other for two bears. Being a gun trader he had ample opportunity to shoot and carry other rifles afield. One time, he thought he had found the perfect deer rifle, a Model 14 Remington. It was light, fast, and easy to carry. He brought it up for his annual hunt with Glade, and in the course of the week, he missed three different bucks with it. Near the end of the week, he switched back to his old favorite and dropped the next buck he saw. The Model 14 is still a nice rifle, but it's not for Ralph!

One fall, there was a big buck hanging around Hodge's Rock Hill. Most of the fellas hunting in that area had seen the buck or shot at him, but for one reason or another, he would always get away. Ralph was hunting up near the rock later in the season when he jumped the buck out of some windfalls. He got off one shot at him and then the buck crossed some fairly open hardwoods giving him some excellent shooting opportunities. It didn't do Ralph any good, though, because his rifle action was all jammed up. He was using a Winchester Model 1895 lever action in 30-40 Krag, a rimmed cartridge. In the magazine you had to lap stack the rims in sequence in order to load each cartridge without a malfunction. Somehow Ralph didn't do this right before starting his hunt that morning. Ralph said, "This buck had a charmed life, and was never meant to be killed, at least not by us hunters!"

CAMP LIFE

During the late'40s and early '50s, there were usually several tents pitched in the Loon Brook area for the deer season. Glade and Ralph spent little of their time around their campsite in the daylight hours. However, after a full day of hunting, or dragging on a buck, they did take the time to occasionally talk to their tenting neighbors and find out who they were. One of their neighbors was a fella by the name of Ralph Gustin. Ralph and his bunch hunted in the area for just a few years.

One evening after the supper was finished, his hunting partners wanted to go into town and have a few beers. Ralph declined the offer and stayed in the tent doing up the dishes. Gustin was a great practical joker, and while doing up the dishes, he thought he would leave the boys a little surprise on their return to camp that night. He got a short length of wire and walked up the trail only a short distance from the tent. Then he stretched it tight across the trail bed, about eight inches off the ground. "This ought to sober them up," he thought, as he walked back to the tent. A few minutes later, he heard a big commotion, and a lot of cursing going on just up the trail. A short while later, a game warden and a state police officer came calling on the tent, both madder than hell after taking a tumble on the forest floor. They wanted to know who put the wire across the trail, but Ralph dummied up. He said, "It's a good thing they didn't find anything out of order around the campsite, or they would have strung me up for sure!"

Ralph Holdridge was cutting a little firewood around the tent just before dark, when he heard a big BA-FOOM. He looked over at the Larkin tent in time to see a huge ball of fire shoot out of their stove pipe. Bill and Paul Larkin were in the camp, and earlier, Bill had tried to get some stubborn wood burning in the stove. He finally threw a little chain saw gas in the stove, but it didn't ignite. He didn't dare throw a match in afterwards, because of the explosive fumes, so he went next door to visit with Glade. Paul went into the tent shortly afterwards, and when he tried to start the fire, the fumes exploded. The blast singed his eyebrows off and knocked him across the tent. Aside from that, he was O.K.

One fall two men from one of the southern tier villages set up a tent not too far from Glade's. It became obvious right from the start that the men liked their alcoholic beverages more than just a little. On a Saturday morning, they came walking in from the road with their rifles and a pack full of supplies. Ralph happened to be outside the tent at that time, and said a brief hello to them. He was sure by their behavior that they had been drinking heavily on their trip up. They were planning on heading right out hunting, and one of them grabbed a quart bottle of whiskey from his pack and stuck it in his hunting parka. "It must have been his lunch," Ralph thought. They grabbed their rifles and headed down the trail in a manor that might be described as less than coordinated.

Late that afternoon, the two of them came back to the tent, stone sober, and dragging a buck. When Ralph walked over to ask them where they found and shot the buck, they said they weren't sure, but it was way back in.

The following morning, Ralph headed up the lower trail on his day's hunt. There was about five inches of snow on the ground, so he followed the skid trail of the dead buck while it was in the trail. A few hundred yards up the trail, he saw where they had dragged it down onto the trail from the east. He continued up the trail for a quarter of a mile, and then left the trail on the east side also. He had only gone 100 yards when he again saw the skid trail of the buck, only heading off in a northeast direction. "Now why in hell are they heading off in that direction?" Ralph thought. His curiosity aroused, Ralph started backtracking the skid trail to the kill site. The trail led him on a zigzag tour through the woods, that crossed itself twice! They had killed the buck only a couple of hundred yards from the upper trail, and not far from the falls on Loon Brook. The hunters must have been pretty drunk and disoriented when they dropped the buck. What should have been an easy pull to the road on a good trail, turned into a lengthy cross country pull until the men sobered up enough to find the trail and head out to the tent!

Ralph was a tough active woodsman right up into his older years. At the age of 67, on dry ground conditions, Ralph and Jim Kling took two bucks together on the same day. Jim took a spike horn and Ralph took an eight-point, which was about a half mile distant from the spike. Jim and his Uncle Dick were dragging out the spike, but Ralph decided he would wrestle with the eight-point by himself. After dragging it only a short way, he made a pack of it, and got it up on his back. He carried it all the way out to the road, passing Jim and Dick early on with their buck. The road was three miles off, and once the deer was stored, he headed back in towards the other two hunters. He met Dave York coming down the trail before too long, and Dave told him, "You must have made a big impression on those other two hunters, because now they're carrying their buck out!"

RALPH'S LAST BLUE RIDGE BUCK

Years later, Ralph was hunting fairly high on the side of Blue Ridge, and ahead of him was a fairly deep ravine. As he approached the ravine, he saw a large buck run down into the ravine and out of sight. He was in a position where he could see most of the other side of the ravine. Ralph brought his rifle up thinking, "Well, you made it in there, now let's see you make it out!" When the buck came up the other side, Ralph had time for one shot. He put the bead on the buck and click! The buck disappeared into the woods on the far side. It was the first time in his life he ever had a factory load fail him. The primer had a nice deep dent in it, so he knew it wasn't the rifle's fault. He slipped in a military round, not fully trusting the factory ammo he had left, and continued on hunting. He went up along the edge of that ravine, and then into some steep terrain just above the hardwoods. While taking a break, a movement in the hardwoods below caught his eye. It was a large eight-point buck that was feeding in his direction. The buck stopped and raised his head, looking up towards Ralph. Since he had a military round in the chamber, he put the bead on the buck's head and touched it off. The buck jumped at the shot, but then stood in one place, swaying. Thirty seconds later, he fell down stone dead. The buck was laying more than three miles in from the road, and Ralph would need some help in getting him out. Late that afternoon, at the tent when he saw Glade, he was asked, "Did you see a buck today?" "Yep, saw two." "Did you shoot one?" "Yeah, I got him alright. He's got eight points." "How much does he weigh?" "Oh, I'd guess about 150 pounds."

The next day when Ralph and Glade approached the buck to begin pulling it out, Glade walked around the buck looking him over. He said to Ralph, "You wouldn't care to up your estimate on his weight a little would you?" That buck weighed right close to 200 pounds, and it took them most of three days in getting it out. It was Ralph's last Blue Ridge buck!

THE LARKIN BOYS

Bill and Kenneth Larkin have hunted the Loon Brook area for close to 50 years now. They are the sons of William and Ruth Larkin of Brookfield, New York. For many years, they ran the family dairy farm along with their parents, and their younger brother, Allen. They were first introduced to the Loon Brook area by their uncle, Clieve Hodges. Clieve first brought the boys up in 1947, and they hunted out of Glade's tent. They started coming up every fall for a hunt after that, and in the early '50s, they invested in their own camping outfit. Ken remembers there being at least a dozen tent camps set up out near the road during the hunting season. There were lots of deer in the woods and enough hunters to move them around pretty good at times.

After the boys started using their own tent, they invited some of their cousin's to come up and try some Adirondack deer hunting. Harry Larkin came up for one hunt, and decided it just wasn't for him. Colin Larkin came up for two or three hunts, and he faded out. Paul Larkin came up, and he really enjoyed himself. He was a regular every year at the tent, and he managed to kill several fine bucks over the years. Paul killed his largest buck, a big eight-pointer, up on the side of Blue Ridge. He had made himself a huge delicious sandwich that morning before leaving the tent. From 11 o'clock on, he was thinking more about eating that sandwich than he was about his deer hunting. He'd found himself a nice broad log to sit on, and was just about to take his first bite when he saw a deer moving through the hardwoods below him. He could see right away that it had a real nice rack of antlers on it, so he got ready to shoot. His first shot hit the buck hard, but the buck moved off down the ridge. Paul gave chase, and a few hundred yards later had the big buck down for keeps. He dressed out the buck and then went back up the ridge for his sandwich. The only trouble was, he couldn't find the log he left his sandwich on! He looked over half the side of Blue Ridge for it, and he could almost taste its succulent flavor! Paul got his buck, but he went back to the tent that day hungry!

THE BOTTLE HUNTER'S BUCK

Ken Larkin is a very conservation-minded fellow, and has a good attitude for keeping a clean wilderness environment. Many campers have come and gone from our Blue Ridge area. Some of these campers leave quite a mess when they arc through with their stay. If Ken happens to find their mess, he will always make an effort to clean it up. There is nothing worse than finding somebody's garbage scattered around the woods! The leavings of the original loggers, at the lumber camp clearings is another matter, though. That's looked on as "History."

When Kenneth wandered through the third lumber camp clearing, along the foot of Blue Ridge, he noticed quite a few bottles in the old dump. Some of them were collectibles, so he planned to return on another day with an empty pack basket. A couple of days later, he was back at the clearing with his basket. He spent most of the afternoon hooking through the old dump and rooting around in any old rubble he could find. The weather had been dark and rainy all afternoon, but Ken had been so interested in what he was doing, that he took little note of it. By late afternoon, he had a pack basket full of collectibles to haul out to the road, so he started heading for the falls on Loon Brook and the trail.

When Ken made it to the falls, the water was so high, he couldn't get across. He decided to head down stream and look for a log to cross on. He was about a quarter mile below the falls, and came up on a small hog back that jutted out into an alder choked beaver meadow. Suddenly, two deer jumped up in front of him and headed for the thicker cover in high gear. Ken brought up his rifle immediately and got the cross hairs onto the closest deer. At that close range, about all Ken could see in his scope was deer hair, so he pulled the trigger. The deer quickly disappeared. Ken didn't notice any horns, but he had a party permit in his pocket, so he was legal no matter what. When he checked the tracks, he found a heavy blood trail heading for Loon Brook. A short while later, Ken was looking down at a beautiful 10-point buck. He hadn't the faintest idea that he had shot at a buck. It was a good day! He'd filled his buck tag, and his pack basket full of old bottles. He had the buck's head mounted, and it now hangs in his summer home in Blue Mountain Lake.

THE MERRY WIDOW DOE OF BEAR BROOK

It was mid-November, and Bill Larkin was hunting along the north side of Bear Brook by one of the big beaver meadows. The beaver meadow hadn't been active in several years, so you could walk right across it in several places. Bill decided to cross over to the foot of the ridge. He had just entered the meadow to cross when he heard the deep guttural grunts of a buck. He looked down the length of the meadow and saw a doe running across with a nice buck right on her heels. The deer were well over a hundred yards away, but Bill swung onto the buck and fired. The buck went down with the first shot, but Bill could see it trying to get back up. He shot four more times at it, emptying his rifle, and missed all four shots.

Bill didn't know it, but Dick Brown and Nick Delorio had all but witnessed the shooting. Dick was in a position to see the downed deer, so he hollered over to Bill, "Why don't you walk over and finish off the buck?" Bill walked over and met Dick and Nick by the buck that was just about dead by then. The first shot had broken its back, putting it down. The buck was obviously courting a hot doe. Unknown to Bill, Nick had shot a spike horned buck about 45 minutes earlier before Bill got his shooting in. He dropped the spike just inside the hardwoods on the north side of the same meadow. The spike horn must have been looking for an opening to get close to that doe, but the big buck held him at a distance. Bill's buck later weighed in at 188 pounds and had eight points.

When Dick and Nick were returning to Nick's spike horn, they almost tripped over my dead nine-point buck. I had shot the buck first thing that morning as he chased the hot doe around the same beaver meadow! After dressing off the buck, I left to go check my fisher traps. I would return later that day to begin dragging it out. They saw my tag on it and guessed what I was doing. Dick got the idea to switch bucks. Leave me the spike and take the nine pointer, just for laughs! They would have done it too, but Nick had to be back in Syracuse that evening, so they dragged out the spike. When I got back from checking traps in the afternoon, it seemed like there were tracks, blood, and skid trails all over the meadow. I couldn't wait to hear all of what happened that day, so I hiked out and helped with the last of the dragging. The only one that didn't get a buck that day was Dick Brown. If he had only tracked that hot doe around for an hour or two after Bill shot his buck, I'm sure that the "Merry Widow Doe" of Bear Brook would have taken care of him too!

A DAY TO REMEMBER

In the fall of 1955, four men were hunting out of Glade's tent at Loon Brook. They included Glade, Ralph Holdridge, Dick Brown, and Dick's 20-year-old nephew, Jim Kling. It was evening, and a strong cold front was pushing into the mountains from the northwest, moving out several days of warm weather that had permeated the region. That night, there were heavy rains accompanied by wind and thunder. This was a much wanted change for the hunters, because experience had taught them that after a dark and stormy night, every deer in the woods would be up and feeding late the next morning. After three days of fruitless hunting, this major change in the weather might be just what they needed.

They were all up and out early. The violent weather had passed, and now they had cooler weather, with slate gray clouds and only a trace of lingering rain. The first one out of the tent that morning was Dick Brown. Dick was a dairy farmer from North Brookfield, who also did a little contract logging on the side. He first began hunting out of Glade's tent back in 1932, when he was 17 years old. On that first trip up, he had taken a 187 pound eight-point buck in on Blue Ridge. He had spotted the buck while it was bedded up in the hardwoods, quite a distance below his position on the ridge. Dick laid across a convenient rock and then made the long downhill shot, killing the buck in its bed. This first successful hunt laid the base work for a long, enjoyable tradition in hunting the Blue Ridge area. On this particular morning, he decided to hunt in the area where he took that first buck, which was a three mile walk from the tent.

About 10 o'clock that morning, Dick was in that area of the ridge, when he jumped several doe, and one incredibly big buck. He got off two shots at the buck, but missed him with both shots. There was no snow, but the leaves were still soaked and showed tracks real good. Dick began to track the buck and, about 45 minutes later, he ran into Glade. He told him of his encounter with the big buck and then continued tracking. An hour later, he jumped out the monster again, and missed him with three additional shots. Dick kept right on the track, and refused to get discouraged. About two o'clock in the afternoon, Dick put the buck out again and this time he connected, putting the big boy down for keeps. When Dick walked over, he could hardly believe his eyes. The buck was not only big in body but sported a large dark rack, with long, wide-spaced, heavy beams, and 10 long, perfectly matched points. Dick sat down and lit up a cigarette to savor the moment and further look over his trophy. Later, while dressing out the deer, he spotted Glade coming his way. They visited a while, and then made an attempt to pull the buck out a ways, but God, he dragged mighty tough. There were some loggers working near Marion River, so Dick suggested that he might try to rent one of their horses to help get his buck out.

That evening at the tent, Dick dominated the conversation, going over every detail of the hunt, and retelling various parts. He was obviously one very happy hunter! Along about 8 o'clock, when the conversation started slowing down, someone asked Ralph how he made out during the day. Ralph said he shot a six-pointer up along Loon Brook. However, they soon found out he was no run of the mill six-pointer. This buck weighed 190 pounds and had long, heavy beams that spread over 20 inches on the inside. The rack had no brow tines, but had two unusually long tines on each side, plus the main beam points. Ralph said he was crossing a beaver meadow when the buck got up from the spruces on the far side, and started up the bank. He never made the top. With two big, heavy racked bucks taken on the same day, the conversation started right in again.

Dick rented a horse from the loggers the next morning, and he and Glade went in after the buck. Getting the horse in to the location of the deer was no problem, but getting the buck up onto the horse's back was! The horse wasn't exactly fond of having a large dead buck on its back either, but after a while, he accepted it. Tying the buck on so the antlers wouldn't jab the horse was another problem, and eventually, that was solved also. On the trip out, the antlers on that buck raked many of the smooth-barked beech trees. For years afterwards, you could see these scars, left by Dick Brown's buck. Once out to the road, the buck rode home on top of Dick's Nash Rambler. He showed it off to family and friends, and brought it up to the hotel where I took a good look at it. It was a very impressive buck, and it was weighed accurately at 212 pounds.

Dick later brought the head and cape over to George Lesser, in Johnstown, to be mounted. However, Dick was a family man, and when the head was done, he didn't have the money to pick it up. George hung onto the head for a while, and finally sold the mount to a hotel for expenses. The hotel was somewhere in the Mohawk Valley, near Herkimer or Little Falls. We later heard that the hotel burned down, presumably with Dick's deer head inside. In later years, how we wished we could have seen that head one more time, and maybe measured it up to see what it would score! Dick had set a full-sized bushel basket right down between the bowl of those antlers, and had often bragged about that fact.

Jim Kling (Dick's nephew) and I were close friends, and constant woodchuck hunting companions. Jim's mother and father, Charles and Frances Kling, owned and operated Kling's Mills, the local feed mill and hardware store in North Brookfield. Jim was five years older than me, and was into all kinds of shooting sports, as well as gun-smithing. Our interests were similar, and we got along great. He was also a good role model for me. His mother would often make the mistake of feeding me, and at times, it seemed like I was at their house more than I was at my own!

The east side of the "Notch" on Blue Ridge where Ralph spent a lot of his time tracking bucks. Photo by Don Adams from 40 ft. up in a white pine tree.

Ralph Holdridge after his "Blue Ridge" days were over and a couple of his many racks. The one on his left was from the one toothed buck. Photo by Bob Elinskas.

*The big beaver meadow on upper Bear Brook looking east. Home of the
"Merry Widow Doe," Photo by Bob Elinskas.*

*Looking northeast from the higher elevations on the west end of Blue Ridge.
Blue Mountain Lake is visible in the distance. Photo by Don Adams
from 35 ft. up a sizeable spruce tree.*

THE "BEAR CAMP"

Jim had taken some small southern tier bucks, but that first season of hunting out of Glade's tent had made a big impression on him. He told me of how Ralph and Dick had taken their bucks, and some of the country that he traversed in looking for his in the "Big Woods." He didn't take a deer up there that first year, but it didn't dampen his enthusiasm any for going back up. While hunting up there that first season, he had stumbled onto the remains of an abandoned hunting camp. It was along the foot of Blue Ridge, and near the head waters of Bear Brook. Jim thought it might still be salvage-able, so we made plans for a trip into the site to see if it couldn't be fixed up into a usable camp. I had only camped in the Adirondacks once before this point in my life, and that was for a few days at Little Brown Pond, which is just west of Raquette Lake. In February of 1956, I turned 16, and shortly afterwards, I had my driver's license and my own car.

In early summer, I took off on a short camping trip into the Adirondacks with a good friend, Don Wyman. Don enjoyed his hunting, fishing, and trapping also, so the mountains were a natural magnet to a couple of kids like us. We camped at Little Brown Pond again and then went farther north to the Rainbow Lake and Osgood Pond area.

While we were at Little Brown, I had a flat tire (one of many on that trip) on my Chevy, so we brought it into Bing's Garage in Raquette Lake to be fixed. While we were at the garage, I noticed a beautiful set of eight-point deer antlers mounted on a plaque and hanging on the wall. When I asked Bing who got the buck, he said, "My wife did!"

Cleo got the deer the year before, in 1955, while hunting off the Sagamore Lodge Road with her husband. She was watching an area of hardwoods that bordered a small swamp. Bing was going to hunt a lot farther in from the road and then return to the road which bordered the swamp. Cleo had been sitting on her watch patiently and figured it was getting close to the time when Bing would be showing up. She glanced down at the swamp again and spotted a big buck coming out of it and heading her way! She let the buck move closer until he stopped, offering her a clear shot. She knocked it down with her first shot and then hurried over to it and shot the buck again, since it still showed signs of life. Bing was already on the road when she shot, so he came right back into the woods to her. They were both as happy as can be at getting him, especially as close to the road as he was. Cleo was a very proud hunter, and Bing hung the buck from the tow truck boom for a while back at the garage, just to show it off.

After the tire was fixed, Don and I stopped at the Raquette Lake Supply Company to browse around and get a few items. There was a mounted whitetail in the window of that store that caught my eye. It was mounted in a sneak style, and the 12-

point rack was beautifully formed, and to me, had a lot of character. The deer had been taken by Dennis Dillon, Jr., while he was hunting up in the Lost Brook region, just east of Sagamore Lodge. "God," I thought, "They take some nice heads up here!"

Late in July of that same year, Jim and I made the trip up to the trail head at Loon Brook and hiked in. We followed the lower trail in, almost to Grassy Swamp, where the trail petered out. We then bushwacked over to Bear Brook, and then hunted up the abandoned campsite. The tent and equipment were in a mess, so we carefully separated them from all the leaves and clutter, and took inventory. We had a heavily rusted sheet metal stove that might work again with some repairs, china, cups, and silverware for six, a well-rusted cast iron skillet, and several pots and pans, all with bear bites in them. There were also two water pails, and a Coleman lamp and stove. The lamp and stove might work with a little clean-up. The 10' by 12' wall tent was chewed and torn in several places, and the canvas walls had been laying on the ground for over two years, so they were moldy and starting to rot in places. The roof, front and back walls, however, had been hanging from the ridge pole, and so they were off the ground. Even though they were torn in places, the material was still sound. After looking it all over very carefully, we decided that with one hell of a lot of sewing, the tent might stand again. With a heavy duty fly over the top of our tent, it might even be serviceable. We decided to give it a try and were all worked up at the prospect!

Jim had heard that a fellow by the name of Lanphear, from Raquette Lake, had owned the camp, so on the way out we decided to try and look him up. Jim was thinking it might be a good idea to offer him something for the remains of the camp, so we wouldn't get any unexpected surprises later when we were using it. At Raquette Lake village, we were steered over to Orrin Lanphear's home on Poplar Point. We told Orrin of the camp we had found and our intentions for it. He knew of the camp right off, and told us that it belonged to Herb Birrell, a wealthy lawyer. Two of his sons had packed it in there for his use, and he seriously doubted that he would ever return for any of the property. When we left Orrin's home that day, we had the secure feeling that the old camp on Bear Brook was now ours!

We pooled our money for the necessary supplies in fixing up the old camp, and made three or four work trips into it before the season opened that fall. The bears had really left their mark on that camp, and since it was located on Bear Brook, we dubbed our tent, "The Bear Camp." It was a great feeling to see that tent standing again, especially with most of the holes closed, and a good fly over it. The original stove and pipe was straightened out, and set up again. We had a supply of half decent firewood cut, and a number of large wooden blocks cut that would be used for seats, table space and cooking platforms. The back of the tent was scraped and covered with plastic for our air mattresses and sleeping bags.

It took us an hour and 15 minutes to hike into it from the road if we moved right along. At first, we used pack baskets to haul our gear, but then we discovered how much easier it was to use a pack board, so the pack basket went the way of the guide boat!

THE ADVENTURES BEGIN

This was a strange new land for me to learn, and although I knew my way into the tent site over the trail, I had never been into the woodlands beyond the tent site. These were unbroken woodlands, and the only landmarks I would see were natural. Jim coached me on using my compass, and explained to me the basic lay of the land. I also had a topographical map of the area and studied it daily. The big landmarks would be the broad north slope of Blue Ridge, and the two brooks that flowed along its base, Bear and Loon Brooks. If I really got messed up big time, I would head cross country out to the road, some two miles distant. My first lone hunts from the tent were relatively short, but as the woods began to open up, and snow cover lay on the ground, I gained confidence and more knowledge with every hike. By the end of the season, I had been all over the surrounding hills, and up to three miles away from camp during day hunts. That first year, I was having more fun in just seeing and learning the country than I was in trying to hunt it. Jim used to kid me about finding my yard long tracks in the snow, heading off one way or another. "You'll never get your eye on a buck hunting that fast," he would warn me.

My very first hunt out of the tent was with Jim. We were to hunt up the slope of the ridge from the tent, keeping a couple of hundred yards between us, and then meet up every so often. As I slowly started hunting my way up the slope in the early morning hour, it was a great feeling to finally be hunting the "Big Woods!" The forest in this area was mostly mixed hardwoods with runs of thick spruce cover every so often, and an occasional windfall to walk around. After about 30 minutes of hunting, I approached a small hardwood flat. A slight movement ahead caught my eye, and I saw the huge gray body of a deer come to a stop, with the head and neck of the animal hidden behind the trunk of a large maple tree. I had a heavy barreled 38-55 lever action rifle that held 11 shots, so I brought up the rifle and got ready to take a shot, should it be a buck. That deer must have stood still for all of five minutes, and by that time, my rifle was wavering all over the place. I was praying for a buck, but it was a doe. It must have winded Jim, because it moved out at a good clip from behind that tree. We hunted up into the higher elevations and saw one deer that Jim thought for sure was a buck, but we couldn't see it well enough to shoot. After this hunt, we both went our own ways, hunting one on one with the deer. We both preferred this method of hunting.

On the third weekend of hunting, Jim killed an eight-point buck up on the side of the ridge and west of camp. The buck weighed about 150 pounds, and the woods were pretty dry at the time. He got the buck almost back to camp that same day, and the next day I began my education on getting out back-country deer. I hunted the morning hours, and then returned to camp for lunch and the pullout to the road. Thankfully, he wasn't a real heavy buck, but it was still a tough, three plus mile pull, and it took us a good three hours to get him out near Glade's tent. When we arrived, we were sweating pretty hard, and there were four tents pitched in the area. With conditions being dry, everyone must have headed for home early, since no one was around. The biggest tent was owned by Tony Dipino. It was an army tent, with a big stove in it, and fixed up comfortably for a good-sized crew. Jim took me over and showed me the tent. I was a little leery about entering a stranger's tent, but Jim said, "Don't worry, Tony's a pretty good Dago!" In the middle of his table, there was a gallon jug with about three inches of Dago Red left in it. Jim said, "Tony always leaves some, in case someone stops in." We both had a big glass full, which wiped out the jug, and nothing ever tasted so good! A weekend or two later, I got to meet Tony and thanked him personally for that cold glass of wine. While dragging deer out on later hunts, we never could get past Tony's tent without a glass of that good Dago Red, and it was always there for us!

Life at the Bear Camp was pretty crude. Most of the time we washed our own plate and cups with the hot coffee left in the pot, and only used soap and water at the end of our weekend hunt. We sat on blocks of wood, and the mice would regularly chew holes in our air mattresses. One night, I awoke to find a mouse inside my sleeping bag. He went all the way down to my feet, and then slowly worked his way back out. Another evening, I heard the tin cover slide off a pot we had set out near our wood pile. I opened the tent door, and in my flashlight beam, I could see our ham bone heading up the trail in the mouth of a large raccoon. About an hour after lights out on another evening, we were awakened by a large beaver. He was chewing down the main tree that held up the south side of our tent! One weekend during a prolonged, and heavy downpour, the creek flowing down the side of the ridge on the south side of our tent overflowed, sending a large stream of water right through the middle of our tent.

Whenever we packed into the tent for a hunt, we would always try to share the weight of groceries, or a guest's heavy pack on his first trip in. On one such trip, Jim Kling, his Uncle Dick Brown, and Dave York, were getting ready for the trip in while out at the trail head. When Jim lifted the packs from the trunk, he noticed that Dick's pack, although full, was noticeably lighter than his or Dave's. While Dick was busy grabbing some extra cigarettes from his glove compartment, Jim slipped a good big rock into the bottom of his pack. Dick packed it all the way in and didn't find it until that evening. Dick bellowed, "How in hell did this God damned rock get into my pack basket?" He eyed his two hunting partners suspiciously! "I knew damn well that pack was heavier'n it shoulda been!" Jim and Dave just grinned sheepishly, but claimed innocence.

THE CAMP EXPERT

Dick was a Bear Camp regular, and since he had been hunting in the region since 1932, he unofficially proclaimed himself the camp patriarch, and expert on everything, including deer savvy! If one of us should comment on a nice buck track we had seen over near Noisy Brook that day, Dick would cut right in and tell us half of that buck's history, just like he knew him on a personal level. It didn't seem to matter much just where or what track you may have seen, Dick was sure to know something about it. Jim was beginning to get his bucks regularly, and had even filled Dick's tag lately. Jim was usually quick to challenge some of Dick's "knowledge" and deliberately get him all riled up, much to the delight of us onlookers. We would still have to give Dick some credit, though, because he had been tracking deer in the area for quite a long time, and knew most of the travel runs of the local bucks. Jim thought Dick spent too much time looking at the track, and not enough time looking for the deer while tracking.

THE MONSTER BUCK

One weekend in late November, Jim, Dick, Dave York and another fella were hunting out of the Bear Camp. At dark, all the hunters were back in camp, and Dick was describing his encounter with a huge buck that he had missed that afternoon. The buck was using a run that was only three creeks east of the tent. Evidently, Dick had gotten a good look at the buck, because he said at least three times during the course of the evening, "You could set a bushel basket right down between the main beams of his rack!" By the time the lamp went out that evening, everyone in the tent was convinced that the monster buck of Blue Ridge was hanging around the lower elevations, and only three creeks east of the tent!

Over breakfast the next morning, Dick was full of plans on how he was going to lay that buck low. Jim hunted way off to the east that day, but by mid-afternoon, he had come a long way back, and found himself in the area of the third creek east of the tent. As luck would have it, he spotted a nice buck moving along the far side of the brook, and dropped it with a single shot. It turned out to be an average-sized buck of about 150 pounds with an eight-point rack, and a spread of about 16 inches. He dressed out the buck, and then dragged it back to camp where he met Dave and Dave's guest. They all looked over the buck, and then put the coffee pot on. A short while later, Dick came into the camp, and as soon as he saw the buck, he said, "That's him! That's the buck I missed yesterday, no doubt about it!" Jim immediately replied, "Well, Uncle Dick, if that's the buck, you're going to have one hell of a job getting a bushel basket down between his antlers!" Everyone started to laugh, and Dick knew that he'd been caught, but even he had to laugh at that one!

YOGI BEAR

Dick loved his hunting and especially his time spent at the Bear Camp. He was a good woodsman, and knew quite a bit about camping and cooking. The bears would occasionally visit our camp while we were gone between the weekends, and on one trip in, we found our coffee pot ruined. Dick showed us how to boil the coffee grounds in a plain pot for a few minutes, then remove it from the stove and add a splash of cold water to settle the grounds. It was good coffee!

On another weekend, we had filled a party permit with a doe and had it hanging in front of the tent on Sunday afternoon. We were all coming in the following weekend for a long hunt, so we were leaving it there for camp meat. We all thought it would be nice to fry up some of the meat for sandwiches before we left, so Dick cut out the tenderloins and a section of a hind quarter. I got our big cast iron skillet, and then discovered that there was no butter, grease, or cooking oil in camp. Dick said, "I'll show you how to cook without grease," and he grabbed the skillet. He put it over a good hot fire, and when the pan was good and hot, he poured in plenty of table salt. Then he used some paper towels to insulate his hand, and rubbed the salt all over the bottom of the skillet until a shiny glaze formed. Then, he dumped out the salt and put in the meat, and the steaks didn't stick enough to talk about!

Those hot venison sandwiches were all the meat we ever got off that doe, because when we returned the following weekend, we learned that a bear had eaten the rest of it right in front of our tent. We named this bear, "Yogi Bear," and he left bear turds loaded with deer hair all up and down our tent creek that fall.

BEAR BAIT

The following year, Jim killed a spike horned buck early in the season, and only about a half a mile above our tent. Due to the late hour in the day, Jim just dressed out the buck, and left him until morning. The next day when Jim returned for the buck, he discovered that it had been moved by a bear and partially eaten. When I got back to the tent that afternoon, Jim told me the story of how "Yogi" was up to no good again this year. However, Jim had a plan. He would return to the deer carcass just before dark, and sit quietly down wind, hoping the bear would return to feed. Then he showed me his new three cell flashlight, and patted his Model 71 Winchester, in .348 caliber, "This will take care of old Yogi Bear!"

Jim returned to the carcass an hour before dark and found himself a comfortable seat down wind. Then he watched the woods grow slowly darker around him. The temperature was in the mid '40s, and the woods were dry, so he was sure he could hear anything coming. His eyes adjusted to the dark, and he could vaguely make out most forms. About 7:30, and without any warning at all, he suddenly heard the popping and snapping of bones coming from the direction of the carcass. Jim couldn't believe that he didn't hear the bear moving through the dry leaves and sticks as it approached the kill. Nevertheless, the moment of truth was at hand.

The carcass was 40 yards off, so Jim quietly got his rifle ready and turned on the three cell light. The light flashed on, and then immediately went out. Jim thought that the light bulb must have burnt out. He tapped and shook the light, but he couldn't get it to work. Meanwhile, the bear had heard Jim's disturbance, and proceeded to circle around and above Jim, in order to catch his scent stream. When the bear caught scent of Jim, he let out an awful loud snort, and went crashing away, back up towards the top of Blue Ridge. Again, there was deer hair in many of the bear turds that fall!

NEVER GO OUT
HALF LOADED

In late October of 1958, Jim, Parks, and myself, were spending a long weekend hunting out of the Bear Camp. On Sunday morning, we realized we were running out of bread and milk, so I volunteered to hike out and get the needed supplies after the morning hunt. On returning to the tent from town, I saw that I still had an hour or so to go out and hunt. I was still using my lever action 38-55 that held 11 shots fully loaded. I wasn't going very far, or for very long, so I just slipped seven cartridges into the rifle, and headed up the slope of the ridge and slightly west.

I got up on the first big terraced flat, where deer sign was fairly plentiful, and just went slow, doing a lot of looking. There was about two inches of snow on the ground, so visibility was good. It wasn't long until the sun started to touch the horizon, and my surroundings began to grow dim. I turned around and started heading back over my tracks towards camp. I didn't go far when I stopped for one last look around. That's when I heard some crunching and sticks popping up the hill near a large rock face ledge. A fat black bear was bouncing down over the ledges and was almost down. He was about 60 yards off, when he stopped briefly, giving me a clear shot at him. I put the bead of my rifle sight right behind his front shoulder and pressed the trigger. The sights looked good when the rifle went off, but the bear just started running in the same general direction that he was in coming off the rock ledges. He had a unique way of running that I would never forget. He would bound up forward, and then kind of rock forward laying all four feet down smoothly, one after the other in a straight line; bound up and rock forward, bound up and rock forward. The action resembled a rocking horse, bounding through the woods, if you can imagine such a thing. Meanwhile, I was blasting away with my 38-55 and all the shooting was starting to confuse the bear. He never stopped running, but just before he was about to go out of sight, he made a half circle to his right and decided to go back up where he had come from. His line of travel was lower, though, and it put him on a course heading right towards me. I let him come closer without shooting, and before I knew it, he was about to land right in front of me. I had the rifle bead right under his chin, and was hoping he wouldn't bowl me down! Then I pressed the trigger and heard the pin fall on an empty cartridge chamber! Damn! I held still and watched the bear's eyes staring past me as he ran under my right elbow. As soon as he went by, I dug out another shell to slip into the rifle, but he was almost out of sight when I got the shot off.

God, I couldn't believe what had just happened! I walked over to where I had first shot at the bear and found a small patch of cut black hair. I followed him down and around his circle, and then back towards me. He started bleeding just before he got to me. I looked at my tracks where I had shot from and the line of bear tracks passing within 18 inches of those tracks. "Man, that was close," I thought. I followed the tracks up the ridge and saw that he was bleeding steady, but not hard. When he got into the thick stuff, I realized how dark it was getting, so I headed back down to the tent. Jim and Parks were more than a little interested as to the what and why of all the shooting they had heard. After the story was told and then retold three or four times, Parks was wondering why I didn't hit him over the head with my gun barrel when he went by. Jim was toying with the idea of going up and tracking him down with a Coleman lamp. They both were a little skeptical about the bear passing within 18 inches of me, though.

The next morning, we all hiked up to the scene and the tracks in the snow told the story. They could see a little packed area where I stood firing at the bear, and eight empty shell casings laying in the snow close by. I stepped onto the packed area where I had shot from and picked up one of the empty casings. Without fully extending my arm, I reached out and dropped a casing straight down into one of the passing bear tracks. Jim said, "Well, I'll be darned." Parks shouted, "Why in hell didn't you hit him over the head with your gun barrel?"

We took the bear's track up the ridge and into the thick black spruce tangles. He appeared to be bleeding out of his right front side, so my bullet didn't go all the way through. We saw where he crawled under a big spruce root for awhile and, after that, the bleeding all but stopped. A half mile later and his tracks were mixing in with another bear's and our snow cover was rapidly melting off. We lost all sign of him shortly afterwards, and I wished him good luck! I'd hate to see any animal suffer a painful, lingering death due to my hand. Ever since then, I have always loaded my magazine to capacity!

DAD GETS LOST

My father, Joe Elinskas, had hunted the Rainbow Lake area, which is just north of Saranac Lake, since the mid '40s. When he saw the number of bucks that we were taking out of the Bear Camp, he wanted to come in and give it a try also. Dad was involved in a serious motorcycle accident when he was a very young man, and he almost lost his right foot because of it. After the foot had healed, he was limited in the amount of walking he could do without the foot swelling and becoming painful. He made the trip into the tent O.K., and the next morning, I put him on a good run that was only a 15-minute hike from the tent and just above the trail. Before I left him, he assured me that he could find the trail and make it back to camp with no problems.

That afternoon, I returned to camp about 45 minutes before dark, and within 15 minutes, everyone but Dad had returned to camp. I hiked up the trail to meet up with him, but couldn't make contact. I got back to the camp just at dark, and he still hadn't come in. We remembered hearing some shooting off in the direction of Slim Pond just before dark, but it wasn't unusual to hear shooting from off that way, since there are other camps in that direction. Dick suggested that we let everything settle down and get some supper, then we'll shoot off a shot and see if we get an answer.

After supper we fired the shot, and way off towards Slim Pond we got an answer. We got a compass out and shot another signal shot, so we could get a good bearing on the answer, but there was no return shot. We got some food together and a half pint of brandy, our flashlights and the Coleman lamp, and headed for the hardwood hill immediately north of our tent. The return shot had come from the west, so we decided to head west in the hardwoods on the north hill, since the traveling would be easier there. A couple of more signal shots were fired up in the hardwoods, but didn't get any answering shots. We traveled as far west as we could before getting into the thick spruce swamps off the western end of that hill.

We were about a mile from the tent and would try one more shot. I plugged my ears for the shot, and afterward, I thought I could hear someone holler way off to the west. Dick shot again, and then Jim could hear it, too. We got a compass bearing on it and headed off through the thick spruce trees. The great windfall of 1950 happened 11 years back, and so there was a lot of new growth and rotted tangles. God, was it ever thick! After a good while of this, Dick fired again, and from the direction of the answer, he guessed Dad was right along Bear Brook. We slowly made our way over to the brook, and then in the alders and meadow grass, we made much better time. We were very fortunate that the beaver meadows weren't active!

Once we headed down the brook, it only took 20 minutes to get to him. He had a fire going and was comfortable enough, but he was very hungry and tired. For a man with a bum foot, he had come quite a distance. We gave him a big sandwich and some cookies. Then, we all took a pull on the brandy bottle. Dad had gotten bored while watching the deer run, so he tried a little still hunting off to the west. When he came down the hill to look for the trail, the trail was east of his location. He kept on looking for it in a southwest direction, until he hit bear Brook. For some reason, he kept thinking that the tent must be down stream. He also thought that firing his rifle during the day might bring some kind of response. When we fired our signal shot after supper, he knew it had to be us, so he fired his last cartridge in return. Those are big woods, so if you want anyone to find you, you'd better have enough shells left after dark so they can figure out your position. Firing during the day is fruitless. Dad would holler as loud as he could after each one of our signal shots. He was very lucky the air was still that night otherwise we would have never heard him. Dad planned on following Bear Brook all the way out to the road the next day, which would have been another big mistake. Bear Brook Swamp is big, and at that time was in one hell of a mess! None of us thought he could have made it all the way out in another day, especially with no food and a bad foot.

It was going to be a tough return trip to camp in the dark, with the Coleman lamp getting low on fuel and our flashlights dim. We decided to stay right there for the night, so I gathered in a large supply of firewood, and the boys cut some armfuls of spruce boughs to sit on. We all kind of hunkered down by the fire and dozed off and on all night. It started to sprinkle a couple of times, but never to the point where we were getting wet.

That night as I sat by the fire, I thought about what I would want with me if I was ever caught by myself in a similar situation. The ability to stay warm and dry would be paramount, so I would have a small, tough, plastic fly with tie off strings, and matches or lighter; something hot to drink, so a metal cup with tea bags, powdered coffee, and bouillon cubes; also, something to eat, like oatmeal, brown sugar, and powdered milk, plus aspirin and a flashlight. I would also spend the night in the spruce trees, so I would have protection from the wind, spruce boughs to sit or lay on, and plenty of dead sticks handy to feed my fire with. I don't like heavy packs, but I've carried these items with me whenever I hunt out of camp alone, and so far, I've never had to use them. We made the slow, difficult trip back to camp at first light, and slept through most of the day. After that, Dad had a new respect for the Big Woods!

NO SALE

In 1957, I killed my first Blue Ridge buck. It was only a modest sized six-pointer, but I had taken him one-on-one and had done everything right, so I was happy with him. I didn't bother the other fellas in camp for help so they could hunt, and I pulled him out to the road by myself on the day after. It was just noon when I got out to my car, so I loaded the buck onto the trunk and went looking for some lunch over towards Indian Lake. The Forest House was about halfway between Blue Mountain and Indian Lake and appeared open, so I pulled into the parking lot and left the car where I could keep an eye on it from the window.

The Forest House was built in 1881 by Samuel Davis, and was used regularly as a stage coach stop. It burned down in 1934 but was rebuilt by the current owner, George Menzies. Shirley Chamberlain, of Indian Lake, bought it in 1949, and that's who I met when I walked in. There were only two other men at the bar when I was there, and they were talking deer hunting with Shirley. I ordered up a nice hot lunch, and while I was eating it, one of the hunters noticed the buck on the back of my car. The fella was from downstate, and he quizzed me a little on how I got my buck. I finished eating shortly, paid my bill, and went out to my car. The fella I talked with followed me out and looked over my buck. Then, he offered me fifty dollars cash for it, and for a 17 year old kid back in the '50s, that was a lot of money. I was briefly tempted, but it was my first ridge buck, and my tag was already on it. I politely refused.

In the late 1950s, Buck Lure began to make a name for itself in hunting circles. Pete Rickard, from the Cobleskill area, was making and marketing it. Word was getting around that, at times, the stuff actually worked! Since it was a new product for hunters, we really didn't know how to use it most effectively. All of us at the camp were still hunters and trackers. If we watched any kind of a run, it usually wasn't for very long. The method we employed was to pin a small rag to your hunting cap, and then periodically soak it with the lure. If it didn't call a buck in, we hoped it might hold an alerted buck's attention long enough so we could get a shot off at him. I'd had some good luck with it in the southern tier, so now we were all giving it a try in the northern zone. Almost everyone in camp had at least one buck lure soaked, foul smelling cap to hunt in, and if that wasn't bad enough, we started pinning soaked rags on our jackets and boot strings also! For all the money we were spending on lure, there were very few times that we could actually say it worked.

THE BUCK LURE, "BUCK"

One such hunt was when my brother-in-law, Dave York, came up to hunt with one of his friends. Dave had been close friends with Jim when they were growing up in North Brookfield. Dave had recently completed a tour in the Army as a Signal Corps photographer. After he was discharged, he dated my sister, "Cookie," and they eventually married. Dave was into southern deer hunting and was a little reluctant to start hunting the big woods out of the Bear Camp at first, but once he started coming up, he became one of the most regular of the Bear Camp hunters. Like all of us, he developed a deep love for the Adirondack wilderness and for hunting its wild deer. Dave was driving up with Delmar Pierson early one morning in November. The two men were going up for a quick two-day hunt. Dawn was breaking when they drove through the lowland stretch of Route 28, just before the Marion River Cabins. A deer was crossing the road ahead, and both men could see that it was a buck with a nice rack of antlers. The deer bolted off into the woods, and Dave was thinking, "This is great! Those bucks are on the move this weekend!"

A few minutes later, the car was parked at the trail head, and after seeing that buck, both men were psyched up for the hunt. They shouldered their packs, and an hour and 15 minutes later, they were crossing Bear Brook, only a few yards away from Camp. With the camp almost in sight, Delmar slipped off the crossing log and went into the icy water right up over his knees. They hurried over to the tent and got a fire started.

Dave left him to dry off and headed straight up the ridge for maybe a half a mile. Then he headed west, hunting one of the bigger terraced flats up on the side of the ridge. There was about four inches of snow on the ground which revealed some pretty active deer sign. About 10 minutes into his hunt on the flat, he spotted a big, lone deer in the distance. He was sure he saw horns on it, but he kept losing sight of it as it was moving north and down the slope of the ridge, and angling over towards Dave every once in a while. The light breeze was also out of the south and moving down the slope of the ridge. Dave lost sight of the deer altogether, so he hunted towards where he had last spotted it. Before he got halfway there, he heard something on his right side, turned and saw the buck coming with his nose in the air and then jump over a windfall heading for Dave who was only a few yards away. Dave dropped the buck as soon as he hit the ground on his side of the windfall!

Dave had soaked his hat with buck lure only a few minutes before, and from all appearances, that was what the buck was tracking down with his nose when Dave dropped him. Dave backtracked the buck and learned that it was the same deer that he had spotted earlier, and on hitting Dave's scent stream, the buck came right up to him. The buck was a nice eight-pointer, so Dave dressed him out and had him back to camp before Delmar even had a chance to completely dry off. Delmar never heard Dave's shot and couldn't believe his eyes when the buck came sliding up to the tent door! Probably the fact that Dave had recently showered and had a clean change of clothing had more to do with attracting that buck while wearing lure. After a night or two in a sometimes smoky tent, no amount of lure would attract a buck!

JAY MANCHESTER & CHARLES DALEY

One weekend there were five of us hunting out of the Bear Camp. We had all left the tent early to begin our day's hunt, but the weather was cloudy, gloomy, and rainy all day. By late afternoon, all five of us were back at the tent, drying off, and enjoying some hot coffee. While visiting, we were surprised to hear voices, coming from outside the tent, especially since it was so late in the day. Dick Brown and one of the others got up and went outside to see who it was. The rest of us remained inside. When Dick returned to the tent a few minutes later, he said it was just a couple of hunters trying to find their way back out to the road. By the tone in his voice and his conversation, it didn't appear that he gave the fellas much help. Dick was always a little protective when it came to seeing other people in "his" hunting area. He said something like, "They found their way in, now they can find their way out!" Not much more was said, but we were all a little shocked at Dick's attitude.

The two men turned out to be Jay Manchester and Charles Daley. Jay was the Agriculture teacher at Waterville Central School in Waterville, New York. Charlie was also a Waterville resident and worked for the local G.L.F. Both men were well liked and respected in the community. The boys had set up a tent camp along the upper Loon Brook trail, about a half mile in from Route 28. On this particular day, they had hiked in to the foot of Blue Ridge and then hunted way off to the west end. They had heard stories of another trail that came into the west end of Blue Ridge from Route 28 and had it in mind, should they find this trail, to hike back out to the road on it. The trail was never found, and a rainy, heavy cloud cover would darken the forest early that afternoon. The two men were soaking wet while retracing their earlier route. That's when they heard voices and then spotted our tent fly. It took quite a while to find the trail with Dick's meager instructions, but it was eventually found, and they reached their tent just after full dark.

The following summer, Jay walked into Lemery's Barber Shop in Deansboro and took a seat to await his turn in the chair. There were several other people in the shop at that time, and one of them happened to be Dick Brown. Dick was carrying on a lively conversation about his deer camp. Then, he started describing how it was right in the middle of the Adirondacks and way back in from the road, where nobody would ever find it. That's when Jay entered the conversation, "Oh, I know where it is!" Dick didn't recognize Jay at all and was a little surprised by this cut in, but returned with, "The heck you do! "Do to!" "Do not!" "Well, I sure do! Charlie Daley and I were in there last fall, soaking wet and close to dark, when we stopped in and asked you where the trail was that led out to the road! You knew we were pressed for time, just gave a vague wave of your hand, and told us to look for the scuffed up leaves! Wouldn't even take a minute and show us where to get started!" Dick's jaw dropped about an inch, and then he didn't say much after that. The conversation was slow to restart, and it sure wasn't on deer hunting after that!

Weekend guests at Jay and Charlie's camp often included Pete Peterson and Robert Brome. Both men were teachers at Waterville Central, and I was numbered in their classes more than once during my tour as a high school student. Pete taught Science and Biology. It was well known by his students that if you could steer the subject of class instruction to bear upon something associated with the Adirondacks, then Mr. Peterson would usually recount several adventures of his from the "Dacks." This would burn up most of our class time, and relieve us of some real dry material or a dreaded test. Pete was a good teacher, despite this occasional sidetracking!

Mr. Brome taught English, and you couldn't get anything past old "Chrome Dome's" balding head, as he was affectionately referred to behind his back, and out of earshot. He ran a tight ship, and everyone participated in his classes. If he caught your mind drifting, you might be given a new name, such as Dunder head, or humiliated in an interesting variety of other ways. He ruled his class with an iron hand, but behind his steely gaze, you could detect a keen sense of humor, and that intangible air, that he cared for each and every one of us. Mr. Brome was one of my all time favorite teachers.

Gun safety was of paramount importance at their tent camp, as well as in the field. One of the rules that they always insisted on was never to carry or swing your rifle, so that it pointed at or passed across another hunter. This was especially important while traveling single file on a trail. They had a guest up one weekend who wasn't very muzzle conscious. Three or four times, he was made aware of, or reminded, that his rifle was pointing at the man in front of him, but it just never seemed to make an impression on him. Finally, Jay, who was walking behind him, pointed his own rifle up and away from the trail in a safe direction, and fired off a round. The blast scared the daylights out of their guest. After he had regained his composure somewhat, he asked, "What the hell happened?" Jay said, "My rifle accidentally went off. Now aren't you glad that I don't carry my rifle like you do?" Instead of taking the lesson, he took offense. When they got back to camp, he packed up and went home. It's far better to have a disgruntled hunter, than a crippled or dead friend.

Jay and Charlie camped at Loon Brook for only a few years. They used to have a 55-gallon drum buried under the floor of the tent to store some of their camping supplies between seasons. It was on its side and had a metal door on the top side fastened with two heavy strap hinges and a strong hasp. One year, a black bear found the drum and uncovered enough of it so that he could work on the door. The bear, in his efforts to get into the drum, had ripped a large piece of metal right off the door. After looking over the damage, Jay thought, "No man with a good set of vise grips could have duplicated that feat!" A determined black bear has some incredible physical power.

A COLD WEEKEND
AT THE BEAR CAMP

Sometime in the late '50s or maybe 1960, Dave York and I spent what was probably the coldest weekend ever in camp. It was the last weekend of the season, and we were going to take the tent down on Sunday afternoon. We hiked in over the trail on a bitter cold and crystal clear Friday evening. When we got to the tent, there was frost all over the inside of it. Real heavy frost! We got a fire going in the stove, but it sure didn't throw much heat. The snow was 8 to 10 inches deep outside, so we went out and banked the tent walls with snow for some added insulation. We took another look at our firewood reserves, and figured at best, we'd have enough for tonight and maybe some left for tomorrow night.

We got a real good fire going, had a hot chocolate, and then slipped into our cold sleeping bags. We had the old mummy style G.I. bags that were filled with duck down. They were generally good for most any night. As long as the fire was going real good, we were comfortable, but just comfortable. As soon as the fire began to idle down, the cold would begin to creep into our bags. I could judge the strength of the fire by the frost line on the tent ceiling. With a good fire going, the frost would retreat to within a couple of feet of the rear wall. When the fire was low, the frost line would be halfway in or better.

I fell sound asleep once, and when I woke up, the fire was all but out. I nearly froze to death trying to get it rejuvenated! Outside in the forest, the trees were really popping and cracking! We slept with our clothes and wool socks on, and covered our lower bags with our hunting coats. Neither of us slept very well that night, and by early morning, we were chopping up the blocks we used for seats in our tent.

Since it was so cold, we decided to hunt out towards the road. We certainly couldn't spend another night back in here with no wood, so we planned on staying in Raquette Lake after hunting. Tomorrow we would hike back in and take down the tent. On the hunt out to the road, I missed a good big buck. We stayed at the Raquette Lake Hotel that night and learned that the Friday night temperature had dropped to 30 below zero on many local thermometers. We both slept warm and toasty that night and took the tent down the following day.

LATER YEARS AT BLUE RIDGE

The years we spent hunting out of the Bear Camp were undoubtedly the very best of our hunting years. It was a time when the older generation of hunters were hunting with the younger generation, and we were all capable, effective, hunters at that time. The decade of the '50s was the last of the really good deer hunting for the Central Adirondacks. Deer numbers seemed to be at an all time high, and good deer sign was everywhere. You couldn't look into any bunch of alders in November without noticing fresh rubs made by some cruising buck. The hardwood flats, or terraces on the side of Blue Ridge, were all hooked up and had many scrapes laid out upon them. The spruce swamps were just as heavily marked with the signs of rutting deer. There was some good hunting to be had in later years, but the hunters who were up during the '30s, '40s, '50s, and beyond, all agree that hunting was never again as good, beyond the '50s. During the later '50s, State biologists were arguing that the deer herd in the Adirondacks was too big, and that their wintering grounds were already overbrowsed. The State began selling party permits from 1957 on, so that antlerless deer could be harvested in addition to a legal buck. The permit consisted of a self-locking metal tag that passed through the jaw of the deer. I learned later that some hunters had figured out how to unlock these tags, and that several doe were sometimes taken on a single tag. Our group took several doe from the Bear Camp area, but it was a long way out to the road with a doe. We would prefer to use this energy on a legally antlered buck. The '50s also ended with a series of tough winters. The party permits, tough winters, a maturing hardwood forest, and an expanding coyote presence, all helped to hold down any future large population of deer.

*Cleo and her big buck
of Nov. 1955. Aldous
family photo.*

*The original bear camp reconstructed from Herb Birrels abandoned campsite.
Photo by David York.*

Dick Brown at the bear camp. Photo by Bob Elinskas.

David J. York and the "buck lure buck." York family photo.

THE SHARP SHOOTER

Early in 1957, my close friend and hunting partner, Jim Kling, entered the Army for a three year hitch. In 1962, I also entered the Army to begin my tour of duty. Jim's tour saw him working with a demolition unit out in California. However, his shooting skills put him on the All Army Team, for much of his three years. Jim shot in the National matches at Camp Perry in August of 1959. He finished 77th in a field of 2275 competitors for the President's 100 Match. In the Crowell Trophy "Master Class," he finished 37th, in a field of 2,076 competitors, with a score of 92-12V. Jim qualified for, and won many competition medals, including the "Distinguished Rifleman" medal. On his wall in a glass case hang 17 of his finest military awards for shooting skills.

ALASKA BOUND

Jim had coached me many times to help me sharpen up my own shooting skills. Especially after my close encounter with the bear! In basic training, I won the Company Trophy as high firer, but that ended my competition in the military. After that, I went to Fort Monmouth, New Jersey to learn photography and photo lab operations. Schooling completed, I was sent to Fort Wainwright, Alaska, in Fairbanks, to serve my foreign tour of duty. I couldn't have been happier with the assignment! During my entire stay there, I spent every hour, day, weekend, and all my leave time in hunting, fishing, and exploring that beautiful state.

After I was discharged, I returned to spend six more years to hike and explore its mountains. On one particular hunt, I was camping alone in the mountains along the Hammond River in the Brooks Range. The area is just north of Wiseman. I had climbed to the top of a predominant peak in order to scope the nearby mountains for Dall Sheep. I was looking for a comfortable place to sit. Then I spotted a nice flat rock that I would move to sit on. When I moved the rock, there was a Hills Brother's coffee can underneath it, with a metal cap on it. Inside was a note written by Bob Marshal. It stated that he had climbed this peak back in 1932 with Ken Harvey and a few others. Some later day area gold miners, who also knew of the can, had also signed their names. I signed my name to the list in September of 1968 and put everything back the way it was.

Bob Marshal was one of the original Adirondack 46ers, with a great love for real wilderness. That Hammond River area was pure and unblemished as I looked it over from my lofty perch. My thoughts at that time must have been much the same as Marshal's were. "Why can't we keep areas like this just the way they are, for all generations of wilderness lovers to enjoy. Just leave it to exist as it is!" Six days later, I was hiking back out after 10 beautiful days in pure wilderness. I had a nice boned-out Dall Sheep on my pack, and several rolls of exposed film to process later. I stopped to spend my last night in a deserted gold mining cabin that was still just barely useable. On a shelf in the cabin was a short, musty, stack of Yankee Magazines. I thumbed through the pages, and some of the pages showed pictures of big maple trees, and an eastern hardwood hillside. I started getting a little homesick just thinking about the farm country I was raised in, and the Adirondacks I had grown to love. As much as I loved Alaska, with all her wilderness flavors, I knew in my heart, that when the time came for me to settle down and start a family, that place would be near the Adirondacks.

I returned to New York State in May of 1970, and worked locally for Joe and Bob Piersma of Brookfield, as a carpenter. In October of that same year, I met Amy Barney who, for me, was special from the first time I saw her. We married in May of 1971, and have been together ever since. We have raised four children, Bob, Dan, Rick, and Suzanne. My wife and my children have been my life's greatest blessing.

Nelson James Kling, top
"Distinguished rifleman" U.S. Army 1959

A young Bob Elinskas in the Brook Range of Alaska with a Dall sheep, 1967.
Photo by Bob Elinskas.

THE BEAR CAMP ENDS

After I left for the service in 1961, Dick Brown, Dave York, Daryl Eaton, and Nick Delorio continued to hunt out of the Bear Camp for four or five more years. Dick used to enjoy hunting the area of the Big Notch, which was over two miles east of the camp location. Dick was getting on in years, so it was decided to move the camp location up onto the side of the ridge, into the hardwoods, and a lot closer to the Big Notch. The new tent site was along a small brook that didn't dry up, and it flowed down the ridge and through what we called the third lumber camp clearing. We informally called the stream, "York Brook," after Dave, since he had picked out the new tent site. When Jim saw this camp a few years later, he didn't like its location, because in his opinion, it screwed up one of the best deer runs on the whole north side of the ridge. Nevertheless, the boys enjoyed some pretty decent deer hunting out of that camp.

There was no prominent trail leading into the York Brook camp, and the boys were still in the habit of hiking into camp on Friday evenings. They would use the upper trail as far as the falls, and then head south, cross country, until they came to the foot of the ridge. Once the third lumber camp clearing was found, they would follow York Brook along its east side to the camp.

On one particular Friday evening, the region had experienced a wet heavy snow that had been driven by a strong north wind. Snow was plastered in a heavy coat, all over the limbs and tree trunks. It also hung heavy on the small saplings and undergrowth, bending them over and making travel difficult in general. Familiar landmarks quickly disappeared or were very hard to recognize. Dick and Dave had been hunting through the week and were in camp. However, Nick Delorio, Bill Tumbacarris, and Dave's son, Scott, were hiking in that evening.

Bill got to the trail head first and began hiking in. He did fine until he started heading cross country south of the falls. It was hard to keep any southward progress going with all the saplings bent over, loaded with snow, and in your face. Scott headed in after Bill, and when he saw Bill's meandering tracks on Smokey Roost, he knew Bill was in trouble. It took quite a while to catch up to him, and when he did, Bill was ready to call it quits right there and build a fire. Neither of these men had spent a lot of years at the ridge at this time. After talking it over, they agreed that following a compass bearing of southeast should bring them to the foot of the ridge. The brook or beaver meadow should then give them some clue to their exact whereabouts. So off went the two hunters again, into the snow laden woods. About 30 minutes later, they met up with Nick, who was also having his troubles. Nick had to agree with their course of action, so off went the three of them. It was just before midnight when the three hunters gratefully entered the warm tent up on York Brook that evening!

ONE CLEVER BEAR

Dave and Scott hiked into the ridge one March just to look things over and get some exercise. While approaching Loon Brook along the foot of the ridge, they came upon a line of bear tracks in the snow that were heading in their intended direction. They followed the tracks out onto the ice of an active beaver pond and over to the resident lodge. They could see where the bear had then dug a sizeable hole in the side of the lodge. Blood on the snow indicated that a kill had been made, then they followed the tracks over into the hardwoods where the bear devoured the beaver. All signs indicated that this was one clever bear. He evidently opened up the hole in the side of the lodge, and then waited in the hole for one of the beavers to return, just like a Polar Bear might by a breathing hole in the sea ice, waiting for a seal to return. Only in this case, when the beaver appeared in the lodge entry hole, the black bear quickly made his move!

THE TENT FIRE

Late in the 1975 deer season, five men were sleeping in the York Creek tent on a bitter cold night. In the pre-dawn darkness, Dave York got up to stir up the fire and throw some more dry wood in the stove. He opened up the draft and damper, and then went outside to relieve himself. In a few minutes he returned and stumbled upon entry. His shoulder hit the elbow on the stovepipe, which hadn't been fastened with screws. The elbow and pipe separated with the hot stack leaning over on the canvas wall of the tent. Almost instantly, the wall of the tent was on fire. Dave grabbed the water pail that was by the door, but there was an inch of ice frozen on top. The flames were up to the ceiling and beginning to burn the fly. Dave began yelling to everyone to get up quickly! He couldn't beat the flames out, and it was spreading incredibly fast! Burning pieces of canvas, and plastic fly began dropping down on everything. The guys made a quick grab for whatever they could, and then rushed out from under the inferno. Scott grabbed a couple of cans of Coleman fuel and threw them out of range of the fire. Their sleeping bags were all burning; a pail with a couple of boxes of rifle ammo in it began popping. The shells were exploding, but instead of the bullets flying, the primers were being blown out. Jim had a clip loaded .45 automatic pistol, and he kept throwing snow onto it. All of the men couldn't believe how fast the fire had spread and how much heat it had generated. It was over quick enough, and by the time the last sparks were put out, dawn was beginning to break.

The men involved in the fire were Dave York, Dick Brown, Jim Kling, Bill Tumbacarris, and Scott York. The men had lost a lot of their clothing and footgear. Dave lost a model 760 Remington pump, Jim's pistol was useless, two wallets were burnt up, all their sleeping bags, and a lot of personal items. One minute they were all sleeping peacefully, and a few minutes later, they were all out in the cold, standing around the stove. Bill had burned the palms of his hands. Dave had lost his eyebrows and singed his hair badly. Aside from this, everyone was alright.

The tops of most of the boots and packs were burned almost to the soles. These were tied on with pieces of plastic and long underwear. There was only one hat and two jackets saved. Most of the men were wearing just long underwear bottoms for the hike out. The temperature that morning was just below zero, and I don't think a motlier bunch of hunters ever walked out of the woods to their cars. They certainly made a sight to behold as they trudged on out.

Out on the trail south of the falls, they ran into Tony Dipino, and two of his hunters. Dave was madder than hell at himself for burning down the tent, and was in no mood to talk to anyone. However, in passing on the trail, Tony and his boys just exchanged the usual, "Hello boys, any luck?" type of greeting, and kept right on going, no mention of their sooty, disheveled appearance being made. Bill was way back and bringing up the rear, when Tony took note and said, "What's this?"

On the way home the boys were in a little better frame of mind and started to laugh about passing the boys on the trail. Here they were in shirtsleeves, all sooted up, and wearing long underwear bottoms and tied on boot soles, and all they got was, "Hi boys, any luck?" "Maybe they see a lot of guys like us hunting out near the road," they jested! Dave hiked back into the burned out tent the next day and took pictures. Thankfully, his homeowners' insurance policy covered a lot of their losses.

RETURN TO BLUE RIDGE

After I returned from Alaska, I learned that my old hunting cronies had a tent full of regulars. I decided that I would be better off and more independent if I hunted alone, at least for a while anyway. At this time, fur prices were beginning to rise dramatically, so I decided to incorporate some trapping into my activities. Amy knew how important it was for me to get away every fall, and she never stood in the way. Her only worry was my safety. She knew that I was a loner, and a far ranger, so she was never sure about where to send help for me, should I ever need it. I would leave her maps of my intended routes, and numbers to call after a certain time, but thankfully, there was never a need.

At first I hunted and trapped in the area of our old family camp at Rainbow Lake. It was good country, but somehow, it just didn't have the same charm for me that the Blue Ridge wilderness did. I decided to set up a small camp on the site of the old Bear Camp. Harry Jacobson hunted in there with me during the first seasons of my return. He left for California the following year, so the next season I tented there by myself. Fisher prices were excellent, so I ran a line of traps while I hunted. I took five nice fisher and a nine-point buck that season. I received up to $200 each for the female fisher, and up to $150 each for the males.

THE TREE STAND

Tree stand hunting was becoming quite popular in the '70s, and some of my friends that used them in the southern tier said that they were very effective. I had tried hunting from a tree stand once while up at Rainbow Lake. However, after only a two hour wait in one, I decided that it wasn't for me. Still, the idea was interesting, so I kept toying with the thought.

Out on the far western end of Blue Ridge, where it falls off towards Sagamore Lake, there is a small swamp that lies on top of a ridge of land that ends over toward the East Inlet Brook. There is a big mud wallow in the swamp that the animals use during the fly season. There is also a big spruce tree that the bears have chewed on for years and years. Beyond this swamp, and on the south side of the ridge, exists a beautiful deer run. It has a mixed hardwood growth on it with a thin ribbon of spruce trees growing among them. The spruce cover was just thick enough to make the deer feel secure while moving through it, and the spruce trees were just thin enough so that if one had a lofty vantage point, he could see quite a lot of the run. The run bridged a favorite bedding area, with multiple feeding areas, and it always had a generous amount of fresh deer sign on it.

The problem with having a stand so far away from your campsite was that you'd never be in it during the most productive hours of the day. The hour before dark, and after dawn, would find you either hiking into or out from it. The thought then occurred to me that if I built a tree stand big enough to lay out a sleeping bag on, then I could watch the last couple of hours before dark and also be there for the first two hours after dawn. This thought intrigued me, so I fooled around with some tree stand designs that could be made from mostly natural materials. I came up with one that I thought would work and made some plans for the following fall.

On the second weekend of the season, I made the long hike in to build and try out my tree stand plan! It took quite a while just to make the hike in from the road. Then it took the rest of the day to gather materials and build a usable stand. I finished work on the stand just as the sun was setting in the west.

Believe me, I was one tired tree stander when I climbed up into it to spend the night! I had side rails tied on so I couldn't roll off, and all the supports were double secured. I was about 20 feet off the ground and had a beautiful view. I didn't expect to see any game this trip, because my scent was all over the slope from gathering materials.

I ate my pre-made supper that had been stored in my pack. I had a sandwich, some fruit, and a soda and watched the woods grow dark around me while eating it. Just at full dark, a full moon began to rise over Wakley Mountain. It illuminated the tree line on the steep southwestern slope of Blue Ridge, and then bathed the woodlands in brilliant moonlight. "God," I thought, "This is incredibly beautiful!" In addition, the Barred Owls were beginning to hoot with their four and five note chant (who cooks for you - who cooks for you all). I could hear several owls, all in different locations.

I slipped into my sleeping bag, and after a few adjustments, found that I was really quite comfortable. "This is like Heaven," I thought, and slowly, my tired body began to drift off to sleep. Suddenly, I was brought back to full awake by the sounds of heavy wings flapping, and very close! Then the air was pierced by a loud, "KOOK KOOK KOOK KOOK KOOOOK!" I fumbled for my flashlight and unzipped my mummy sleeping bag. When I turned and looked, I saw a huge barred owl, not four feet away from me, and it looked like he was ready to do battle. "KOOK KOOK KOOK KOOK KOOOK!" Boy, was he ever loud! "Get to Hell out of here!" I shouted. But, he answered right back, "KOOK KOOK KOOK KOOK KOOOOOK!" I suppose that meant, "Get the Hell out of my tree!" The owl kept up his verbal barrage, and I looked in vain for something to throw at him, but I needed everything I had up there. Zipped up in my army mummy bag, I must have looked like a huge grub to that owl when he first spotted me. I started to laugh at the humor of my situation. Fifty million trees are standing in this region, and I have to build a tree stand in "His" tree! He sat there scolding me a good five minutes. I got back in my bag and zipped up, and eventually, he flew away.

I slept peacefully until around 3:00 a.m., when a gentle breeze began to blow, and then a moderate wind. My tree platform began to sway, and then creek. I knew I was safe, but still you wonder how much of this before it weakens? Then I began to think about a rainy or snowy evening, and that wasn't very appealing at all. When dawn broke, I decided to leave the tree stand to the owl. A nice, warm, dry, wall tent is more my style!

A WOMAN'S INTUITION

On a Friday evening, I was doing some last minute packing in preparation for setting out a small line of fisher traps at Blue Ridge. The fisher season had already been open for two weeks, but I don't like to trap for them while there is still a chance to get one that isn't in prime condition. I also like to trap later because my vacation time is better spent both in running the line and hunting in conjunction with trapping. I had the car all packed for a 4:30 a.m. departure and was getting ready for a hot cup of mocha when Amy told me that the weather forecast called for rain tomorrow, with temps in the low 40's. "Yes," I said, "I know. Shouldn't be any problem." "Well, did you pack a change of clothes?" "Well, no. I've got my wool shirt and jacket, wool pants, Lacrosse boots. I've been wet before, more than a few times. I know how to dress!" "Well, you should have a change of clothes along. At least carry them in your car so I don't have to worry!" I grabbed a paper bag and put in a change of pants, shirt, wool socks and half sarcastically, underwear, which I showed her, and ran them out to the car. I was a little irritated that she should tell me what to pack. I've been trapping, hunting, fishing, and camping all over the place for over 30 years, and figured I had my lessons learned. One of the lessons, by the way, was to just do the little things she asks and get on with what I was doing!

By 6:45 the next morning, I was at the trail head with a pretty hefty pack, and a four-and-a-half mile hike ahead of me. First light revealed a slate gray sky, with temperatures in the mid-30s. There was no snow on the ground, and the forest floor was moderately dry. "A good day for doing what I had to do," I thought, and I started in from the road. My pack may have been heavy, but my heart was light, since I looked forward to every day I could spend out in these woods! Today, I planned on setting a string of five sets for Fisher off towards the west end of Blue Ridge. They would be along some small swamps and hillsides that Fisher sign consistently showed up on every year. I like to use the double spring #220 conibear trap because it kills the animals quickly, causing a minimum of suffering. I also like to set two traps at each site, because many times a pine Martin or a Blue Jay will find the bait before the Fisher will. Then the Fisher will have a risk-free meal, or avoid the set, being suspicious of the dead martin or Jay. My favorite set is a mostly weatherproof cubby, open on two ends, with a trap at both openings.

At a point about 3 miles in, I left enough traps and bait for two complete sets. I would take them cross country on my way back out to the road to two already constructed cubbies. By 12:30, I had three new cubby sets all baited and set, and was almost back to where I had left the traps and bait for the two final sets. I stopped for a breather near the top of a small hardwood ridge where I could look down its gentle slope towards a swamp. I mentally reminded myself to keep a sharp eye out for deer, since this was a good place to see a buck. I grabbed a sandwich out of my pack and was wolfing it down when I felt a temperature drop, and sensed a change in the weather. It wasn't raining yet, but I could tell it wasn't far away. I finished off my sandwich and hadn't taken two steps when I saw a buck turn and run down the slope only 60 yards off. My rifle came up quickly, but there was no chance of a decent shot. He appeared to have a small, light colored rack, probably around a six-pointer. He wasn't spooked too bad, so I slowly started after him, and that's when the rain started, slowly at first.

I left the buck for another day, and got back to my traps and bait. It was raining steady now, and a whole lot harder. It was a cold rain that I could feel soaking through my woolens. The next two pre-made cubbies would be quickly set, and I wanted them made today so I would have this whole line out. The rain didn't really bother me because I'm usually warm enough in woolens, even though wet. Besides, I've had some of my best hunting on rainy days. Before I got to my first cubby set, a good old Adirondack cloudburst of cold rain came down on me. After that, I could feel the water running down the crack in my rear end! While setting the last trap at the first cubby, the cold rain, turned to a slush rain mixture. The last set was only a quarter of a mile away, and now it was pouring down a cold gray slush that was beginning to coat everything, even my woolen hat, jacket, and pants. I hurried over to the last cubby site and made up the set as quickly as I could. I was soaked right through to the bone, and bending over and stretching one way and another while setting the traps seemed to work the coating of slush ice on my clothing right down into the skin. I could feel a deep chill building within me — something I'd never felt before as long as I was active in my woolen clothing. The trail out was only a mile away now, and then another mile out to the car on the trail. I ate both my candy bars and set off for the trail as fast as safety would permit. There was a good two inches of the cold grey slush on the ground. A bad fall or mishap now could be fatal.

The sticky grey slush was building up on all the trees, breaking off weak limbs, and bending over saplings. I had about an inch of it on my jacket, and it permeated my gloves and pants. It wouldn't brush off, it would just make a smear. I got out to the trail, and then pounded my way out over a slushy trail, in a slushy downpour. For all my exertion, it felt like the chill was getting worse, since my clothing seemed to have lost its ability to insulate me. I got out to my slush covered car, and with fingers almost too numb to turn the ignition switch with, started the car. My body was shaking almost uncontrollably with the cold. I put the heater on high, even though real heat was still minutes away, and began removing my slush-laden clothing. The soaked clothing came off with a great deal of difficulty, since it was plastered to my body. The bag of dry clothing I had grudgingly put in the back seat was now thankfully grabbed and, with each piece that I put on, I thanked God for my wife Amy!

By the time I was dressed in dry clothing, the heater was just starting to put out a few B.T.U.s. When I left the parking area at the trail head, I was still shaking with the cold, and would for several miles. I stopped at Sixth Lake, at Drake's Inn and had a shot and a beer, just to take the edge off, something I never do! Then I had a big bowl of soup, and a hamburger with onions. When done, I got a coffee for the road, and headed for home to thank my wife. The experience showed me that after over 30 years of hiking and camping in the woods, that there are still lessons to be learned!

BEECH BARK DISEASE

The decade of the '70s saw our mature Beech trees being seriously afflicted with "Beech Bark Disease." The majestic trees are eventually killed by the sequential activities of an insect and a fungus. The disease is of European origin, and it first made its appearance in North America, in Canada, during the 1920's. Eventually, it spread throughout all the Maritime Provinces, most of New England, Eastern Pennsylvania, and then the Adirondacks. The disease didn't seem to bother young Beech trees to any extent, but damage to mature trees was quite extensive. I can clearly recall driving through the Central Adirondacks in summers during the '70s. Some of the hardwood hillsides had to consist of 10 to 15% minimum of dead Beech tree crowns.

In late fall, while walking my lengthy trap lines, I would frequently have to pass under numerous dead Beech crowns. When the wind was gusting, I would always keep my guard up watching for falling limbs or trees. Twice during these years, I've come very close to being hit or possibly killed. On one occasion a large Beech fell to the ground and broke into several pieces with a mighty loud thump. I was standing in that exact spot only seconds before, when I heard the approach of a heavy wind gust and decided to move along. Another time, I was descending Blue Ridge on a violently windy day. I heard a sharp crack behind me, and looked quickly to see a large dead Beech tree leaning my way. I sprinted ahead, but didn't escape the top most branches from whipping me on the calves of my legs!

THE SMOKEY ROOST TENT

    My brother-in-law, Dave York, made a major career change in the mid '70s and moved to Missouri. This opened up a permanent slot in the tent with Dick Brown, Daryl Eaton, and Nick Delorio, so they invited me in. By the late '70s, the number of tent campers in our area had dropped off considerably. The older generation of hunters were beginning to weaken, and the younger generation didn't share the same enthusiasm for deep woods hunting that the old timers did. After the York Creek tent fire, the tent site was moved again. This time it was located on the west side of Smokey Roost, near Grassy Swamp. Dick was getting older, so it would be easier for him to make the hike in to this tent. Glade and Ralph ceased setting up their tent during this period also, and started making shorter hunts out of our tent. A few years after this, the Larkin boys, Bill, Kenneth, and Paul, started hunting with us also. All of us fellows got along great together, but our tent could only sleep five in a pinch. If ever there were any hard feelings to arise, it would be with too many people heading for camp on the same weekend, and having someone getting squeezed out.

DICK'S ROAD BUCK

In our travels between home and the trail head, we would often see more deer than we had in the woods all weekend. It wasn't unusual to see a legally antlered buck among these road-seen deer. They were always nice to see, but beyond that we weren't interested in potting any of them when we had waited a whole year to hunt the deep woods.

Dick was a good enough hunter, and always enjoyed his days afield out of the tent, but for one reason or another, he always wanted to drop one of these road-side bucks. He would often talk about it, and you got the idea that he might even be a little obsessed with it. We didn't like the idea, because we didn't want to get involved with the law and a fine, and also the fact that it just wasn't hunting!

Whenever Dick drove up, he would always have his .308 and a few shells handy. Over the years he's had several opportunities, but either the buck would disappear before the shot, or traffic would approach, etc. On one Friday morning, late in the deer season, Dick, Daryl, Glade, and Ralph were driving up through the mountains, heading for the trail head. A considerable amount of snow had fallen during the previous two weeks, and several new inches had fallen the night before. There was almost no traffic on the road, and the snow banks were high along the road edge. While traveling through the lonely stretch of road between Eighth Lake and Raquette Lake, Dick spotted a deer in the distance, and it proved to be a very nice eight-point buck! The buck was in the middle of the road, so Dick got the car as close as he dared without spooking it. The buck didn't seem to be concerned about Dick's car at all. He had been walking down the road away from the car, and now he turned around and started walking towards Dick's car. Glade said, "Gosh, he sure seems to want to cooperate." Dick grabbed his rifle, and two shells, then graciously offered Ralph the shot. Ralph replied, "Thanks, but no thanks." Meanwhile, the buck left the road and was now standing up on top of a cutbank, broadside, and looking back at the car, only 60 yards off. Ralph said, "You can't ask for much better'n that!" Dick aimed, fired, and the buck bolted off into the spruce trees without any sign of being hit. Dick ran right over feverishly checking out the track for any sign of a hit, blood, cut hair, anything! It was a clean miss. The guys started laughing hysterically at Dick and broke his balls all weekend, and then some! After that incident, Dick's rifle started riding back in the trunk, where it belonged.

HUNTING PROBLEMS

In the fall of 1986, Dick, Jim, Daryl and I hiked into our tent camp for some mid-November deer hunting. I was only up for the weekend, but the other fellas were going to hunt for most of a week. Dick had purchased a new Winchester, model 94 Big Bore lever action rifle. It was a .375 caliber and it shot a big 250 grain bullet at 2550-feet-per-second muzzle velocity. Dick thought it would make a pretty good deep woods deer rifle, and he was hoping his nephew Jim would "christen" it for him, by taking a buck with it. The rifle hadn't even been fired yet, but the dealer had bore sighted it after the sale, and said he'd had no complaints on his sighting in jobs yet.

Jim had been a little reluctant to join Dick on this hunt because Jim lived alone, and there was no one to look after his dog, "Skippy." Skip originally came to Jim from the family of David and Karen Mustee in New Hartford, N.Y. at the age of 8 weeks. His breed was a mix of blue tick and walker blood. It wasn't long before he grew into a sizable dog. He would have made an excellent coon hound, but Jim kept Skippy for companionship, not hunting.

Skip accompanied Jim on all his back woods walks, and was well-mannered in the woods. He always stayed close to Jim, and never attempted to follow some fresh inviting scent off on his own. You would never guess it while looking at him though. He was a big healthy dog that had "Let's go hunting" written all over him! Dick talked Jim into going by telling him to bring the dog into the tent with us.

Saturday morning dawned with a cold rain coming down that soon changed to a wet snow. Jim took the new Winchester, and he and Skip headed south from camp, and up on the slope of Blue Ridge. Jim worked his way up the ridge to where it became noticeably steeper, and then hunted east. Skip was at his side or within 50 feet of him all the while, checking out interesting scents with his talented nose. Jim wasn't far off from the Old York Creek tent site, when he spotted a spike-horned deer moving slowly down the ridge above him. It was only 70 yards off in fairly open timber. The .375 came up, the trigger was pressed; snap. A misfire? Jim cranked in another round; snap. The damn rifle wouldn't fire, and the buck took off!

Jim gathered up the two shells that didn't fire and noticed that the firing pin dents in the primer were very light. He hiked back to the tent and took the rifle apart. It appeared that the hammer spring wasn't strong enough to do the job it was supposed to do. Jim hunted around the camp site and came up with a couple of washers to put behind the hammer spring in order to beef it up. He then reassembled the rifle and tried it out. This time it worked perfectly, so he fired a few more rounds, and fine tuned the sights. By the time this was completed, the day was mostly shot.

When the alarm went off the next morning, Skippy went around to everyone and gave us all a big kiss. "God," we thought, "If a warden ever walks in here and sees this dog, we'll all hang!"

There was about four inches of snow on the ground now from yesterday's snow showers. It was still gray skies, and a cold raw breeze was blowing. Jim hiked back up onto the ridge with Skippy. When he got to the area where he had seen the spike horn, he saw a fresh set of deer tracks running hella de hoot down the ridge. They appeared to be the size of yesterday's spike. Jim was thinking about what might have scared the buck down off the ridge so bad. Another hunter was unlikely. A coyote, maybe, but he hadn't seen any coyote sign around yet. A bigger buck was a good possibility, so he started backtracking the deer up the ridge.

Jim was moving up slowly, doing a lot of looking. After about 100 yards of this, he spotted a movement behind a large blowdown. He could make out parts of a deer, and then after another movement, he could see an eye and a forked antler. The breeze was starting to shift towards the buck, so Jim put the front sight bead just behind and a little lower than the eye, and let the bullet fly. It was a clean miss, because Jim had assumed that the deer was facing one way, when in fact, he was facing the other.

The buck kept most of his cover between him and Jim as he made his escape down the ridge. Jim could see right off what was happening, so he ran towards the low end of the blow down cover, just in time to make one of his "partridge type" shots at the fleeing buck. He walked over to the track and saw fresh blood on the snow, thinking, "Look's like I'm going to have a buck on the ground shortly!" He put Skippy on a leash, not wanting him to follow the fresh blood trail ahead of him.

Jim followed the trail down the ridge in a northeast direction, and then north and northwest for a good 45 minutes. The buck had traveled almost two miles before he put him out again. He got off two shots at him as he went out, hitting him both times. Jim tracked the buck for a good 20 minutes more and noted that the buck had fallen five or six times during that period. The buck was entering the thick spruce trees bordering one of the big beaver meadows along the foot of the ridge. The track was heading west along the southern edge when Skippy started pulling on his leash looking north, out towards the meadow. He was very insistent, so Jim walked out to where he could see the meadow. Just as he got there, Jim saw the buck's head rise from out in the brook in the middle of the meadow. He quickly shot the buck in the neck ending the buck's suffering. Just for the record, when Skippy pulled Jim out towards the open meadow, it was the only time he actually aided Jim in getting the buck, and that was by only shortening the end of the hunt.

The buck's troubles were over, but Jim still had plenty of his own to contend with. The badly wounded buck had circled the end of the beaver meadow and then walked out into the inlet stream and lay in water up to his ears in an effort to lower his body temperature. There was still a little water backed up in the meadow from the old beaver dam, and the buck was lying in two feet of ice cold water. In addition, the air temperature was steadily falling, and Jim had his leather packs on, which were already soaked through. Jim waded out to the buck and then pulled him through the grass and muck onto the higher ground along the north side. The buck was big, wet, and very heavy. He was later weighed at just under 220 pounds. Jim never got a good look at the rack until he actually killed him. It had 10 perfect points on wide heavy beams and was a hard won Adirondack trophy. The buck had been hit four out of the five times that Jim had fired at him. The second shot had burned the buck's testicles and entered the paunch, going up into his right side. The third had hit the buck high in the ribs, but too high to do a lot of damage. The fourth had broken the buck's right hip. The fifth had broken his neck. The middle three shots were some tough shooting, but Jim is a capable man, and that's what put the buck in the beaver meadow for the last shot.

After dressing off the buck, all Jim wanted was a warm tent and a hot stove. Over supper, he told Dick and Daryl of his adventures with the buck. The next morning they hiked over so that Dick could have a look at him. The rack wasn't as big as his Uncle Dick's big 10-pointer, but Dick thought this buck's body was bigger and rangier. Dick took off for some hunting around Smokey Roost, and Jim worked on dragging out the buck. He got him over to one of the small hummocks above the falls on Loon Brook, and left him for the day.

The following morning, Jim and Dick began hiking over to the buck again. On the way over, they crossed what appeared to be a decent sized buck track. When they reached the skid furrow of Jim dragging the deer, this track came up and sniffed of the furrow. After hiking along the furrow, the track again approached and sniffed of it again. The buck was taking an awful lot of interest in this skid trail!

The two men began hunting along the skid trail looking for the interested buck. He had come up to the trail four or five times, just before the knoll the buck was laying on, so they stood there for a while watching the skid trail. After several minutes, they could see a deer heading for the skid trail, and it was a buck! It was decided that Jim would do the shooting, so using a .243 he shot the buck through the lungs. The buck started running in circles, so every time he would come around, Jim would shoot him again. He went down shortly, and when they looked him over he had four shots through the lungs in a four inch circle. This was a 160 pound buck with a decent rack. It took them an extra day to get them both out to the road, and they sure looked good in the back of Dick's El Camino! It was Dick's last Blue Ridge Hunt.

OVER GUNNED?

Jim Kling was an excellent gunsmith. He also built several fine rifles and stocked them with wood that he had personally cut, sawed, and dried. One of these rifles was a .458 Winchester magnum. He used the 510 grain bullets in it, and in my opinion, the rifle, when fired, killed on both ends. I was with Jim when he took it out to fire it for the first time. It wasn't at a rifle range, but a remote back forty pasture. There was a wet area in the pasture, with several small, gray rocks showing above the mud. The rifle hadn't been sighted in yet. This was just a quick curiosity trip to see how the rifle felt when fired, recoil wise, etc. Jim picked out one of the stones that was about 100 yards off and touched off the round. I can clearly remember him missing the stone by a good eight inches and seeing a bushel basket full of mud being plowed up into the air by the big slug. It was mighty impressive! Jim said the recoil was a little excessive, but fired it twice more before offering it to me. I was a little apprehensive after watching Jim rock with the recoil, and seeing the mud fly, but I took my turn. I only fired it once, and didn't miss my intended target by much, but that recoil on a 165 pound kid told me that once was enough! Jim made some adjustments on the stock to lessen the effect of the recoil and took the rifle up to Blue Ridge a few times. He killed three bucks with it on those trips, and I'm sure you've already guessed that the three bucks were only hit once!

Our warm and comfortable Smokey Roost camp. Photo by Gerry Chesebro.

Three Smokey Roost regulars. L to R Bob Elinskas, Bill and Ken Larkin.
Photo by Gerry Chesebro.

The author and a nice Blue Ridge buck. Photo by Mike Keith.

A prime Fisher brought big money in the late '80s. Photo by Sue Elinskas.

THE POWER OF PRAYER

The following stories involve me personally, and circumstances that I believe had some spiritual influence. The experiences for me were blessings in more ways than one. They were like little reminders to me that someone of a greater power was watching over me as I journeyed through this life, and that he was willing to help me at times when the need was unselfish, and the plea was sincere. I am a Catholic, and I firmly believe in Jesus. I've read the Bible from beginning to end, and I go to church regularly, except during hunting season! If you want to argue about that, I'll tell you that God made the Sabbath for man, not man for the Sabbath, so you can figure out your own answer from there on!

The first incident happened at Rainbow Lake in Franklin County. I used to hunt the area every fall until the ice froze the lake to the point where I couldn't use the boat. I was hunting out of our old family camp, that had been sold a few years back to Frances Kling, Jim's mother. She had given me permission to use the place whenever I wanted, just maintain it. During this particular fall, I was warned that her son and daughter-in-law, Jim and Linda, might show up to use the camp late that fall. This was good news for me, since I would look forward to seeing my old hunting buddy again and get caught up on past events.

Amy used to accompany me on some of these hunts up to Rainbow Lake. The camp was warm enough, and we would bring our two young boys and our beagle up, also. One snowy Friday evening, we pulled into the boathouse driveway to see a strange car with out of state plates parked there. The camp was on an island, and a quick check revealed the boat was gone. I drove past our boathouse driveway and hiked over to where I could see the camp. After hollering and waving my light briefly, I got their attention, and Jim came over in the boat to pick us up. We visited for a few hours, and then we all turned in for the night. Amy and I and the kids had the downstairs bedroom. There was a sleeping loft, but it was very cold, so Jim and Linda elected to sleep on the hide-a-bed in the living room.

The following morning, I was up before dawn and gone. I hunted right through the morning with no luck. Just after noon, I found myself not far from the boat. I almost never go back to camp for lunch, but since we had guests, I thought it might be a good idea to see how things were going. While going in the back door of the camp, I gave Amy a good scare. Our guests were in town shopping, and she really hadn't expected me until dark. Over a sandwich and a hot cup of tea, she told me she got along well enough with Jim and Linda, but she didn't really know much about them, so it was hard to converse at times. Also, she was breastfeeding our youngest son, Danny, and the kids tend to wake up early. With Jim and Linda sleeping late in the main room, and her trying to keep the kids and the dog quiet, she was very uncomfortable.

I went back to my hunting up on Buck Hill around 2:30, but I couldn't get my mind off Amy. I loved my wife very much, and my heart went out to her. Suddenly, my hunting activities didn't seem so important to me. I lowered my head and said with all the heartfelt sincerity that I had, "Lord, help me get my buck, so we can end this and call it a season." I opened my eyes and thought, "I hope he heard me." It wasn't 60 seconds later that a beautiful eight-point buck came ghosting along through the hardwoods. One shot through the lungs and he was down. I knelt down and thanked the Lord first thing. There was no doubt in my mind what had just happened! For the benefit of the agnostics out there, I will admit that I was on a good run in the middle of the rut, but that's all you get!

I pulled the buck down to the boat, and had him back to camp before dark. We enjoyed another good visit that evening, and after church on Sunday morning, we headed for home. I stopped at the Long Lake Hotel to have the buck weighed. The buck went 176 pounds, and Amy overheard an onlooker say, "Look at this guy. He takes his wife, and kids, and even the family dog, and he gets a nice buck!"

SUZANNE'S BUCK

When our children were young and growing, and up until they were well into high school, we made it a practice of kneeling down and saying our bedtime prayers together. In the fall of the year, I would encourage the kids to pray so that Dad would get his deer that fall. One fall, after our youngest child, Suzanne, had started praying with us, I asked the kids to pray so that Dad would get his deer. Well, they did, and I hung up two nice bucks that fall. After the season ended, Suzanne continued her prayers with, "And I hope Daddy gets a nice big buck!" I explained to her that God had helped me put two deer in our freezer, and that hunting season was over until next year. "Well then, I'm going to pray for next season!" she said. She sure did! Every night from then until the following season opened, she ended her prayer's with, "And I hope Daddy gets a nice big buck!"

The following fall on opening day, I was packing a heavy load of trapping supplies back in towards the big notch on Blue Ridge. The weather was unseasonably warm, in the mid-60's, with a clear blue sky and a hot sun burning down. I was about four miles in from the trail head and working up a pretty good sweat. I hadn't heard a shot all morning, and I really wasn't looking for deer, because I figured any respectable buck worth his salt would be laying nice and comfortable up on some shady ledge in the spruce trees, and a lot higher than I was going on the ridge that day. It was also very noisy walking in the woods through a thick carpet of dry leaves. I was climbing a steep slope in the wide open hardwoods that led up to a series of ledges, when I heard this crash, crash, crash! I turned and saw this huge buck running along and about to cross my back trail only 30 feet behind me. Two quick shots from my 742 Remington 06 put the buck down quickly.

As soon as I walked up to him, my first thought was of Suzanne's prayers. Again, I knelt down and thanked God for his blessing! The buck had a large 10-point rack, and four days later weighed in at 192 pounds. Normally when I get a buck in that far, I'll bone him out and bring him out on a packboard. However, this was Suzanne's buck, and I wanted to show her how her prayers had worked. I was in to camp alone that weekend, so I was only able to pull that buck as far as the divide along the foot of the ridge, between Loon and Bear Brooks. I was going to need some help in getting him all the way out, so when I got home, I asked my neighbor, David Pavese, if he would give me a hand.

David was a big, strong guy in his early 20's who liked to hunt deer, but didn't have much experience in the Adirondacks yet. He enthusiastically agreed to give me a hand. Monday morning found us in the divide, snaking the buck out of the spruce trees. The nights were cold, so the meat still had a good chill in it. Dragging was pretty tough, so we cut a pole and tied the buck tightly to it, so that he didn't sway when being carried. We picked up some foam pads at the tent, so the poles wouldn't cut into our shoulders too badly. We got him almost to the first crossing on Loon Brook in this fashion then we resorted to pulling again. He was a heavy buck to pull on those dry leaves. We met Anthony Dipino near the crossing, so he helped us get up the steep bank with the deer. By the time we made the road, we were almost as dead as the deer was! Suzanne got to see the fruit of her year of praying, and David got his first taste of pulling Adirondack deer. Evidently it didn't scare him off, since he is now a regular at the tent and has pulled a few of his own deer out.

A LACK OF FAITH

Many Christians believe in praying to the Saints to intercede for them in asking favors of our Lord. These Christians don't worship the Saints, as many believe. They are only asking for their intercession with our Lord. I, personally, pray to the Saints very little, since I prefer to deal directly with Jesus, but I do believe in the community of Saints. Many Christian hunters of old used to pray to the patron Saints of the hunter, Saint Hubert and Saint Eustace. My wife, Amy, is a strong believer in praying to certain Saints for enlisting certain types of help. For instance, Saint Anthony is the one you would pray to for finding something that is lost, and Saint Joseph is the one you would pray to if you needed financial help. She swears by this, and I have to confess, I've seen it work for her remarkably well!

One fall, I was telling Amy about a particular buck that I had located but could never quite get my eye one. The buck used to bed up on a little hardwood knoll that was surrounded by windfalls and thicker growth, but on its east side, was a fairly open black spruce swamp. I could approach the knoll from that direction quietly, but every time I did, something would go wrong: an unexpected shift in the wind, two doe winded me off to my right, a new windfall blocked my quietest entry route. There was always something. Whenever I was over that way, I would give him another try anyway. Amy told me, "Why don't you pray to Saint Anthony? He'll find you that buck!" "I thought he was mostly to help you find lost items?" "Well, you can't find that particular deer, can you?"

The following Saturday, I was again hunting through the small swamp, heading towards the hardwood knoll. The knoll was just nicely coming into sight, when I remembered my wife's words about Saint Anthony. I closed my eyes and said, "Saint Anthony, if you can help me find this buck, I'd sure appreciate it." I said it sincerely enough, but I had my doubts. I took another step and saw a nice buck turn and jump over a thick blowdown. My rifle came up, but not quite in time for the shot. I couldn't believe it! That darn buck was standing 50 or 60 yards away from me all the while, and I couldn't see it! Well, Saint Anthony showed me the buck, but not quite long enough to get it. When I told Amy about it Sunday night, she said, "If your faith had been stronger, you would have gotten the buck!" I guess she was right!

"DON'T TEMPT ME"

It was late November, and I was in the process of pulling out my fisher traps for the season. Both the deer season and the fisher trapping season were almost over. I had put in a lot of miles during the last three weeks, running my lengthy trap line and looking for a good-sized buck. I had worked some long hours on my regular job recently, and evidently, my resistance had fallen. I could feel a bad cold starting to take hold in my body. I had close to a six-mile trip in one way in order to get to all of my trap sites that day. I wasn't going to haul any of the traps out, just spring the traps and hang them up until next year, but I had a big male fisher, and some other gear that I wanted to haul back out to the road. To make matters worse, there was a good eight inches of snow on the ground back in along the ridge, so you had to put a little effort into getting where you wanted to go. By the time I had worked my way back in to the end of my line, I could feel myself getting a little feverish from my building cold infection.

My trap line was all pulled. Two weeks before this, I had killed a dandy buck and filled my tag, so all I wanted now was to hike out to the road, go home to a hot bowl of soup, take some cold medicine, and go to bed. I really didn't want any deviations, but being only human, I knew I was subject to temptations. Before I took my first step towards the road, I sincerely prayed, "Lord Jesus, please don't show me any big buck today, because I'm probably just stupid enough to shoot it!" With that said, I started knocking off the miles back to the road and my car.

All went well until I got into the area of the divide along the foot of the ridge. There were fresh tracks ahead in the trail. A closer look around showed me that they were both big deer, and one of those deer was absolutely huge.

It looked like a doe and a huge buck to me, and my adrenaline was beginning to flow, making me forget all about any cold symptoms. The big track was wide spaced and heavy, with a lot of toe drag. Even with my cold building, I could almost smell his rank musk from his tarsal glands. The tracks were steamy fresh. They had to be almost in front of me! I slow poked up the trail—rifle at the ready and on full alert. A slight movement ahead and to my right froze my movement. It was the doe, and she had just swung her head towards me. Moving my eyes only, I searched the spruce cover for any sign of the buck. The doe waited a minute and then nervously moved ahead and then into some thicker cover. I waited for the buck to make his move, and then sensed a movement close and off to my right. I swung my head in time to see the huge body of a deer, from the shoulders back, disappearing into the heavy spruce cover. He was gone, and then I remembered my prayer. It was a good thing I didn't see that bucks rack because I was pretty stupid at that moment!

Later on, I came down with one of the worst cold infections that I ever had, so

I felt that God was really looking out for me. I couldn't help but ponder afterwards how classic that Adirondack experience was. Here I'd been all over that country for the last six weeks, deer hunting and trapping, and most of it done with snow on the ground. I thought I'd seen just about every deer track that there was to be made in that country. Then on the last day of my season, this great big track appears right in the middle of it all, and I think, "How did I miss seeing his track?"

ONE LAST LOOK?

Back in the '50s, when I first started hunting the Blue Ridge area, I was up on the side of Smokey Roost looking off towards the side of the ridge. It had been a dry weekend, and although there were lots of deer around, they were hard to see. As I looked off towards the ridge, I wondered if after my life on earth was over with, that maybe our Lord would bring me back to this point in time and show me where all the legal bucks were hiding on this day. Of course, I was only fantasizing, but I could envision a huge red column or beam rising above the hardwoods over every buck in the area. I was wondering how many beams I would see, and where each one would be. It was a natural curiosity for a young hunter. Now I'm getting to be an older hunter, and God has blessed me with many healthy years of hunting activities. Over those years, he has shown me where all those deer were bedded, and where they were most likely to be found on such a day. When I close my eyes for the last time, I don't believe my spirit will want to return for one more look, I'll just thank God for the many wonderful days he blessed me with to explore this magnificent wilderness area.

I ended my season with a prayer and a buck, very close together! Buck is hanging from the Long Lake hotel scales. Photo by Amy Elinskas.

The buck Suzanne prayed for. Opening day on a hot sunny morning. Photo by Bob Elinskas.

THE CAMERA TRAPPER

The idea of setting a camera trap for deer first came to me from reading an article while I was in the Army. The author had described how he had taken pictures of several animals with the use of a trip line and a shutter pushing device. I didn't save the documentation, but I remembered his trap design and thought some day that I would also give it a try. Years later, when I was again hunting the slopes of Blue Ridge, I would occasionally look at the tracks of some big, cruising buck, and think, "Boy, I'd just love to get a look at this guy!" It was then that I remembered the article on camera trapping. The author had used a mouse trap for his shutter button pushing device. When the trip line was pulled, it set off the mouse trap, and the trap jaw or wire would push in the shutter button, then bingo, the camera would go off. However, when I tried it on my camera, the mouse trap struck with such force that my shutter spring broke. The repair cost me $60 and that dampened my enthusiasm for a camera trap.

In the summer of 1984, I attended a photographic display of night time deer pictures. The deer pictures were taken by the late Hobart V. Roberts around the turn of the century in the southern Adirondacks. This exhibition, which was at the Rutger Gallery in Utica, rekindled my desire to camera trap. I redesigned the shutter pushing device and put my camera in an open-faced box, designed to keep most of the weather off from it when it was placed in the woods.

In November of 1985, I packed my first camera trap into the woods. The camera was a Yashica "D," twin lens reflex, film size 120 for color prints, and ASA of 400. The camera had a tilt-a-mite flash attachment on it, and I used M 3-B flash bulbs. I set the trap in along Bear Brook, where it was unlikely to be found by another hunter. I had the lens pointed towards a game trail that was showing good signs of current use. There was also a small buck hooking nearby. The trail was exactly 11 feet away from the camera, so I set the lens opening at f-11, and the shutter at 125th, and said a prayer to our Lord for success.

This trap was only good for one exposure at a time and had to be manually reset, including the trip lines, which were of four pound test monofilament fishing line. I checked the trap four times during the season, and each time it had been sprung, giving me a total of four exposures for my first season. Two of the exposures had been on snow, so I could read the tracks to see what their reaction to the flash was. There was no sound to the flash or camera to speak of. So when the flash went off, the deer would instinctively bound off for three or four jumps and then stop to wonder what had just happened. Then they would go back to feeding or whatever they were doing.

Of my first four exposures, the first was set off by the wind blowing some long-stemmed ferns around, the second was of a young deer bounding up the trail in high gear, and the third was of an adult doe on snow at night. The fourth shot answered my prayers. It was of a fat and sleek four-point buck, striding up the trail in the dark of night. It was a beautiful picture, and I thanked God for a successful "first" season!

My experience as a fur trapper helped me a great deal in placing my camera traps. However, the best placed traps won't work if you have poor equipment. In the next few years, I learned what would work with some degree of dependability, and what probably wouldn't. Some of these "lessons" cost me some fine buck pictures. Sometimes a properly set trap in a good position can be undone by variations in the weather. Rain, snow, or frost on a lens can ruin your pictures. Moisture can ruin your flash attachment. Heavy, wet snow or icing can weigh down your trip lines and can set off your trap. One time, I returned to a set to find that the tree the trap was attached to had blown over and the camera was now pointing skyward, totally exposed to the weather!

That first buck picture was a real morale builder for me. I began to realize that, with a little effort and a small investment in materials, I would get to see some of those monster bucks that came off the top of Blue Ridge after dark and cruised the lowlands for doe during the night. About three miles east of our tent site and up on the side of Blue Ridge is a big basin notched into the side of the ridge. We have all hunted it, and we simply refer to it as the "Notch." Most of the Notch is made up of mature hardwood forest. There are some slashings and spruce cover within the basin also, but not to any great degree. The higher country that surrounds the basin is made up from dense growths of spruce, birch, and alder. Almost every mature buck within walking distance will choose to bed up in this lofty hideout, and it's not very often that they will leave it again until after full dark. The top of the ridge in the back of the basin is also the lowest elevation along the length of Blue Ridge. Cruising bucks will often cross over from the south side to the north side in this saddle, and vice versa. Many times I've seen some very impressive buck sign in this area.

In the fall of 1986, I brought a camera trap into the back end of the Notch with a firm determination to get a look at one of these night time cruisers. High up on the southwest side, I found the sign I was looking for. Several attention getting hookings on four- and five-inch trees, a couple of small pre-rut scrapes, with heavy three-inch long deer tracks on them, and enough tracks showing in the leaves to help me figure out a good trap site. I like to look for a good funnel set. Big bucks like heavy cover, and will stay in it wherever they can. In this area, he was using a ribbon of spruce growth to access the lower elevations of the Notch. I found a reasonably open area he crossed just above the spruce trees, and set my camera trap on a small tree that was just in front of a rock ledge. If the buck used this travel lane again, he should trip the camera at 12 to 13 feet away from the camera. I left the camera in there for two weeks and visited it four times while checking on it. I had three exposures in all. One was set off by the weather, another by a doe, and the last by a big-bodied 10-point buck. I loved that picture! It was just as I had imagined a big buck might look, as he slowly made his way down the slopes of Blue Ridge from his daytime bedding area. Every guy in camp got an enlargement of that picture, and he's always referred to as the "Notch Buck."

I've been camera trapping for many years now, and nothing gives me more pleasure than running a small line of camera traps. I'm actually hunting with a conflict of interest. During the late '80s, and early '90s, our deer populations fell to their lowest levels ever. There wasn't a lot of deer sign anywhere. Quite often when I would find signs of a decent buck, I would quietly set one of my camera traps, and then leave that area, hoping I wouldn't see him until I had a chance to get his picture.

In camera trapping you get the picture of the animal in whatever pose or activity it was doing at that instant when the camera goes off. There is no posing! The pictures are always interesting, and sometimes funny. There are few pictures worthy of enlargement; but they are out there. If you ever decide to try camera trapping, be persistent, patient, and always try for a reasonably close shot.

Several years ago, they came out with a commercial camera trap that uses an infrared heat sensor to trip the camera with. It is much better than the old trip line system that I started with. I use these new camera traps now with a fully automatic camera. The traps will take up to 36 exposures automatically without being revisited.

My first camera trap buck picture. Photo by Bob Elinskas.

"The Notch buck" one of my favorites. Photo by Bob Elinskas.

Most buck pictures are taken after dark. This is a rare daylight trip.
Photo by Bob Elinskas.

COYOTE

When I first started hunting the Central Adirondacks in 1956, some hunters were talking about the presence of Coy-Dogs in the mountains. They were coyotes, but this wild dog appeared to be a lot bigger than his western cousin, so it was thought to have crossbred with some domestic dogs along the way — hence, the name Coy-Dog. That's the way it was explained to me, many years ago, and at that time, we figured it was just somebody else's guess. As far as we were concerned, Coy-Dogs were still just a rumor since none of our hunting group had come across any sizeable dog tracks in our hunting area.

We were not even aware of the first positive signs of coyote that were slowly showing up in our hunting area until years afterward. Ed Welch of Cooperstown was hunting out of his grandfather's camp at Loon Brook, back in the very early '50s ('51 or '52). It was late in the season, and there was a few inches of snow on the ground. Ed was about a half mile into the woods from the highway when he came upon the tracks of three or four dogs that were trailing a bleeding deer.

In the summer of 1952 when Ed Goulet was cutting out the fire break trail through the Blue Ridge Wakley Mountain Valley with his crew, they would frequently hear the sounds of coyotes howling.

In 1952, Elva Brown saw a coyote in her pasture that was so big, she would swear it was a wolf.

Our own group of hunters at Glade's tent, and also the Bear Camp, didn't notice any sign of them at all until well into the '60s. Even then, we never considered them much of a threat to deer. After I returned from Alaska and married, Amy and I bought a lake front lot on Rainbow Lake, in Franklin County. We spent most of our weekends and vacations up there enjoying the lake and working on our camp. I hunted in that area some through the mid-1970s, and the deer population remained stable enough to provide some good deer hunting. Then in the last half of the '70s, the coyote population began to explode. People were frequently seeing coyotes along many of the area roads. Residents living along the old Mohawk and Malone rail bed, which is now a power line right of way, were complaining of coyotes howling almost every night, seemingly right in their backyards! A local dairy farmer had a newborn calf killed while it was out in the pasture with its mother. Jim Kling, who lives in the area year round and hunts every fall, said that the deer population fell to darn near zero in just a few years. Coyote tracks were all over the place!

While this was going on in the Rainbow Lake area, the north side of Blue Ridge showed only a modest amount of coyote sign, and hunting populations of deer remained good. However, in the Cedar River country on the south side of Blue Ridge, in the very late 1970's, the coyote population began to rapidly increase.

Dick Fletcher, who owns and maintains Wakley Lodge and Golf Course, told me how bad it got. He said that in the spring, the golf course would be like one big unclean dog kennel. The amount of coyote scats laying on the greens and fairways was incredible. He noticed that they would all be loaded with deer hair and bone fragments. In addition, he used to have a good white rabbit population, but not anymore. A snowshoe rabbit had become a rare sight. The deer population along the Cedar River was experiencing a major decline.

Elva Brown feeds the deer near her farm every winter. She personally watched the numbers of deer showing up for winter feeding decline. She also saw some of the injuries inflicted on the deer by a large and aggressive coyote presence. One of her does that she was feeding daily showed up trailing some of her intestines from an ugly wound in her side. She lasted two more days until the coyotes pulled her down for keeps. In addition, the surviving does were losing a huge number of their fawns in the spring. One fall, a local hunting camp took two healthy bucks that had almost been hamstrung by coyotes. The bucks were still able to run when shot, but their hind quarters were very severely bitten.

In the mid-1980s, I was regularly hunting a three mile length of Blue Ridge along its north side. Just about every year, I was filling my tag with a respectable-sized whitetail. When snow cover was on the ground, I would regularly see the sign of three or four big bucks when they traveled to and from their bedding areas up towards the top of the ridge. In 1985, coyote numbers began to dramatically rise. Deer numbers began to fall, even though our winters were easy to normal. In addition, signs of the real big bucks almost vanished. The coyotes that were moving in seemed to know that the rut-weary big bucks could be killed fairly easy. The bucks with the best chance for survival were the one-and-a-half and two-and-a-half year olds.

The deer population continued to decline to very disheartening levels. When you have hunted an area for a good number of years, you become familiar with all the places that deer or deer sign are likely to be found. When you hunt through these areas on a two day old snow cover and don't see enough deer sign to comment on, things are really bad! The existing deer population was reduced to pockets of deer, and they usually weren't far from heavy spruce cover. Deer became extremely hawky, and hard to stalk. If you did happen to get your eye on some before they spotted you, your observance of them made you acutely aware of how fearful and watchful, they were of the coyotes.

Coyotes hunt deer hard in the winter months. They usually start by chasing whatever fawns survived from the previous spring. Then, when the rut gets well under way, they'll start dogging the biggest bucks and wear them down. Snow depth and winter conditions dictate their success rate for the remainder of the winter. The coyotes get a big bonus in May and June, when the surviving does give birth to their fawns. During the late '80s and early '90s, very few fawns in our area saw their first fall. Coyote scats, whenever found in early summer, would usually reveal some remains of another unfortunate fawn. Royce Wells, of McCane's, shot a coyote one summer that was carrying the remains of half a fawn in its mouth. Its belly was swollen with the remains of the other half.

An interesting phenomenon occurred during this period of heavy coyote predation. A small percentage of the deer population moved into close proximity with human habitation, in order to avoid the pressure being put on them by the coyotes. Those deer living in and around villages and year-round residences survived much easier than their deep woods cousins. Those deer took a major hit and suffered huge losses. Meanwhile, the high visibility of deer around villages and home sites led people to believe that deer were just as plentiful, if not more so, back in the deep woods. Central Adirondack deer hunters knew how bad it was getting. I don't know how many conversations I overheard in coffee shops by hunters saying that there were damn few deer left in the woods!

Adirondack hunters complained bitterly to the state for some kind of relief, but to no avail. There were some informational meetings held by state biologists. At some of the meetings, it was announced that the current Adirondack coyote population was estimated to be one coyote for every nine square miles. I'm not positive how that figure was arrived at. Usually, a biologist will have a limited study area to observe, test, and draw conclusions from. Normally, I have a great deal of respect for their work. Maybe in their study area that figure was close to being correct. However, in the Blue Ridge wilderness area during those years, that figure was pure bullshit!

Coyote populations seem to fluctuate dramatically from one region to another. Jamie Roblee, of Blue Mountain Lake, is a very active coyote trapper. In late fall and early winter, he covers a lot of country in the Central Adirondacks. His own experience with coyotes has shown him that there can be incredible numbers of coyotes in one district, and relatively few in another. It makes a big difference to him on where to set his traps. His biggest coyotes have weighed in at 45 pounds, and a close personal friend of his has taken two that went 58 and 59 pounds. Those are big coyote! In talking over the local coyote population explosion, we both agreed that the winter of '90-'91 seemed to be the worst!

In 1995, the coyote population began to suffer from a mange infection. In April of that year, I got a picture of a coyote in one of my camera traps. There was dew on the camera lens when the picture was taken, so the picture wasn't very clear. The coyote seemed to have a bobbed tail. I thought he might have lost his tail in a fight, or maybe some weird accident. During the summer, I learned from friends that they had seen coyotes with bald spots on them. In early fall of that year, I saw a coyote along the road that was so bald, he looked like a giant Mexican Hairless! Remembering my earlier camera trap photo, I thought, "Maybe that's what he had, a mange infection!" Coyote populations were down that winter, and down even farther the following winter. For the first time in many years, we began seeing a decent number of fawns surviving into their first winter.

Most of us know that some predation is always beneficial to wildlife groups. We prune a fruit tree so it will bear more fruit, and we thin out our carrots and similar root vegetables so they will have room to expand into large, healthy plants. The same holds true for our Adirondack deer herd, but not to the extent that the coyotes did to it. We could all live with the one coyote for every nine square miles figure. In the summer of 1995, a mother coyote and two of her pups were killed by a motorist on the Cedar River Road. The three coyotes lay dead along the road for three or four days. According to local residents, there wasn't one drop of remorse felt by anyone in the whole valley!

The last Adirondack wolf was supposed to have been shot back in 1899, although some of the dates on this seem to vary. The earliest reports of coyotes showing up in the Adirondacks date into the 1920s. That's only a little over 20 years where nothing official, or of any significance, was reported on a wolf or a coyote presence. In the early 1970's, I was reading electric and gas meters for Niagara Mohawk Power. In the Village of New Hartford one day, while I was reading the meters along the west end of Genesee Street, an older man came out of one of the houses, and we visited briefly. He had some mounted animals on display in his front window, so I inquired about them. He told me that one of them was a life-size mount of the last wolf taken in the Adirondacks.

Having heard that, I went in to take a good look. The size of the animal was what impressed me the most. Having spent several years in Alaska, I was familiar with the Alaska or Yukon timber wolves. They come in various colors, but the big males will weigh over 150 pounds. Even the females will average between 80 to 100 pounds. The color of this mounted animal was faded considerably, and the mount, in general, was in poor condition. In my opinion, the animal might have weighed 60 pounds at the most, when alive. It was about the size of a good, big, present day, Adirondack coyote! This always made me wonder if there ever really was a Gray Wolf presence in our Adirondack Mountains.

Coyotes love venison!. Photo by Bob Elinskas.

GLADE GETS LOST

November 9, 1985, found me fully awake by 4:00 a.m. and heading out to my car in the garage. I didn't get a good night's sleep. I turned in a little late, and then about 1:00 a.m., our neighbor let his dog out, and the dog barked constantly for the next hour. After breakfast and a couple of cups of java at the O.K. Corral in Remsen, I felt more like putting in a good day as I drove north towards our trail head. There would be five of us in camp this weekend. They included Glade Keith and his son, Mike, Ralph Holdridge, Ken Larkin, and me. There was about five inches of fresh snow on the ground when I got to the trail head, and a lot of it was sticking to the trees. I was into the tent by 7:20, and met Mike as he was starting down the trail. Everyone else in camp was off to an early start. I told Mike that I would be heading out towards the Big Notch that day and would see him later on for supper.

The snow was hanging heavy on all the undergrowth, making for very poor visibility. Sometimes the deer will take advantage of this extra cover, and spend time in the more open hardwoods. There was little sign in the hardwoods along the foot of the ridge, as I headed southeast towards the basin of the Big Notch. High up on the ridge, just where it starts a sharp sweep into the Notch, I came across the tracks and recent bed of a massive buck. His tracks were wide spaced, blocky, and showed lots of drag, and his bed stunk of rank musk and urine. After he left his bed, he dug a few ferns, and I could see where his wide-spaced antlers had dug into the snow on either side of his head. I followed his tracks into the back of the Notch through the open hardwoods. Near the back of the Notch, the buck began following what appeared to be another sizeable buck track. More fresh tracks were noticed, so I was on full alert with my rifle ready for quick action. The deer were heading into some heavy cover, so it was getting tough to see any distance ahead. Suddenly, I caught a movement and spotted a deer moving up the ridge to my right. I couldn't see its whole body, but I'd seen antlers with tines. I knew it was a smaller buck than the one I was trailing, but I had traps to check and miles to go. I put the bead on his shoulder when he hit the next opening and dropped him. The buck had no brow tines and turned out to be a big five-point in good condition. I didn't waste much time in getting him all boned out. I laid the meat out upon the snow. I would return for the meat and head with my big pack tomorrow.

I had two more fisher traps to check, so I took some of the bones and entrails for bait, and left. About 200 yards below the kill site, I began seeing lots of fresh deer tracks. There were all sizes, traveling single and in groups. The big buck I had tracked into this basin got into one hell of a fight with another big buck. That buck lost, and was now bleeding badly from his front shoulder. He also had a bad limp. If the visibility wasn't so bad, I would have followed him a while. By the looks of things, there were several bucks present, and at least one hot doe at this party. That big buck cleaned house and drove them all off. It really must have been something to see! I was almost sorry I dropped the buck I did, but the snow made hunting conditions pretty bad. I was very lucky to see the buck I got.

There was nothing in the last two sets that I checked, so I freshened up the bait and made the long hike back to the tent. I had one last set to check out along the west trail, but I was exhausted. Between no sleep and a long day in the woods, all I wanted was a warm tent, a hot cup of coffee, and a comfortable chair for a while. It was very late in the day, and a few minutes later Ken came in and told me that I had a large dead fisher in the set down the trail. Ralph and Mike came in after that, so we all coffled down and visited while darkness settled in. Glade wasn't in yet, and we were getting concerned, but he was always in the habit of getting in at dark or after dark. The weather had warmed up, and the snow had melted off the trees in the last half of the afternoon. We were expecting a major rain storm to move in on us during the night. Mike wanted to see the fisher, so thinking Glade might be returning by the west trail, we grabbed our lights and headed down the trail. We didn't bump into Glade, so I removed the animal from the 220 conibear, and we hiked back to the tent.

On our arrival at the tent, we were disappointed to learn that Glade still hadn't returned. We fired a signal shot for him, and the answer came from a northwestern direction, off towards Bear Brook Swamp. Ken and Mike grabbed their lights and headed off towards Hodge's Rock so they could get a better bearing on where he was firing his shots from; then they would go out and get him. After getting up to the rock, they fired off another signal shot. Glade answered, but Ken and Mike had a difference of opinion on just where it came from. Ken thought it came from way off to the west, beyond our West Hill. Mike thought it came from a more northwest direction, and not so far away. Then it was discovered that neither man had brought a compass with him. They had both assumed that the other man had one on him. Ken knew the country, but he was a little timid about hiking off into the darkened woods without a compass on him. They decided to come back to the tent and get a compass.

When the guys came back to the tent without Glade, we were all disappointed. I quizzed Ken on where he thought Glade's shot came from, and he was reasonably sure it came from an area beyond the West Hill. Mike wasn't so sure, but Mike hadn't hunted that much up here. If Glade was somewhere off the end of the West Hill, we had a rough trail that would take us to the far side of it. It was decided that Mike and I would hike out to the other side of the West Hill and fire another signal shot, and we would compass line over to him. The storm front was beginning to move in on us now, and it was raining out fairly hard when we got down to the end of the West Hill. We fired off the signal shot, but the answering shot seemed to come from way off, out near the road. "God," I thought, "He sounds like he's heading for the road!" We talked about heading cross-country for him, but he sounded an awful lot closer to the road than he did to us. If I hadn't come up short on sleep, I would have headed right out to him, but I already had about 15 miles of hiking under my belt, most of it with a pack on and through snow. I was running out of juice! We hiked back to the tent, and Ken and Mike took off for the road. A little over an hour later, we could hear some shooting going on but couldn't figure it out. Meanwhile, the wind and rain ruled the night.

About two hours later, Ken and Mike returned. They never got any answers from their signal shots out at the road, so they went into Raquette Lake and alerted the ranger there, Gary McChesney. Gary agreed to meet the boys at the second crossing of Loon Brook at first light. When we heard this, we went outside and shot off another signal shot. I had it in my mind that if we received any answer at all, we would head right off into the woods and not stop until we found Glade. Our signal went unanswered. We fired another one with the same result.

When you lose touch with someone that needs help, it's a sickening, depressing feeling. Kenneth felt worse than any of us, if that were possible. He knew he screwed up by not striking right off for him when he was up by Hodge's Rock. Now there were no answering shots, and all the possibilities of what might have happened to an 81-year-old man started running through our minds. Nobody slept worth two cents that night, and all the while, a steady downpour of rain fell. About 4:00 a.m., Kenneth woke up in a puddle of water. The drainage ditch around our tent had plugged up with leaves, sending a stream of water into our tent.

The rain stopped just before dawn, and just as dawn was breaking, we fired off a signal shot. To our delight, it was answered right away from the same northwest direction it had come from the night before. Mike and I headed right for Hodge's Rock, while Ken went down to meet the ranger at the second crossing. Ralph stayed at the tent. Should Glade come in on his own, Ralph would fire off a signal to let us know he was back. When we got up to the rock, we fired off another shot, and the answer came from the lower slopes of the hill we were on. We weren't sure if it was Glade or the ranger coming in, so we went down to the base of the hill, and Mike and I circled the swamp that was at its base. We met up at the lower end of it, and then heard Ken and Gary coming through the hardwoods. We flagged them over, and asked them if they had shot. When they said no, I told them that he's got to be right close by, because he answered two of our signal shots. We spread out, heading west, and began to holler for Glade. A short while later I heard an answer coming from the spruce trees below us, and then we spotted Glade. He had spent the night only a few yards from where we had just found him.

He had been hunting just west of his present position. When the hour got late and darkness began to fall, he wasn't sure just exactly where he was. Before he knew it, it was just too dark to go anywhere. He found himself a big log to sit on and stayed there. When the signal shots started up, he would answer them but he was down in the thick spruce trees with a little 250/3000 Savage. It wasn't a big boomer, so with the wind and rain, that's why he sounded so far off. Glade answered four of the signal shots, but they sounded like they were coming from all around him, which in fact, they were. He only had seven shells with him on the hunt that day, so he decided to keep three shells for the next day. That's why he didn't answer later that evening.

Glade has an excellent attitude. He never gets excited about anything. He just resigned himself to spending that night sitting on the log. He had all woolen clothing on, and fortunately, the temperature remained in the 40's. Glade told us that he could make out vague images of the surrounding trees, but that was about it until dawn. He said his ass got darn good and sore from sitting on that log. Glade said that the one thing that impressed him the most was that the night seemed so gol' darned long! He thought it would never end. He got up and tried to walk, but stumbled right away, so he got right back on the log and stayed put until dawn.

We had a hot thermos of coffee for him and some food. He drank and ate everything right down. After that Glade, Mike and Gary headed out to the road. We were all grateful that things turned out as good as they did. Ken, Ralph, and I got caught up on some much needed sleep after that. The next day with all the snow melted off and temperatures in the 40's, I didn't know if my boned out meat would be any good. I made the hike up into the Notch to find that there was still snow on the ground up there. My boned-out meat was still on snow and had a good chill in it. It turned out to be one of the best eating bucks I had taken in several years!

THE "DEER ALERT" DEVICES

Early one November morning, Bill Larkin and I were driving north on Route 28, heading for the trail head. Dawn had broken, and we could now see well enough to turn off our headlights. Bill had just bought himself a new Chevy conversion van, and we were discussing its merits as we drove along. Bill told me that he had just added some new "Deer Alert" whistles to the exterior of his van in order to help prevent a possible deer-van collision. I asked him if he thought they would really work. He said that since he put them on two days ago, he hasn't seen a deer, so he couldn't be sure.

We were in the area of Eighth Lake at that time and hadn't gone a mile more, when we spotted two deer just up the road. Both deer were on the pavement, one on the right side and one on the left side. Bill was driving, so when he saw the one on the right was a good big buck, he drove right up to within 20 feet of it. Neither deer moved, and the buck kept his full attention on the doe in the other lane. The buck was an easy 170-pounder, with an eight-point rack that had about a 17-inch inside spread. The big, gray doe seemed completely oblivious to either the buck or our van, but she made the first move. She casually walked off the pavement, took a leak, and then entered the woods. The buck gave Bill and I a token glance, and then followed the doe off into the woods. As our van began moving back up to cruising speed, I said, "Well, now you know how well your new whistles work!"

SPEEDING ON THE LOON BROOK TRAIL

On a warm weekend in early November, four hunters were in attendance at the Smokey Roost tent. They included George Gay, Tony Gulisano, Bill Larkin, and me. It was Saturday night and a strong cold front was bearing down on us. The Adirondacks were under a high wind warning. David Pavese was supposed to be hiking into the tent after dark so that he could hunt with us on Sunday. The wind and the rain had been building in strength since late afternoon. Now it was 7:00 p.m., and the wind gusts were getting tremendously strong. You could hear the bigger gusts approaching through the hardwoods, sounding like a huge air force bomber flying low over the tree tops. We could hear trees and heavy limbs hitting the ground quite regularly. When one of those big blasts reached our campsite, we would all be a little nervous just imagining what would happen if a tree or heavy limb came crashing through the tent roof. The cold front was well forecasted, so we were sure that David must have cancelled his plans to hunt with us.

About 8:45, we could hear rapid footfalls approaching our tent, and then David burst through the tent flap and into the tent. He was wearing a back pack that had to weigh 75 pounds, and he was soaked from both rain and sweat! He was obviously all pumped up from the hike in, and it took him a good 15 minutes to calm back down and get into a more normal breathing pattern. Dave's wife, Karen, had dropped him off at the trail head. The hike in to our tent site from the road is about a 55-minute trip one way if you walk at a normal gate. If you want to put in some speed and step right along, you can make it in about 45 minutes. Dave made it into the tent from the road that night, with a heavy pack, rifle, flashlight, and wet eyeglasses, in under 35 minutes! Dave told us that he didn't realize just how bad it actually was until he got into the woods. He said there were trees and limbs coming down all around him, and some of them were awful damn big! He was already committed to the trip in, so he figured the quicker he got in, the less chance he would have of getting hit. Dave is a professional trucker, so he put his rear in gear, and the pedal to the metal! The morning news reported that wind gusts of over 70 mph were recorded!

THE STOLEN BOAT

As we travel life's journey, we become aware that our trip is one big learning experience. There isn't a one of us that hasn't done something that we really regretted afterward. However, if we learn from our mistakes, and make the effort to correct them, we build character and elevate our values.

A few years ago in April, after the woods had opened up, Don Adams, myself and one of our junior hunters, decided to try for some early season trout. We planned on making a major bushwack hike, and try fishing some of the remote fish-bearing ponds that lay between Blue Mountain Lake village and Blue Ridge. The weekend we selected to go on turned cold, but the skies were clear and sunny. Even though the ponds were now likely to be frozen, we decided to go anyway, just for the hike. The day trip proved to be very enjoyable. I got to see some new country, and also see some that I hadn't visited for many years.

While we were approaching one of the last ponds, we found a 10-foot aluminum Jon boat hidden up under the undercut of a huge boulder. The boat was about 200 yards away from the water, and the boat and oars were painted camouflage. Don and I didn't say much about the discovery, because we knew that many of the fishing ponds in the back country had a boat or two hidden back in away from their shorelines. If the boat is not locked up, and no one is around, you use it and don't abuse it, and return it to its place. If the owner, or another fisherman shows up, you give him his boat, or save a part of the day for the other fisherman to use the boat. It's an unwritten rule!

About three weeks later, our junior hunter made the hike back into that pond with one of his peers. They used the boat, had a good time, and caught some fish to boot. About three weeks after that, I learned that they had also carried out the boat! It was now in his backyard and painted black.

Oh God, I really felt bad about that! How I'd wished that I had taken the time to explain how things worked concerning back country property. All of our hunters were surprised and disappointed that he took the boat, but we didn't push him for its return. When I talked with him about it later on, he told me that he regretted taking it, and that he planned on returning the boat. In the spring of the following year, he and his younger brother drove up to the trail head leading into the pond with the boat on their truck. It was close to a three mile hike into the pond, and half way in they met a stranger on his way out. The stranger stopped to talk with the boys, and complimented them on their boat. When he asked them where they got it, our hunter explained that he had taken the boat from the pond the year before after using it. However, he felt guilty taking it and was now returning it. The stranger then admitted that he had recognized the boat as being his when he first stopped to talk with them. He told the boys he was very thankful to see that they were returning it. The boat was returned to the pond, and our hunter felt a lot better for having done it. The stranger was first class in dealing with the boys, and also left them a note on their truck thanking them again.

*Once coyote populations began to drop, these spring fawns
had a much better chance to survive. Camera trapped by Bob Elinskas.*

RETURN OF THE MOOSE

In the first half of the 19th century, the Adirondack region supported a modest-sized moose population. There was no legal protection for the animals, though, so as the human presence grew in the mountains, the moose numbers dwindled until there were no more. The last moose of record was in 1861.

In the first half of the 20th century, Adirondack Moose, in general, were non-existent. Then, in the 1970s, an occasional lone bull would be spotted during the fall rutting season. These sightings began to slowly grow in number, until I began to anticipate when the first moose sightings would begin. By the mid-1980s, there were also reports of cow moose being sighted. The cows were year round residents, and many of them were accompanied by calves. Our long absent moose herd was beginning to re-establish itself.

In our hunting area covering the drainages of Loon and Bear Brooks, there was little Moose sign to be found. In the early '80s, we learned from some neighboring tenters that they had found some alders that had been all slashed up by a moose. They were probably right, but there were no tracks present to reinforce their guess.

In the fall of '92, while packing in some supplies for the upcoming season, I spotted the unmistakable track of a moose in some mud near the second crossing of Loon Brook. A few days later, a young bull was spotted walking along the shores of Raquette Lake. On that day, Gerry Lanphear was visiting in his living room with his grandson, Jamie Roblee. His picture window gives him a nice view of the lake at Poplar Point. The Moose was walking knee-deep in the shoreline water when it came into view, and suddenly Gerry realized that he was looking out his window at an Adirondack Bull Moose. He said to his grandson, "There's a moose in the lake!" Jamie thought he said, "Goose." When he got up to look, he said, "That's not a goose, it's a God damned moose!"

They got right on the phone and began calling friends and relatives. Before long, it seemed like half the town was over on Poplar Point looking at the moose. Even some of the school children were brought over for a look. The moose cooperated fully by walking down the length of Gerry's driveway, and then did a little turn around on Route 28. He walked back down the drive and wound up 12 feet in front of his picture window again. Shortly afterwards, he left for parts unknown, but he caused quite a stir for a short while on Poplar Point.

In the fall of '96, my nephew David S. York, and his hunting partner, Ron Syr, of Utica were hiking into their tent site, which is about halfway up the north slope of Blue Ridge. It was early October, and their tent wasn't set up for the season yet. When they got within 70 yards of the small tent clearing, they noticed a movement within it.

A young bull moose that had been feeding on ground plants raised his head and looked their way. Both men were a little shocked at seeing a moose in their hunting area. It takes a little getting used to. The young bull's rack spread out to just beyond his ears, and then curved back into two small palms without any points. The moose was aware of their presence but didn't run off. Instead, he calmly fed off in a westerly direction. It was the first time that any of our tenting groups had actually seen a moose on our side of Blue Ridge. That same fall, there were many moose sightings in the Cedar River drainage, on the south side of Blue Ridge, especially in the Cedar River Flow area. It was good to see the moose coming back. A change we could all live with!

There's a moose in the lake!
Photo compliments of Ralph Harding.

THE LATEST ADIRONDACK DEER CENSUS

In 1957, my father and my older brother, Tom, bought a small camp on Rainbow Lake. The lake is just north of Saranac Lake village, in Franklin County. Having a summer camp in the family began a tradition of spending many weekends and summer vacations in the Adirondacks. My father was a skilled carpenter, plumber, and electrician. He greatly enjoyed working on the camp when he wasn't fishing and hunting. The camp necessitated many a trip from our home in North Brookfield to Rainbow Lake and back. Over the years, the number of trips made has grown to a very sizable figure.

I have always had a strong fascination with deer, and early on, my brother also did. We used to regularly count the number of deer spotted on each trip, one way. Our normal route would be to take Route 12 north to Alder Creek, then 28 North to Blue Mountain Lake, and then Route 30 to Paul Smith's College. Our camp was only four miles east of the college. Almost all of our trips would be either early in the morning or very late in the day. All of the deer we counted were Adirondack deer, because south of White Lake, we seldom saw any deer at all. During the late '50s, a good average number of deer spotted on a one-way trip was about 28 deer. If deer seemed scarce for whatever reason, then the number of deer seen would average around 12 to 15. In the 1950s, we always saw deer!

On one trip up in the fall of 1957, Tom and I were heading for camp late in the evening. Around midnight, we were north of Long Lake on Route 30. We were near the second left that leads over to Sabattis, when we saw a buck cross the road ahead of us. I was driving my '55 Chevy Bel Air, and it had two spot lights on it. There was no traffic, so I brought the car to a stop and switched the spotlight on. The buck was standing just inside a spruce tree line, and when the beam illuminated him, we were amazed to see an identical twin standing right behind him. Both bucks were good sized four-pointers, and they sure made a memorable sight.

On another trip, Dad, Tom, and I were just leaving for home after a weekend of hunting. It was after dark, and we were just pulling onto the Rainbow Lake Road from the camp access road. As we turned onto the road, our headlights swept a farmer's field across the road, and several pairs of eyes reflected back at us. Tom positioned the car so we could see what was in the field, and then switched his high beams on. Several doe, and three antlered bucks were illuminated. Two of those bucks were real monsters. The two big bucks got nervous right away, and began to move out. It was a grand sight to behold, and one I can clearly remember to this day!

We still have a family camp on the shores of Rainbow Lake, so we are still making many trips to and from. I still count deer, but their numbers are way down. In recent years, a good number of deer seen will number 8 to 10. A poor trip will number zero to two or three deer spotted. These are average numbers, and you have to realize that on rare occasions 20 or more deer might be spotted, or maybe no deer would be spotted for three or four trips. Again, I only count park deer. It's interesting to note that many more deer are now spotted outside the park, south of White Lake, than there ever was even inside the park. On some trips from Alder Creek south on Route 12, I've counted over 100 deer. Within the Adirondack Park, though, if you use my road seen deer figures, it will tell you that our deer numbers are only one third or less of what they were in the 1950s. Of course, there are some variables, but I hunted deer in the '50s, and I hunt deer now. From what I can see, my figures aren't very far off!

"METHUSELAH"

Among the seasonal tent hunters that have visited the Blue Ridge Wilderness, Glade Keith has got to be the "Methuselah" of all of them. Glade is entering his 95th year at this writing and is still quite active. In his older years, his hunts at the ridge have grown considerably shorter. His last hunts have been little more than day trips, but still he was able to hunt in to the foot of Blue Ridge some three miles in from the road and then out again in the same day. Since 1925, he has made it up for 67 seasons.

His last visit was at the age of 92. I didn't see him that day, but when I got back to the tent, I noticed the letters "G K" written in the snow outside on our wash-up table. He had come in with his son, Mike. The two had hiked in as far as the second crossing of Loon Brook and then split up to hunt with an agreement to meet at our tent around 3:00 p.m. I visited with Glade a few weeks later and he told me of his hunt that day. After he left Mike, he began hunting up the slope of Hodge's Rock Hill. He was about halfway up the hill when he came across the fresh track of a big lone cruising buck. "God," he said, "I was tempted to take right off tracking him cross country! The only thing that stopped me was the thought of how mad Mike would be if I was two miles or more from the tent come 3 o'clock."

These remarks came from a 92-year-old hunter! I couldn't help but ask myself, "Why does the spirit of the hunt last so long in some individuals, and with others it burns only a few years?" Certainly it couldn't be the need or desire to have a little venison. I personally believe it's the pride one feels in taking an Adirondack buck, and the experience of hunting it in some truly wild and beautiful country. So as long as the hunter remains healthy, he will return.

The Adirondack bucks of today are much more difficult to take than they were in the first half of this century. In the old days, it wasn't uncommon to hear hunters talking of hunting "way back in" where the deer were undisturbed, and hopefully bagging a big old stupid buck. Today's deer, thanks to the coyote presence, are all very much disturbed and watchful. Taking one of these bucks on a regular basis has got to be one of the most difficult challenges facing hunters today. This is why most hunters head for the easy pickings in New York's southern tier. For those of us with a deep love for the Adirondacks, we will keep coming back season after season to visit some of our favorite wild haunts one more time. Glade's southern tier dairy farm is prime deer-hunting country, but he only rarely hunted deer there. When it came to bagging a buck, his heart was north, in the Blue Ridge area!

Glade died on January 15, 2001, at the age of 96. His close friend and hunting Ralph Holdridge died 4 months later at age 93.

continue to hunt out of a remote tent site at Blue Ridge. The tradition lives on!

Good Hunting

Glade Keith at age 90 by Hodges Rock. Photo by Gerry Chesebro.

"End of the Tracks" by Bob Elinskas.

BIBLIOGRAPHY

Adirondack Golf Courses	J. Peter Martin
An Adirondack Resort	Harold K. Hochschild
Adirondack Railroads Real & Phantom	Harold K. Hochschild
Adirondack Steamships on Raquette Lake and Blue Mountain Lake	Harold K. Hochschild
Albany Times Union	21 Dec. 1958
Alaska Magazine	June 1992
The Browns	Gertrude M. Brown
The Brown's & Neighbors of Cedar River	Elva Brown
The Carry Railroad	Richard Sanders Allen
Clinton Pennysaver – Collector's Corner	Barbara Crane 91
Cornell University	Registrar
"Durant"	Craig Gilborn
E.S.F. Quarterly Fall 92	Rainer H. Broche
The Forest Preserve of N.Y.S. in the Adirondack and Catskill Mountains	N.J. VanValkenburgh
Hamilton County News	16 March 1972
Hamilton County News	29 April 1976
Hamilton County News	22 July 1976
History of Hamilton County 1965	T. Aber & S. King
Life & Leisure in the Adirondacks	Harold K. Hochschild
Lumberjacks & Rivermen in the Adirondacks	Harold K. Hochschild
N.Y.S. Conservationist	Dec. Jan. 1951
N.Y.S. Conservationist	Feb. Mar. 1951
N.Y.S. Conservationist	Dec. Jan. 56-57
N.E. Regional Climate Center	Cornell University
The News World	20 March 1982
Raquette Lake "A Time to Remember"	Ruth Timm
Sports Afield Oct 92	Lionel Atwill
Township #34	Harold K. Hochschild
True Magazine "The Search"	Carl Kaufmann
U.S. Weather Service	Washington, D.C.
Daily Press	31 Oct. 1914
Press	16 Aug. 1951
er Dispatch	5 March 1932